Paradoxes of Modernization

WITHDRAWN
UTSA LIBRARIES

D0742697

REDIGITIZED
FROM BEST
AVAILABLE
COPY
UTSA LIBRARIES

Paradoxes of Modernization

Unintended Consequences of Public Policy Reform

Edited by
Helen Margetts, Perri 6, and
Christopher Hood

OXFORD
UNIVERSITY PRESS

OXFORD
UNIVERSITY PRESS

Great Clarendon Street, Oxford ox2 6DP

Oxford University Press is a department of the University of Oxford.
It furthers the University's objective of excellence in research, scholarship,
and education by publishing worldwide in

Oxford New York

Auckland Cape Town Dar es Salaam Hong Kong Karachi
Kuala Lumpur Madrid Melbourne Mexico City Nairobi
New Delhi Shanghai Taipei Toronto

With offices in

Argentina Austria Brazil Chile Czech Republic France Greece
Guatemala Hungary Italy Japan Poland Portugal Singapore
South Korea Switzerland Thailand Turkey Ukraine Vietnam

Oxford is a registered trade mark of Oxford University Press
in the UK and in certain other countries

Published in the United States
by Oxford University Press Inc., New York

© Oxford University Press 2010

The moral rights of the author have been asserted
Database right Oxford University Press (maker)

First published 2010

All rights reserved. No part of this publication may be reproduced,
stored in a retrieval system, or transmitted, in any form or by any means,
without the prior permission in writing of Oxford University Press,
or as expressly permitted by law, or under terms agreed with the appropriate
reprographics rights organization. Enquiries concerning reproduction
outside the scope of the above should be sent to the Rights Department,
Oxford University Press, at the address above

You must not circulate this book in any other binding or cover
and you must impose the same condition on any acquirer

British Library Cataloguing in Publication Data
Data available

Library of Congress Cataloging in Publication Data
Data available

Typeset by SPI Publisher Services, Pondicherry, India
Printed in Great Britain
on acid-free paper by the
MPG Books Group, Bodmin and King's Lynn

ISBN 978-0-19-957354-7

1 3 5 7 9 10 8 6 4 2

Library
University of Texas
at San Antonio

Acknowledgements

We would like to thank all presenters and participants in the seminar series 'Unintended Consequences of Public Policy Reform' hosted by the Oxford Internet Institute and the ESRC Public Services Programme in Oxford during 2007–8, for valuable discussions and development of issues covered in this book. We are very grateful to the OII and the ESRC for supporting and funding these seminars. We thank Nesrine Abdel Sattar for her work on the bibliography, Klaus Goetz for some valuable discussions on modernization and Josep Colomer, who found the painting for the front cover. Finally, we thank all those people who have helped us with the book — without necessarily intending to.

Contents

Contents

List of Figures

List of Tables

Contributors

Perri 6 is Professor of Social Policy in the Graduate School of the College of Business, Law and Social Policy at Nottingham Trent University. His recent books include *Institutional Dynamics of Culture* (ed. with G. Mars, Ashgate, 2008), *Public Emotions* (ed. with S. Radstone, C. Squire and A. Treacher, Palgrave, 2007), *Beyond Delivery* (with E. Peck, Palgrave, 2006), *Managing Networks of Twenty First Century Organisations* (with N. Goodwin, E. Peck and T. Freeman, Palgrave, 2006) and *E-governance* (Palgrave, 2004). He is well known for his work on joined-up government, consumer choice in public services, privacy, and data protection, and on social networks, and has published articles in such journals as *Political Studies, Public Administration, Journal of Public Administration Research and Theory, Policy and Politics, Journal of Social Policy,* and *Journal of Comparative Policy Analysis*. He is currently researching how different styles of political judgement result in decisions that produce different types of unintended consequences.

George Boyne is Professor of Public Sector Management at Cardiff Business School, Cardiff University. His main current research interests are organizational performance, executive succession, and structural change in public services. His recent books include *Public Service Performance: Perspectives on Measurement and Management* (Cambridge University Press, 2006) and *Theories of Public Service Improvement* (Oxford University Press, 2009). He is President of the Public Management Research Association, co-editor of the *Journal of Public Administration Research and Theory* and a member of the ESRC Research Grants Board.

H. George Frederickson is the Edwin O. Stene Distinguished Professor of Public Administration at the University of Kansas. He is President Emeritus of Eastern Washington University. Frederickson is the author or co-author of *The New Public Administration, The Spirit of Public Administration, The Public Administration Theory Primer,* and *Measuring the Performance of the Hollow State*. His most recent book, *Social Equity and Public Administration,* was published in January 2010. Frederickson is a Fellow of the National

Academy of Public Administration and serves on the Academy Board of Directors. He is Editor-in-Chief of the *Journal of Public Administration Research and Theory*. Frederickson has received the Dwight Waldo Award, The Charles Levine Award, The John Gaus Lecture Award, and the Distinguished Research in Public Administration Award. The Lifetime Award for Contributions to Public Administration Research of the Public Management Research Association is named in his honour as is the *Public Administration Times* Best Article Award.

Jeanette Hofmann is a researcher at the Centre for the Analysis of Risk and Regulation at the London School of Economics and the Social Science Research Centre Berlin. Her work focuses on global governance, particularly on the regulation of the internet, and on the transformation of intellectual property rights. She holds a PhD in Political Science from the Free University Berlin. In 2009, she co-edited *Governance als Prozess* (Governance as process), an interdisciplinary collection of contributions to governance research.

Christopher Hood has been Gladstone Professor of Government and Fellow of All Souls College Oxford since 2001 and was Director of the UK Economic and Social Research Council Public Services Research Programme from 2004 to 2010. Before that he held chairs at the London School of Economics and the University of Sydney, New South Wales, and was a lecturer at the University of Glasgow for fourteen years. His publications include *The Limits of Administration* (Wiley, 1976), *The Tools of Government* (Palgrave Macmillan, 1983, updated as *The Tools of Government in the Digital Age*, 2007, with Helen Margetts), *The Art of the State* (Oxford University Press, 1998 and 2000), and *The Politics of Public Service Bargains* (Oxford University Press, 2006, with Martin Lodge). His latest book, *The Blame Game*, is due to be published in 2010 by Princeton University Press.

Oliver James BA (Oxon.), MSc, PhD (LSE, London) is Professor of Politics, Department of Politics, University of Exeter, UK. His research interests include citizens and users' interaction with public services — especially satisfaction with public services and political participation, reform of public organization, and regulation of the public sector. Recent publications include (with G. A. Boyne, P. John, and N. Petrovsky), 'Democracy and Government Performance: Holding Incumbents Accountable in English Local Governments', *Journal of Politics*, 71/4 (2009) and 'Evaluating the Expectations Disconfirmation and Expectations Anchoring Approaches to Citizen Satisfaction with Local

Public Services', *Journal of Public Administration Research and Theory*, 19/1 (2009), 103–27.

Peter John is the Hallworth Chair of Governance in the School of Social Sciences at the University of Manchester, where he is co-director of the Institute for Political and Economic Governance. He is known for his work on public policy and urban politics, and he is author of *Analysing Public Policy* (1998) and *Local Governance in Western Europe* (2001). He is currently working on two main projects: one applying the experimental method to the study of civic engagement and collective action, the other mapping the decisions of British government since 1911.

Justin Keen has been Professor of Health Politics at the Institute of Health Sciences, University of Leeds, since 2001. His research interests include the politics of information technologies in healthcare, the coordination of care delivery, and health and social care policy. Since 2008 he has also been director of a National Institute for Health Research programme, whose purpose is to 'bridge the gap' between the worlds of research and clinical practice, with the aim of improving the use of research evidence in the NHS.

Tim Leunig is Reader in Economic History at the London School of Economics, and visiting International Fellow at the University of Lund. His academic publications include *Time is Money*, an analysis of the value of time savings generated by the invention and use of the train in the nineteenth century. As well as his academic work, he is the author of public policy papers for various think-tanks, and writes for the *Financial Times*, *Prospect Magazine*, and *Inside Housing*.

Helen Margetts is Professor of Society and the Internet at the Oxford Internet Institute (OII) and Fellow of Mansfield College, University of Oxford, before which she was Director of the School of Public Policy at UCL. A political scientist specializing in politics and government on the internet, she has authored and co-authored a wide range of books, articles, and policy reports, including (with Patrick Dunleavy and others) *Digital-Era Governance* (Oxford University Press, 2006); (with Christopher Hood) *Tools of Government in the Digital Age* (Palgrave Macmillan, 2007); and *Government on the Internet* (a joint LSE-OII study for the NAO, 2007). She is editor of the new journal *Policy and Internet* (Berkeley Electronic Press).

David Marsden is Professor of Industrial Relations at the London School of Economics and a Research Associate of the Centre for Economic

Performance. He did his doctoral work at the Laboratoire d'Économie et de Sociologie du Travail (CNRS), Aix-en-Provence, and developed a lasting interest in comparative analysis of labour markets and labour institutions. His books include *The End of Economic Man: Custom and Competition in Labour Markets* (Wheatsheaf, 1986), published also in French and Spanish, and *A Theory of Employment Systems: Micro-Foundations of Societal Diversity* (Oxford University Press, 1999), published also in Japanese. His recent research includes studies of pay and incentives in Britain and France, and a number studies on the effects of performance pay and of absenteeism in the British public services. He has also worked with the ILO and the OECD on public-service pay questions. He is currently working on a book on a comparative theory of human resource management.

Nicolai Petrovsky is an assistant professor in the Martin School of Public Policy and Administration at the University of Kentucky. His main research interests are the performance and responsiveness of public organizations in democratic countries. Before coming to Kentucky, Nicolai worked for three years at Cardiff University in Wales on a research project about leadership turnover and performance of English local government. Nicolai has published in journals including the *Journal of Politics*, *Public Administration*, and *Defence and Peace Economics*, and contributed a chapter to the Oxford University Press book *Public Service Improvement: Theories and Evidence*.

Devi Sridhar is a Postdoctoral Research Fellow at All Souls College Oxford, and Director of the Global Health project at the Global Economic Governance Programme, Department of Politics and International Relations, Oxford. She is also visiting faculty in health policy at the Public Health Foundation of India. She is the author of *The Battle Against Hunger: Choice, Circumstance and the World Bank* (Oxford University Press, 2008) and editor of *Inside Organisations: South Asian Case Studies* (Sage, 2008). She is currently working on a book on the politics of global health with a focus on public health policy in India.

Edmund C. Stazyk is an Assistant Professor with the Department of Public Administration and Policy in the School of Public Affairs at American University in Washington, DC. His research focuses on the application of organization theory and behaviour to public management, public administration theory, and human resources issues. More specifically, much of his research examines organizational and individual performance with an emphasis on bureaucracy and employee motivation—particularly public-service motivation. He also works in the areas of organizational design, ethics, and human capital.

Yorick Wilks is Professor of Artificial Intelligence at the University of Sheffield, and is also a Senior Research Fellow at the Oxford Internet Institute. He studied maths and philosophy at Cambridge, where he got his Ph.D. in 1968. He has published numerous articles and six books in artificial intelligence concerned with language processing, and has most recently edited *Close Engagements with Artificial Companions* (Benjamins, 2009). He is a Fellow of the American and European Associations for Artificial Intelligence, a member of the EPSRC College of Computing, a member of the UK Computing Research Council and on the boards of some fifteen AI-related journals. He was founding Coordinator of the EU 6th Framework integrated project COMPANIONS (4 years, 15 sites, 1.3m euro) on conversational assistants as personalized and permanent web interfaces.

I

Understanding Modernization's Paradoxes

1

The Drive to Modernize

A World of Surprises?

Christopher Hood, Helen Margetts, and Perri 6

The persons and objects of [the social world] must be weighed and counted, marked out and identified, subjected to the brightness of the public light, the better to be seen by the public eye. Only then could they be controlled and security made possible; and only then might the mad reign of contingency be brought to a close.

(Bahmueller 1981: 44)

So in all human affairs one notices, if one examines them closely, that it is impossible to remove one inconvenience without another emerging.

(Machiavelli 2003: I.6, p. 121)

Introduction

Why did the formidably clever people who developed the internet set it up in such a way that it would be so highly vulnerable to cybercrime? Why has fifty years of expensive railroad 'modernization' in Britain ended up with many passengers taking as long to reach their destinations as their grandparents or even great-grandparents would have done on the same journeys? Why do pay-for-performance schemes invented by highly quali-fied economists to improve Civil Service management so often end up by demotivating the workers for whom they were meant to provide incen-tives? Why do state-of-the-art nutrition programmes devised by the world's brightest scientists and development economists fail to take account of elementary features of how life is actually lived in developing countries?

In short, how is it that, after two centuries or so of modern social science that might have been expected to advance the age of reason by making the social world more knowable (as the first epigraph promised), do surprise and paradox still so commonly attend interventions in social affairs? Is there even something about 'modernization' in some sense that produces a particular type of surprise or paradox, as some have claimed? Or do those continuing surprises and paradoxes suggest that modernity (whatever that much-used word means) makes little difference to human ability to predict and control the social world? And how precisely do those surprises and paradoxes come about? Those are the questions this book aims to explore.

Obviously, everything turns on what exactly is meant by the siren terms 'modernization', 'surprise', and 'unintended consequence'. The next two chapters delve into those issues, before we go into eight cases of public policy initiatives and practices that can be considered 'modern' in some sense, and explore what unintended or unanticipated effects — happy or otherwise — they produced. Those cases include efforts to modernize railroads, to introduce more effective ways of rewarding public servants, to rank and rate municipal governments and universities to put more pressure on them to perform effectively, to relieve poverty in developing countries by combining modern nutrition science with development economics, and three developments and applications of modern information technology — all eminently rational, serious, up-to-date practices and policies. As we shall see, one of those applications can be interpreted in some senses as having done more or less 'what it said on the tin' (in the well-known words of the Ronseal advertisement) and we shall go into why and how that seems to have happened, but all the other seven cases produced results that were unintended or unanticipated in some way for at least some of the key actors involved.

Why Did We Write this Book?

We wanted to write about the surprises, paradoxes and unintended effects of policies or practices that can be considered 'modern' for at least three reasons. One is simply the abiding fascination of any tale that involves surprise for some or all of the characters involved, when something turns out differently from what they anticipated or intended. And that perhaps applies particularly when the tale involves apparent blind spots on the part of clever people or powerful corporations doing things that seemed like a good idea at the time, or conversely involves developments that were far more successful than anyone expected.

That theme is probably as old as human story-telling, and it draws poets and novelists as well as historians and social scientists. There is something deeply intriguing in looking in retrospect at 'yesterday's tomorrows' — futures that never quite arrived, such as the early-twentieth-century vision of future improvements in office productivity to be gained from training workers to write with both hands at once, as students are taught to play the piano, or of the mid-twentieth-century expectation that nuclear power would produce electricity so cheap that it would hardly be worth charging for it. How could anyone have believed *that*? And such retrospection has a particular hold over our attention when the characters involved can be seen — or see themselves — as 'moderns', with powers to predict and control the world that are presumed to be far superior to those of the unenlightened past. So it is not surprising that such turns of events have been much written about, in well-known works such as Pat Moynihan's (1969) *Maximum Feasible Misunderstanding*, David Halberstam's (1972) *The Best and the Brightest*, and James Scott's (1998) *Seeing like a State*, to name only three classic analyses from the last forty years or so. How do organizations that are supposed to be functional embodiments of modern science or business practice come to produce outcomes that are so far from what was apparently anticipated or intended?

However, a second reason for writing this book is some puzzlement about some of the standard answers to that question. As we shall see in the next two chapters, there are vast literatures, almost too voluminous to review, on the subject of 'modernity' and 'unintended consequences', and even some analyses about the sort of unanticipated or unintended consequences that go along with modernity. One of the best known examples is the work of James Scott (1998), mentioned above, who argues that what he calls 'high-modernist' state-planning schemes commonly go awry because their features of centralism and standardization tend to ignore or discount practical, tacit, locally specific knowledge in favour of the sort of general and theoretical knowledge that central managers have. He introduces his book with the dramatic case of those eighteenth-century German scientific foresters, with undoubtedly enlightened and highly prescient notions of how to calculate 'sustainable yield', who unintentionally killed the forests they were trying to manage. Why? Because their efforts to render the forests easily countable (by growing trees in serried ranks without the statistical ambiguities of disorderly clusters or fallen trees among the living ones) turned out to destroy the very ecosystem that is needed for healthy forest growth, in a classic example of what Sam Sieber (1981) calls 'functional disruption'.

The former USSR has also provided rich material for this sort of analysis, for example in the 1986 meltdown of the Chernobyl No. 4 nuclear reactor — ironically caused by a safety test that went disastrously wrong — that has been linked by writers like Piers Paul Read (1993: 455) to the meltdown of the Soviet state itself, founded as it was on a belief in social salvation through science and engineering (physical and social) rather than outdated religion or other traditional ideas. The so-called 'New Public Management' changes of the 1980s and 1990s — ostensibly designed to improve the performance of traditional public bureaucracies by the appliance of up-to-date managerial ideas — have also subjected to a similar type of analysis, with several analyses of the paradoxes and unintended effects that can be bound up in such changes (for instance Maor 1999; Hesse et al. 2003; Hood and Peters 2004).

These accounts have much to offer in helping us to understand how apparently well-planned, rational and 'evidence-based' projects can lead to surprising results. Yet these studies tend to focus on the negative results and the failures (perhaps because negativity bias means humans give more attention to such information) rather than on the successes or on the positive or happy surprises that can arise from attempts to 'modernize'. Many such studies tend to select on the dependent variable, making it hard to assess what role 'modernity' (which as we shall see in the next section is a term that means different things to different people) plays in such outcomes. Moreover, they leave open the question as to whether the disappointing surprises identified by Scott and others really stem from modernity as such or from a failure to be *sufficiently* modern. But the latter issue is central to what-to-do debates about such outcomes: is the answer to abandon 'modernity' in some respects, or to apply a better or developed form of it?

Our third reason for writing the book is that there is a gap that needs to be filled between detailed single-case studies of particular events or interventions and the broad generalizations of much of the writing about modernity and unintended consequences. What we therefore aim to do in this book is to combine a critical analysis of the notions of modernity and unintended consequences with a set of specimen examples taken from different public service domains — railroads, health, education, crime, development, municipal services, Civil Service management, information technology. Of course, that range of specimens cannot be seen as a statistically representative sample in any sense. Therefore, its usefulness as a test of theory can only lie in disconfirmation and a limited exercise in qualitative comparative analysis. But it is nevertheless sufficient to allow us to go beyond the idiosyncrasies of a single instance, to compare across different episodes and cases, and to go deeper than the use of brief examples typically allows. So it enables us to develop theory and to explore the sorts of mechanisms that operate between intention and outcome — how it is that those surprises come about.

To do so, we first need to grapple with the beguiling language of 'modernity' and 'unintended consequences', both of which turn out to be surprisingly fuzzy and slippery. What exactly are 'modernity' and 'modernization'? Jean Monnet (1978: 259) famously observed that 'modernization is not a state of affairs but a state of mind'. So are these terms anything more than a rhetorical claim to be up-to-date and part of some wave of the future? Do they have specific connotations that do not necessarily go with the here and now, such as a rejection of traditional religion or a preoccupation with quantification (as in the epigraph, describing Jeremy Bentham's eighteenth-century vision of social science)? And if modernity is any more than a synonym for 'current', are there characteristic types of paradox or unintended effects that go with it, or are such things to be seen as universals across space and time? Further, as we shall see in Chapter 3, there are perplexing issues of method, concerning matters such as what we take to be threshold conditions of 'surprise' and whether it is ever — or at least normally — possible to say exactly who intended or anticipated what in any moderately complex institutional context.

Modern, Modernity, Modernism, and Modernization

Because we are concerned with paradoxes of modern public policy initiatives and reforms, the terms 'modern', 'paradox', and 'public policy' recur throughout the book. The first two will be expounded at greater length in subsequent chapters but some of the issues at stake merit some discussion at the outset.

The notion of 'modernization' is a central but perplexing issue in social science and history, as is discussed in the next chapter by Helen Margetts. The dictionary definition of the adjective 'modern' is 'of or pertaining to present or recent times'. According to Jürgen Habermas, the word in its Latin form 'modernus', which means 'just now', was used for the first time in the late fifth century 'to distinguish the present, which had become officially Christian, from the Roman and pagan past' (Habermas 1985: 3). It seems to have come as a loan-word into European languages from the sixteenth century. Its first appearance in English for which a written record survives came in 1500, when it was used to mark the contemporary period off from medieval and ancient times. Drawing on Robert Merton, Ralf Dahrendorf (1988: p. xiii) traced an influential early use of the abstract noun in English to George Hakewill in 1627: 'Yea, but I vilifie the present times, you say, whiles I expect a more flourishing state to succeed: bee it so, yet this is not to vilifie modernitie, as you pretend.' In the form of a noun, the word was central to an intellectual debate (*la querelle des anciens et des modernes*) in France in the late seventeenth century, where the 'moderns' were associated with a belief in the possibility of literary progress beyond the imitation of the great writers of antiquity (DeJean 1997). The word does not seem to have emerged into German until the early eighteenth century and a few European languages (such as Gaelic) even today have not imported the Latin word to supplement their indigenous terms for 'new'.

The words 'modern', 'modernity', 'modernization', and 'modernism' are often used almost interchangeably, but can have different meanings to different observers. Historians tend to use the word in its adjectival form 'modern' rather than its variants, and use it to identify a specific period in time from 1500, with 'early modern' conventionally denoting a period from around 1500 to 1800 and 'modern' a period starting sometime during the eighteenth century. The latter term is thus used to indicate the 'age of Enlightenment' and critical ideas, a move from religious to secular values, a shift away from medieval modes of political and economic organization and the decline of Christian theocracy, feudalism, and serfdom. Although it has often been criticized,[1] that conventional periodization remains in common use among historians, and until recently philosophers used to be taught that 'modern philosophy' began with Descartes.

By contrast with the adjective, the nouns 'modernity' and 'modernism' seem now most commonly to be applied in English to a later period than that conventionally denoted for historians by the word 'modern'. Those nouns seem to be normally applied to nineteenth- or twentieth-century cultural, intellectual, or sociological developments, although the term modernism was evidently in use as far back as the eighteenth century according to Samuel Johnson's famous dictionary. There are also debates, into which we will not enter here, on the precise connotations of these nouns as applied to the visual arts. Some present-day sociologists, notably Anthony Giddens (1990), Ulrich Beck (1992), and Bruno Latour (1993), have used the noun not to refer to a specific time period (as with the historians' conventional usage) but to an epoch or cultural milieu

---

[1] For instance Jürgen Habermas (1985: 4) claims, 'People considered themselves modern during the period of Charles the Great in the 12th century as well as in France of the late 17th century ... the term "modern" appeared and reappeared exactly during those periods in Europe when the consciousness of a new epoch formed itself through a renewed relationship to the ancients.'

'conceived of as novel and different from, and possibly better than, the present and the past' (Therborn 2000).

The word used as a verb, 'to modernize', and its associated verbal noun 'modernization', seems to be even more theoretically and normatively loaded than either the noun or the adjective. Perhaps that is because the verb is usually transitive[2] (*x* modernizes *y*). Some readers will no doubt have had experience of being 'modernized', in the sense of being subjected to changes in work practice, physical structures, or organizational routines that are described by their promoters by that verb. And perhaps it is because the use of the verb is so often freighted with presumptions of progress and one-way social development (a 'process of long-range cultural change accepted by members of the changing society as beneficial, inevitable, or, on balance desirable' in the words of Ward and Rustow 1964: 3). The word has been in use in English at least since the mid-eighteenth century, meaning 'to adapt to the requirements of modern times; make modern'. The verbal noun 'modernization' seems to be rarely applied to art (Therborn 2000: 54), but figures much larger in sociology. Its German form *modernisierung* was a central concept for nineteenth-century German sociologists such as Karl Marx, Max Weber, and Ferdinand Tönnies, all of whom saw modernization as a specific type of social change brought about by industrialization.

Indeed, many of the classic nineteenth-century sociologists and political economists had some sort of vision of modernity and modernization as connoting a fundamentally different form of social organization from what had gone before, whether that involved a new proletarian working class rather than the peasants and artisans of an earlier age (Marx), or a new form of bureaucracy as a central way of organizing society and government (Weber). Émile Durkheim is also often seen as preoccupied with social modernization, particularly in his work on *The Division of Labour in Society*, although he made very sparing use of the words 'modern' and 'modernity' even in the chapters on the development of what he called organic solidarity (book 1). For Simmel, modernity was characterized by a tragic and irresolvable conflict between aspirations and established forms, never adequately settled by resort to purely instrumental practices (Simmel 1955; Levine 1971: 375–93). The term continues to fascinate sociologists up to

---

[2] Some sociological writing uses the verbal noun to denote a grand macro-social process without a single animating agent, but that ultimately implies a process of agency involving the transitive use of the verb: 'Modernization, whatever else it might mean, is change brought about by active agents affecting other people and social institutions, be they former "elites", "entrepreneurs", or "innovators" of variable background' (Therborn 2000: 59).

the present day: for instance, Anthony Giddens (1998: 15) uses it to denote a continual process that extends to the current moment ('an historical condition of difference; in one way or another displacement of everything that has gone before') and sees a major shift from what he calls 'social modernization' to 'reflexive modernization'.

But all these ideas of modern, modernity, and modernization are fraught with problems. The various definitions of social modernization do not add up to a single well-founded concept. The notion of fundamental difference from earlier societies is historically problematic (as shown by Creel's (1964) argument that all the features Max Weber claimed to be associated with modern bureaucracy could be identified in Han China 2000 years ago). Giddens's claim that modernization involves 'displacement of everything that has gone before' and 'de-traditionalisation' (Heelas *et al.* 1996) sits uncomfortably with Hobsbawm and Ranger's (1983: 4) observation that tradition as a self-conscious, managed, and socially discrete practice is something that has probably increased in importance in recent times rather than diminishing. The conception of modernization as a continual process with no terminus, advanced by Giddens and some other contemporary sociologists, contrasts with the view that modernism or modernity has some end point. Examples of scholars who take the latter position include Jürgen Habermas (1985: 6) who sees an end point but does not specify it, cryptically claiming that 'Modernism is dominant but dead', and the military scholar Mary Kaldor (2001), who describes the Cold War as 'the final stage of what has come to be known as modernity' — which presumably implies that modernity came to an end in the last decade of the twentieth century.

Indeed, the development of the idea of 'post modernity' (which dates back at least to Frederico de Onis's *Antologia de la poesia española e hispanoamericana* of 1932, according to Hassan 1987: 85 and then developing much more widely in the 1930s and 1940s) has added to the conceptual confusion. For those who profess to be postmodernists, 'Modernization is not the final stage in history' (Inglehart 1997: 6), and indeed the rise of advanced industrial society has led to another fundamentally different shift in basic values where 'postmodern values become prevalent, bringing a variety of societal changes' (ibid.). But it is not very clear what these postmodern values might be (for Ingehart they include equal rights for women and democratic political institutions). Writers such as Giddens (1990: 45–6) deny the usefulness of the concept outside the arts: 'Postmodernism if it means anything is best kept to refer to styles or movements within literature, painting, the plastic arts, and architecture. It concerns aspects of *aesthetic reflection* upon the nature of modernity.'

Postmodernism has been debated as an academic approach to public administration (for example by Rod Rhodes 1997) and for public administration postmodernists such as Peter Bogason (2004: 236), postmodernism connotes conditions of fragmentation, chaos, spontaneity, and adhocracy in contrast to the planning, reason, and global visions said to be associated with modernity. But there does not seem to be any consensus on what postmodern society might look like, what postmodern values might be, or how postmodernization as a social process might work. And when it comes to public policy and public service reforms, even the exponents of post-modern public administration tend to concede that those reforms, for better or worse, seem to be animated in practice by some sort of modernist vision, even if postmodernism might be considered to be a better way of characterizing present-day developments in the field.

So is modernization, the term we are using in this book, simply a syno-nym for what was cutting edge up to a century or so ago, but is now old-fashioned, like steam engines? Or does it have a different analytical mean-ing? We use the term here in two senses. One, the weak sense, reflects the position of those languages that have not imported the Latin word into their vocabulary, and takes 'modern' as a synonym for 'current' or 'contem-porary'. All of the cases we are concerned with in this book can be consid-ered 'modern' in that loose and undemanding sense — they were all considered or claimed to be shiny, up-to-date, and state-of the art in some way at the time when they were introduced.

But we also use the term in a more specific sense developed by Helen Margetts in the next chapter, which is distinct from simply what is current and which also seems to apply to all the cases considered here. Dislocating modernization from time and other developments specific to the present day, Margetts argues that if modernization means anything more than that in public policy, much of it comes down to three basic elements, which she defines as processes aimed at (i) economic efficiency and individual incen-tivization, (ii) integration, interconnectedness standardization and forma-lization, and (iii) specialization, expertise, scientific advancement, and technological innovation. All of the cases considered here fit that more specific definition of modernization as well, in that they all involve at least one of those elements, or 'pillars' as Margetts calls them. And that, as we shall see later, allows us to use the cases to explore tensions between these different elements of modernization and trace the way that they combine in shaping policy outcomes.

11

Unintended Effects, Paradoxes, and Public Policy

The notion of unintended effects of human action is something that has fascinated historians at least since the days of Thucydides. The unintended self-destructive effects of the pursuit of luxury preoccupied Ibn Khaldûn (1967: 285–9) and the notion of unanticipated consequences became an important theme in social science from its outset. To take two well-known early examples, in the eighteenth-century Scottish Enlightenment Adam Smith pointed to social benefits that could unintentionally result from individual profit-seeking behaviour and David Hume (in his *A Treatise of Human Nature*) interpreted institutions such as justice as the unintended consequence of individual human actions.

But Perri 6 points out some of the complexities of this idea in Chapter 3. Something can be anticipated without being intended (as in the case of pre-nuptial agreements providing for the distribution of property in the event of the marriage breaking down), and in some cases vice versa. The threshold conditions of what is to count as unanticipated or unintended raise some perplexing issues, for example when decision-makers are weighing up issues of risk. If thirty years ago I had estimated the probability of the collapse of the Soviet Union within ten years at 0.001, should that be counted as a lack of anticipation, or just a less than perfect risk judgement? What if I had put it at 0.4? And how should my lack of anticipation be compared with that of someone who made no probability assessment at all and for whom the event was an 'unknown unknown'?

Furthermore, the methodological issues of how we can ever firmly establish intention or anticipation in retrospect are daunting too. In their own lives, most readers will know individuals who in retrospect profess not to have been surprised by turns of events that the rest of us never expected. And at a more institutional level, careful forensic research often if not invariably reveals a range of players with different anticipations and intentions, raising issues about whose are the views that are to count most heavily when we decide whether or not the issue concerned is to be counted as a case of unintended consequences. Moreover, the various different mechanisms or pathways that can produce unintended or unanticipated effects — many of them (such as self-fulfilling or self-defeating prophecy) noticed by writers such as Robert Merton (1936) and Sam Sieber (1981) — suggest that we need to be cautious about positing any single cause or pathway of unintended or unanticipated effects in public policy. In media commentary and common speech we often hear of 'the law of unintended effects', but as we shall see, the cases we examine here show that the definite article in its singular form does not seem appropriate. Nor is it obvious that causation of unintended consequences is particularly lawlike.

Closely related to, but not the same as, the notion of unintended or unanticipated effects are a number of other terms such as irony, paradox, and surprise. Irony, in that common meaning of the word that denotes an incongruity between what might be expected and what actually occurs, for example when revolutionaries adopt and develop the very practices they denounced in the previous regime (as in Tocqueville's (1949) famous characterization of what the French Revolution produced in the extension of government bureaucracy), is almost a synonym for the notion of unintended or unanticipated consequences, and throws up the same sort of analytic problems. 'Paradox' is a term of art for logicians, for whom it strictly means any plausibly true statement that entails a contradiction (such as 'I always lie'), and more broadly in its dictionary definition denotes an apparent contradiction that may nevertheless be reconciled, as in a puzzle or a riddle such as 'the son on the roost and the father unborn'.[3] But we use the term here in a looser sense to denote something that goes contrary to opinion or expectation, and thus is closer to the notion of surprise, happy or otherwise.

We are concerned here with a particular group of paradoxes (in that loose sense) that arise from initiatives and practices that involve 'modernization' in the two senses discussed earlier. As we have already noted, we are by no means the first to explore that issue. Indeed, many of the classical writers on modernization who were referred to in the previous section pointed out some of the surprises and unintended effects that went along with the process. For instance, Max Weber thought modernization produced an 'iron cage' or shell (*stahlhartes Gehäuse*) that could trap individuals in an over-bureaucratized social order (see Hamilton 1991: 294). Karl Marx thought the development of modern capitalism was a process full of surprises and contradictions. Georg Simmel declared that the modern cultural struggle against social forms was doomed to fail yet also destined to persist (Levine 1971: 392–3). To the extent that his (originally 1893) *Division of Labour in Society* can be interpreted as an account of a shift to 'modernity' (which is debatable: see Miller 1996), Émile Durkheim stressed that the

---

[3] A Gaelic riddle literally meaning the smoke of a fire that has not yet kindled and more generally used to denote any enterprise that is loudly heralded before it has come properly into existence.

shift to organic solidarity exhibited as many deformations as segmentary organization and spent much of his life analysing the corrosive effects of organic solidarity such as *anomie* and other pathologies associated with the growth of individualism. Many later writers, from James Scott to those who adopt a 'postmodern' view of public administration, as noted earlier, have had much to say about the way that projects carried out in the name of modernization can lead to disappointment, deterioration, and uncertainty, contrary to what their proponents expected or anticipated. But what we will show in the cases that follow is that the effects of modernizing reforms are not always negative, that surprise does not always come in the same form, and that when we look at modernization as something involving the three basic elements identified by Helen Margetts, those elements can sometimes reinforce and sometimes clash with one another.

Finally, we are concerned here with modernizing reforms and initiatives that relate to public services in some way, rather than with other aspects of human activity. Not all of the initiatives we are concerned with here come from government bodies with the special legal powers of the state at their disposal — one of our cases consists of a ranking of US universities by a newspaper. Some of the internet developments we describe are only loosely connected with government in a narrow sense, and indeed some of the early developers of the internet evidently saw the new medium as a sort of *imperium in imperio*, providing a common social space that would or should be somehow beyond the reach of government. But they all comprise efforts to change the way that public or common services are provided or operate, using one or more of the three basic elements of modernization that Helen Margetts identifies in the next chapter.

It may be that modernizing reforms that apply to public services have features that are not shared with other manifestations of modernity and modernization that were discussed earlier, for example in art and literature. We do not explore that issue here (to do so would require a detailed comparison of public policy cases with instances of development in the visual arts, music, dance, or architecture). But perhaps it may be that the 'modernist project', if we can still call it that, is more tenacious in public services and public policy than it is in some other parts of life. In modern art perhaps, the spirit of innovation and experimentation that defined the early days of modernization has been easier to keep alive. But it does seem that initiatives and reforms applied to public policy often tend to be rebadged or repackaged versions of the same basic drive to subject common or public services to the sort of processes signified by the first epigraph to this chapter. As with the old joke that, whoever you vote for, the government always gets in, many public service initiatives and reforms seem to comprise either variations on a theme (just as some management scholars, such as Huczynski 1993, see apparently different management fads as different ways of packaging the basic ideas of 'scientific management' a century or so ago) or attempts to drive each of the elements of modernization identified by Margetts to ever greater heights. Instances of the latter include attempts at ever more advanced applications of information technology, just as Tocqueville saw the French revolutionaries extending and refining the tools of the Bourbon bureaucracy.

So What? What can we Learn from Examining Paradoxes of Modernization in Public Services?

Observing how modern initiatives and practices play out in public services has its own intrinsic fascination, as has already been noted. But it also leads to at least three related conclusions that emerge from the next two chapters and will be discussed further in the final chapter.

First, what even a limited number of cases, such as those investigated in this book, shows, is that there is no such thing as a single 'law of unintended consequences' when modernity in some form meets public services, commonly invoked though that idea is. Not all policies and practices seem to produce such consequences to the same extent or by the same route. Nor do all unintended consequences take the form of unpleasant or negative effects. Some arrive as happy surprises.

However, one common thread running through the three elements of modernization identified by Helen Margetts in the next chapter is that of an aspiration to more effective control of social outcomes (by interventions that aim to step up integration, efficiency, and scientific advance), as highlighted in the first epigraph to this chapter. And to the extent that efforts at increased control are what modernization initiatives embody, the theory of control systems (cybernetics) may give us a clue to how and why surprises develop. Control is conventionally defined as the ability to keep the state of some system within some specified sub-set of all its possible states — for instance, keeping a car somewhere on the road instead of upside down in a ditch. The science of cybernetics began to develop some seven decades ago as an attempt to formulate general propositions about control (see Wiener 1948) and more than fifty years ago, one of the most distinguished cybernetic scientists, Ross Ashby (1956) formulated its perhaps most important discovery as the 'law of requisite variety': The law states that control is only

15

possible if the variety (number of possible states) of a controlling agent matches that of the subject of control — meaning for example that if you want to control the behaviour of eleven people in red jerseys you will need at least the same number of people in green jerseys (see Beer 1966). Much of cybernetic theory has been concerned with how such requisite variety can be achieved in complex social situations, and the idea has been applied by social scientists to the design of bureaucracies (see for instance Dunsire 1978) and of institutions more broadly (such as Schwarz and Thompson 1990). Applied to attempts to intervene in public affairs using elements of modernization as defined by Margetts, the requisite variety condition implies that any such initiative has to be able to incorporate a sufficiently broad range of elements of modernization to avoid the surprises that are likely to arise from relying on only some of them, and that it has to be able to relate to a sufficiently broad range of social behaviours and attitudes to match the variety of the social world at which it is aimed. We shall return to this 'requisite variety' idea at the end of the book.

A second conclusion is that applications of high-technology are associated with unintended consequences in several of the cases we relate here and that chimes with a large body of writing about the way that new technologies produce such effects, such as Edward Tenner's (1996) *Why Things Bite Back* and James Chiles's (2001) *Inviting Disaster*. But while gripping tales can be told by such best-selling authors about the negative unintended effects of new technology, some big technological developments can produce happy surprises to many people, as our case of the World Wide Web suggests. Nor does it necessarily seem to take a hi-tech project to produce positive or negative surprises.

Third, as the cases we describe show, policies or practices that can be considered 'modern' can produce unintended or unanticipated consequences through a number of characteristic pathways, not a single one. Indeed, the main value of looking across a range of cases such as those that follow is that it leads us beyond the obvious and trite conclusion that 'the best laid schemes . . . gang aft agley' (go often askew)[4] to greater understanding of the various different ways in which that can happen.

---

[4] In the oft-quoted words of the penultimate verse of Robert Burns's poem *To a Mouse: On Turning Her Up in Her Nest with the Plough* (Nov. 1785).

2

Modernization Dreams and Public Policy Reform

Helen Margetts

As noted in the previous chapter, from the sixteenth century onwards, variants on the word 'modern' have been scattered liberally across writing, thought, and speech about economy, state, and society. This chapter considers the history of the concept of modernization and the role it has played in public policy reform. The aim is to disentangle from a huge body of thought (there are 300,000 articles and books on Google scholar with the word 'modern' or one of its variants in the title) the key 'pillars' of modernization that would allow us to define a public policy reform as 'modernizing'. Such a definition allows us to characterize our cases in modernization terms, setting up a number of possible sources of the paradoxes discussed. The discussion thereby contextualizes approaches to public policy reform within more general intellectual and social trends. Modernization is an implicit theme of much of public administration and holds attractions for policy-makers and academic analysts alike, yet rarely is it discussed explicitly in relation to public policy reform.

Many bold claims have been made for modernization. Empirically, it has been claimed as a profound social change sweeping across the world over a period of around 300 to 500 years, as well as a snapshot characterization of the present time. Normatively, it has been prescribed as a formula for societal and state development for almost every country in the world at one time or another. Rhetorically, it has been used as a justification for profound policy changes at all levels of government, from Soviet collectivism to public transport systems.

Modernization has received a great deal of theoretical social science attention. The 'theory of modernization' or the 'modernization school' appeared in the response of American political elites and intellectuals to the post-Second World War era (Tipps 1973) and 'contrasted sharply with the theories of historical evolution and social change which prevailed in Western thought during the 1920s and 1930s' (Huntington 1971: 290), which emphasized a pessimistic view of the future of society, disintegration, and cyclism in human affairs. As with the other variants on 'modern' discussed in the Introduction, modernization analysis is generally applied to the large-scale historical change occurring from the seventeenth to nineteenth centuries in Western Europe, spreading to North America (Parsons 1971), with some arguing it starting earlier, around 1500 (Rustow 1964), or later in the eighteenth century (Bendix 1977) and others (such as Huntington) indicating quite specific time periods for different countries. These early modernization theorists identified industrialization, secularization, urbanization, and democratization as the key elements of change. They associated modernization with ideas of progress and of making the social world more intelligible, suggesting a break with 'traditional' ways of doing things and the end of the reign of contingency; 'the essential difference between modern and traditional society, most theorists of modernization contend, lies in the greater control which modern man has over his natural and social environment' (Huntington 1971: 286). Perhaps more than the other variants on modern, modernization is often viewed as a continual process and therefore can be considered, as with modernity, to have no end point, unless it is a transition to 'postmodernization'.

The scope of this chapter, in contrast, is both modest and ambitious. It does not attempt to verify the validity of the claims made for modernization, nor to develop the 'theory of modernization', but rather to discern from them analytically some meaning of the word that may be used to identify characteristics of a modernization reform, characteristics that might prove to be associated with surprise, disappointment, and other unintended or unanticipated consequences. For 'reform', defined here as 'an improvement or change for the better', we take the literal dictionary definition in order to include policy 'actions' or changes which were not intended, or at least not intended to alter the institutions or practices which they did eventually change. The search for a definition of modernization that might be applied to public policy reform is at the same time ambitious, in that none of the vast array of previous work on modernization appears to have produced it.

Proponents and scholars of modernization make three distinct claims. First, they locate modernization as an empirical development, in different times in different places, but during some period from the sixteenth century. Second, modernization is presented as a normative prescription for development of either state or society. And third, modernization has been used by some political leaders or public policy reformers as a justification for some reform or revolution. Likewise, critics of modernization turn to each of these claims; some take issue with modernization as an actual empirical development, in particular arguing over the time period and whether the process is still continuing. Some question the normative prescription, arguing that it imposes Western values on the developing world, for example. Third, some question the rhetoric of reform, arguing that reforms carried out in the name of modernization have little in common either with each other or the rhetoric used to justify them. Proponents and critics of modernization in all these categories are discussed in this chapter.

Politicians and policy-makers using the rhetoric of modernization to justify certain types of reform (arguably the concept's most influential role) are likely to borrow from across the full spectrum of modernization writing, and so are discussed in the first section below. The next section draws out from the most basic and earliest discussions of the term 'modernization' three possible candidates for the characteristics or 'pillars' of modernization reform: efficiency, integration, and specialization. The next three sections look at the work of analysts, proponents, and critics of three broad types of modernization: social modernization emerging from societal trends, such as changes in belief and value systems; state-centred modernization, where the state drives social change; and modernization of the state itself, geared at creating a more efficient and productive state. The final section considers whether the three characteristics of modernization (efficiency, integration, and specialization) have survived the analysis and how they might be used to classify a reform as 'modernizing' and be identified as possible sources of 'paradoxes of modernization' discussed in this book.

The Attractions of Modernization for Policy-Makers

Modernization (and all its variants) have at various times held huge attraction for policy-makers. Although not always explicit, in terms of using the word 'modernization', other synonymous and associated words lend themselves readily to the promises of politicians, particularly the words 'new', 'change', 'revolution', or 'transformation'. Cynics would say that these images of modernization are most often used by politicians as a justification for political actions that they wanted to carry out anyway. A more sympathetic view would be that at times politicians have believed in their own rhetoric, seeing modernization as holding the key to certain types of societal improvement. Either way, through the rhetoric of modernizing policy-makers, modernization can become a self-fulfilling prophecy. If reforms are carried out in the name of modernization, they tend to get categorized as such retrospectively by commentators and scholars. This link between reform rhetoric and reform is a two-way process, because there is a long tradition of policy-makers taking advice from and using the language of modernization theorists, particularly during the last fifty years.[1]

Machiavelli (1469–1527), argued by some to be the founder of modern political thought (Strauss 1995), was perhaps the first thinker to make modernization[2] sound attractive to policy-makers, with his belief of the importance of human agency (*virtu*) in political affairs and his instruction book for would-be political rulers, *Il Principe*. The book argued for innovation rather than conservatism, rejecting the authority of divine and natural right, and discussed how knowledge can be exploited to bring greater order into human affairs. The book makes claims about the efficient administration of monarchies, promoting the benefits of change and attempts to make progress in technology, economics, and military power.

Various reforms from the sixteenth century onwards can be characterized as modernization, although the word was not used explicitly. Peter the Great, for example, famously 'immersed himself in the problems of modern shipbuilding' in the late seventeenth century (Cracraft 2003: 81) and carried out a 'Petrine revolution in naval architecture', bringing Dutch shipwrights from Archangel and laying down the foundations of the Russian navy. Although it is clearly possible to characterize such moves as 'modernizing', it is only during the 'later modern era' that modernization makes an explicit appearance in the rhetoric of policy-makers. In Britain in the late nineteenth century, the 'New Liberalism' ideas of T. H. Green, L. T. Hobhouse, and J. A. Hobson included an emphasis on harmony rather than class or sectional conflict; a view of capitalism as a hindrance to freedom when unrestricted; and a belief in change and social reform in order to improve the lot of everyone, not just the well off or the working class. These ideas shaped reforms such as non-contributory old age pensions and

---

[1] During this time of course, 'non-modernizing' or even 'anti-modernizing' rhetoric has also been attractive to politicians, as in the appeal to a return to traditional values and the glory of the imperial past.

[2] Machiavelli does not appear to have used the word 'modernization' or 'modern', but does discuss 'new forms of government' and 'transitions' to 'liberty' and makes an argument for adapting oneself to the times.

the National Insurance Act of 1911 and progressive income taxation in the 'People's Budget' of 1909 through the premierships of Asquith and Churchill. In other parts of Europe, 'new liberals' established social reform organizations such as the Social Policy Association (1873). In France, radical politicians such as Bourgeois were influenced by Durkheim in arguing that the greater division of labour was leading to a more complex interdependence, requiring the removal of barriers to social mobility. Later in the USA, the ideas of John Dewey, himself influenced by Hobhouse, were incorporated in Roosevelt's New Deal.

Modernization as a justification for policy reform is particularly observable in the USA, the country itself deemed by some proponents of modernization to define the modern world. Many US presidents have been associated with the US progressive movement, 'the political movement that addresses ideas, impulses and issues stemming from the modernization of American society' (Harriby 1999), which claims that particular strides towards progressivism were made under Theodore Roosevelt, William H. Taft, Woodrow Wilson, Franklin Delano Roosevelt, and Lyndon Baines Johnson.[3] However, we can only expect explicit justifications through 'modernization' and links between theory and practice from the 1950s and 1960s, when modernization was developed as a concept and theory. In the 1960 US presidential campaign, Kennedy appeared inspired by modernization when he spoke of a 'New Frontier' of 'unfulfilled hopes and dreams, a frontier of unknown opportunities and beliefs in peril. Beyond that frontier are uncharted areas of science and space, unsolved problems of peace and war, unconquered problems of ignorance and prejudice, unanswered questions of poverty and surplus.' US foreign policy (in Vietnam and Latin America for example) was publicly justified in terms of modernization, in ways that Latham (2000: 5) argued 'articulated a common collection of assumptions about the nature of American society and its ability to transform a world perceived as both materially and culturally deficient'. Indeed, Latham pointed to the pervasiveness of modernization theories in the decision-making processes of the early 1960s, as a 'cognitive framework' through which policy elites interpreted their actions and the place of the USA in the world.

At a similar time, across the Atlantic in the UK, both Labour and Conservative governments claimed the mantle of modernization for public policy reform. In a Party Conference speech in 1963 the Labour prime minister

---

[3] These presidents are 'claimed' by the progressive movement itself, although some of them, notably Roosevelt and Johnson, were at times dismissive of the legacy of the progressive era.

Harold Wilson spoke of the technological revolution (in a way that evoked the industrial revolution if not modernization specifically) as a way to move to a 'new Britain' which, 'forged in the white heat of this revolution will be no place for restrictive practices or for outdated methods on either side of industry...those charged with the control of our affairs must be ready to think and to speak in the language of our scientific age' (Williams, 2009: 91). This technological revolution would be furthered by 'refashioning Whitehall into an instrument for stimulating economic growth based on applied science [a new Department of Economic Affairs buttressed by a new Ministry of Technology], all staffed by a new breed of gritty, better-trained production- and management-minded officials that could rise in a Civil Service open to all the talents' (Hennessy 2001: 293). Wilson 'pilloried the Conservatives as reactionary incompetents... incapable of grasping the significance of "science"' (Williams 2009: 89)[4] and emphasized a break with class structures and privilege; 'we are more interested in the monthly trade returns than in Debrett... more concerned with modernizing the machinery of government... than in altering the layout of Burke's Landed Gentry' (Hennessy 2001: 304).

Modernization was promoted particularly enthusiastically and even explicitly by political leaders on both sides of the Atlantic in the 1990s; speeches were peppered with the words 'new', 'modern', and dazzling images of the twenty-first century and a decisive break with the past. In the USA, President Clinton proclaimed, 'Now we work to modernize government...so that again it is a force for progress and freedom in the new era' (speech at the seventy-fifth anniversary of *Time* magazine, 3 Mar. 1999). His vice-president Al Gore launched a programme to 'reinvent government', stating 'It is time to get rid of the old way of managing the federal government... What's needed instead is an entirely new model of leadership based on clear sets of principles, flexibility, innovation, accountability and customer service.' In the UK, somewhere between the mid-1980s and the mid-1990s, the Labour party became 'New Labour' and modernization made a particularly explicit appearance. At the first party conference after its election in 1997, the new Prime Minister Tony Blair told delegates:

Modernization is not the enemy of justice, but its ally...Progress and justice are the two rocks upon which the New Britain is raised to the heights. Lose either one and

---

[4] A little harsh given that Edward Heath as a minister in Douglas-Home's government abolished retail price maintenance as a restrictive practice in the 1963–4 session, a move opposed by many in the parliamentary Labour Party.

we come crashing down until we are just another average nation, scrabbling around for salvation in the ebbing tide of the 20th century. That is why we changed the Labour party — to make New Britain. (Press Association, 30 Sept. 1997)

The new government was soon described as 'the government that promises in almost every breath to modernise Britain' (*The Times*, 11Mar. 1998), as Anthony Giddens, the sociologist author of several books on modernity, was advising Tony Blair on his 'Third Way' for British politics, standing for 'a modernised social democracy, passionate in its commitment to social justice and the goals of the centre-left, but flexible, innovative and forward-looking in the means to achieve them' (Blair 1998: 128).

Technology and scientific advancement have played a particularly strong role in these transatlantic visions of modernization. For Clinton, the twenty-first century would be 'many things new: a time of stunning leaps of science; a century of dizzying technology; a digital century; an era in which the very face of our nation will change' (speech on the seventy-fifth anniversary of *Time* magazine, 3 Mar. 1998). With regard to administrative reform, Al Gore announced more modestly but in the modernization tradition: 'With computers and telecommunications, we need not do things as we have in the past. We can design a customer-driven electronic government that operates in ways that, 10 years ago, the most visionary planner could not have imagined' (NPR 1993: 121–2). By the end of the decade, the populist writer Alvin Toffler was advising both Democrats and Republicans on how to achieve the full transformative potential of information technology. In the UK in 2005, the Cabinet Office announced its strategy for *Transformational Government* (Cabinet Office 2005), with a foreword by Tony Blair indicating a faith in modernization as a development and a strategy:

The world is changing around us at an incredible pace due to remarkable technological change. This process can either overwhelm us, or make our lives better and our country stronger. What we can't do is pretend it is not happening. Government has to respond to keep up with the hopes and aspirations of citizens and business, to remain efficient and trustworthy. That is why I asked for a strategy on how we can use technology to transform government services.

Modernization is alive and kicking in the inspiration of political leaders in the twenty-first century too. In the USA, the election of President Barack Obama on the mantra of change via an extremely sophisticated internet campaign, drawing unprecedented numbers of people into the campaign through video-sharing, online fundraising of small internet-based individual donations and community-based networks, would fulfil many of the criteria of the most fervent hyper-modernists. The word 'change' replaces 'modernize' in much of what he proclaims, but the idea of meeting the challenges of an uncertain future with the tools of modernization is a key theme of his agenda, particularly the application of scientific and technological innovation to tackling climate change. In April 2009, for example, he pledged to spend more on scientific research and development than at the height of the space race, and proclaimed 'in no area will innovation be more important than in the development of new technologies to produce, use, and save energy — which is why my administration has made an unprecedented commitment to developing a 21st century clean energy economy, and why we put a scientist in charge of the Department of Energy' (speech at the National Academy of Science, 28 Apr. 2009).

These snatches of modernization rhetoric from politicians illustrate how their visions are founded on both hopes and fears of the future. On the one hand, the future is presented as uncertain, even frightening (as in Kennedy's 'new frontier') and modernization is put forward as a tool to pin it down, to erase the nightmare, to 'shape the future by embracing change not seeking to defy it' (Blair 1998: 33). On the other hand, modernization is presented as the way to attain an exciting, efficient, or equitable future. In both these visions (often presented simultaneously by their proponents, as in the Kennedy speech) the past is generally presented as unsatisfactory and modernization reform as a necessary way to escape from it, as typified by Clinton's administrative reforms — 'We are determined to move from industrial age government to information age government . . . the failure to adapt to the information age threatens many aspects of government' (NPR 1993: 122) — Wilson's threat to 'restrictive industrial practices' and need for 'the language of the scientific age', or Obama's fears of environmental decay. Such rhetoric is thereby compatible with the idea of a break with the past that characterizes modernization, but ironically in recent times the break is with industrialization, the very phenomenon that has, in the past, been seen to start the modernization process. In this sense, the modernizing rhetoric highlights the need to identify characteristics of modernization that may be dislocated from a specific time or place, the task of the next section.

Pinning Down Modernization and Public Policy Reform

Having identified modernization as the best candidate for discussing public policy reform, the next task is to define 'modernization reform' for the purposes of this book, identifying the key characteristics which would earn a reform this title. Looking for a definition of modernization is an extremely frustrating process, as elaborated by (for example) Therborn (2000). Some of the most distinguished proponents of modernization theory are inclusive to the point of banality: 'modernization is a multifaceted process involving changes in all areas of human thought and activity' (Huntington 1968: 52) or (even more unhelpfully) modernization involves 'the institutionalisation of doubt' (Giddens 1990: 176). Discerning what is common to scholarship on and reform in the name of modernization can be difficult, and indeed some scholars of the topic surrender:

the popularity of the notion of modernization must be sought not in its clarity and precision as a vehicle of scholarly communication, but rather in its ability to evoke vague and generalized images which serve to summarize all the various transformations of social life attendant upon the rise of industrialization and the nation-state in the late eighteenth and nineteenth centuries. (Tipps 1973: 199)

In fact, some have argued that modernization has no 'specific intrinsic content' because classical modernization theory never united around any concrete specification of a modern society, polity, or culture (Therborn 2000). Where traits of modernization are identified, they are often contradictory; modernization has been associated with both individualism and decentralization (Parsons 1971: 122) and 'increasing subordination of the individual to the Leviathan state' (Inglehart 1997: 74). Defining modernization at the level of individual reforms is particularly challenging, as most modernization theorists aggregate the various facets of modernization (industrialization, economic growth, rationalization, structural differentiation, political development, social mobilization and/or secularization or some other process) as sources of change operative at the national level; 'theories of modernization are fundamentally theories of the transformation of national states' (Tipps 1973: 202). Indeed, the concept has been relegated by some as a way of interpreting the world and a programme for changing it, rather than a means of explanation (Therborn 2000; Tipps 1973).

To characterize reforms in terms of modernization and to use this characteristic as an explanatory variable, therefore, is to be brave and hypothesize some characteristics that seem to have reached universal agreement without descending to tautology. To do so, I draw on the origins of the word 'modernization' and the work of the earliest modernization theorists; societal change including the replacement of family and community with the individual; a break with traditional and religious values and beliefs; the identification of man's greater control over the natural and social environment as the essential difference between modern and traditional society

25

(Huntington 1971: 286); and the association of modernization with industrialization. I have sifted through the various lists or 'traits' associated with modern societies provided by proponents of modernization theory: Parsons (1967) for example identified four 'evolutionary universals' which characterize modern societies: a differentiated, predominantly universalistic legal system, money and markets, bureaucratic organization and the pattern of democratic association (Parsons 1967: 490), which are vital to further evolution. Using just these basic 'first' (in chronological terms) principles of modernization theory before so many protagonists entered the debate, it is possible to identify three clusters of characteristics that might be hypothesized to define a modernization reform. These will be considered under each heading in the following sections.

First, *economic efficiency* emerges from the link between modernization and the economic transition from subsistence economies to technology-intensive industrialized economies and *individualism* derives from an emphasis on individuals and self-orientation, rather than families, communities, and collective orientation as the basic unit of society. In emphasizing the importance of economic transition in societal development, modernization accounts both observe and promote the primacy of economic *incentives* as a key driver for political organization and social change.

Second, modernization implies a move away from a fragmented society, based on association with place and clan, towards a more integrated and interconnected society. A modernization reform, therefore, can be hypothesized to involve *integration and interconnectedness*. Social integration also results from the higher density of population that results from industrialization; economic integration results from the 'two-way flow of goods and services between towns and villages'; while political integration emerges from the 'high degree of *centralization* associated with modernized societies' (Levy 1967). The emphasis of early modernization theory on the development of and commitment to the nation-state, implies a level of integration beyond towns, villages, or immediate locality. *Standardization* also emerges from many early modernization accounts, in part from the characteristics of early forms of industrialization in comparison with other modes of production; that is, the concentration of labour and machinery and the standardization of processes to provide economies of scale. Indeed, integration, interconnectedness, and standardization can be viewed as mutually dependent. For example, the standardization of Greenwich Mean Time across countries relies crucially upon each country involved knowing what Greenwich Mean Time is, on their agreement to standardize and their knowledge of how other countries are operating.

Third, modernization involves an emphasis on *specialization, scientific advancement, expert knowledge, and technology* in economic, political, and social life. These emphases emerge particularly from the 'greater control over the environment' that modernization theorists argue is based on 'the expansion of scientific and technological knowledge' (Huntington 1971: 286) and institutional adaptation to 'the unprecedented increase in man's knowledge permitting control over his environment, that accompanied the scientific revolution' (Black 1966: 7). Specialization is associated with scientific advancement, the division of labour associated with industrialization, the disappearance of tradition, custom, sovereignty and religion as governing principles, and the move from ascription and 'closed status systems to open, achievement-oriented systems' (Tipps 1973). An emphasis on technological development as a way to achieve modernization is also present; Levy claims that 'a society is more or less modernized to the extent that its members use inanimate sources of power and/or use tools to multiply the effects of their efforts', identifying 'technological indicators of industrialization' (Levy 1966: 7). I interpret technology broadly here, using the word to include material objects of use (such as machines, hardware, or utensils) but also systems, methods of organization, quantification, and techniques.

Before moving on to a discussion of modernization theory, I make a basic distinction between three types of modernization, which vary in their perspective on the role of the state in modernization. First, 'social modernization' is a perceived empirical development stemming from transitions in society; there will most likely be implications for the state (in developing a response to a social phenomenon, such as rising crime, for example), but political institutions are reflecting or reacting to societal trends rather than pushing them forward. In contrast, proponents of 'state-centred modernization' see pressures for modernization originating from the state itself trying to modernize society (for example, in the provision of universal access to technologies such as electricity or the internet). Third, modernization reforms can be geared at the state apparatus itself, for example with the aim of improving efficiency, described under 'modernization of the state' below. These distinctions are an organizing device, a question of emphasis rather than an absolute categorization. There are complex feedback loops between society and state in any development that may be labelled modernization, with the causal pattern of developments difficult to follow. For example, the internet was developed within the state, originally for state actors to use and with the military aims of the state in mind, but was gradually taken over by society as a serendipitous social innovation, eventually provoking governments to use it, provide access to it (in some cases), and possibly regulate it, as discussed in two of the chapters of this book.

Social Modernization

Social modernization, therefore, is used to refer to developments or theories where modernization appears or is deemed to spring from society — with implications for the state, but with a separate origin. Those who write about social modernization tend to perceive modernization as an empirical development within society or the economy and are less likely than those writers discussed in the subsequent two sections to be prescriptive in terms of pushing modernization forward.

The 'theory' of social modernization has its origins in the arguments of French philosopher Condorcet and the sociologist Durkheim. Condorcet argued in the eighteenth century that economic change would bring change in people's moral and cultural values and continuous progress and improvement in human affairs. Émile Durkheim, in the *Division of Labour in Society*, described how 'primitive' societies would make the transition to more economically advanced industrial societies, developing over time much like a living organism. This process of 'social evolution' was defined in terms of progressing from 'mechanical solidarity', where there is little integration and the need for the use of force to keep society together, to 'organic solidarity', where people are more integrated and interdependent. Under this view, societies develop from traditional cultures with a low division of labour to greater levels of complexity, with increasing levels of population density, specialization of tasks, and social differentiation.[5] Some theories of modernization rest on the idea of modernization as a process of human development, in which people's basic values and beliefs are changing in ways that affect political, sexual, economic, and religious behaviour (Inglehart and Weizel 2005). Some, following their own interpretation of Durkheim, see society itself as the unit of analysis, in a process of social evolution or cultural evolution (Service 1975) where 'modernist culture has come to penetrate the values of everyday life; the life world is infected by

[5] Experts have argued that modernization theory (particularly that of Talcott Parsons) has misrepresented Durkheim (who in fact rarely used the word) and his view of societal evolution and the state is far more sophisticated than such a thumbnail sketch could possibly provide (see 6 2003), but his work is certainly viewed by many as being at the foundations of social modernization.

modernism' (as Habermas 1985 characterized Daniel Bell in *The Cultural Contradictions of Capitalism*).

Economic efficiency emerges from these accounts due to the key role played by economic development, through the argument that as countries move from subsistence economies and become richer, they modernize. Modernization is frequently identified with industrialization and changes in economic structure and production which were deemed to be more economically efficient. In England, for example, Perkin (1969) found 'the origins of modern English Society' in the 'more than Industrial Revolution of 1780–1880', 'a social revolution with social causes and a social process as well as profound social effects', including the demise of the old pre-industrial aristocratic society. *Individualism* in social modernization emerges from growing emphasis on self-expression (Inglehart 1997) and attempts to define 'the modern personality' (independent, active, interested in public policies and culture) (Inkeles and Smith 1974). The sociologist Max Weber, in analysing the ways in which modern society was different from earlier forms of social organization, also focused on individual agency as the key to social change, arguing that ideas, values, and beliefs (particularly religious beliefs) were vital to and strongly characterized the development of Western society.

Social *integration* also emerges from these perspectives, particularly through higher densities of population and urbanization resulting from industrialization. Social mobility is another feature of 'post-aristocratic' governing principles and in the later stages of industrialization geographical mobility provides links across classes, groups, and cultures, leading to greater social integration (Durkheim's organic solidarity).[6] *Standardization* is also present in many social modernization accounts, as countries become more like each other; Levy (1967) for example labelled modernization a 'universal social solvent' that dissolves the traditional traits of developing countries, and Ferdinand Toennies (1887) described modernization as a process of standardization and unification, where smaller societies are absorbed into a more unified large modern society, pointing towards modern accounts of globalization, where 'we all increasingly live in one world, so that individuals, groups and nations become interdependent' (Giddens 2006). *Formalization* in social modernization accounts comes from Weber's view that as people moved away from traditional beliefs grounded in

---

[6] Durkheim's organic solidarity involved integration but not cohesion, which Durkheim viewed as unnecessary to sustain viable social organization if interdependence can be institutionalized among those who are classified as dissimilar from each other.

superstition, religion, custom, and long-standing habit, 'modern' society was marked by the rationalization of more and more areas of life, from politics to religion to economic activity. The main organizational vehicle for this rationalization was bureaucracy, a hierarchical arrangement which Weber saw as the only feasible way to organize human beings on the large scale necessary to organize industrialized society. Bureaucracy would allow the control of the world through calculation and the systematization of meaning and value into an overall, ethical, consistent view (Gerth and Wright Mills 1975: 55; Roth and Schluchter 1979: 14–15; Kolb 1986: 10–11), with the paradox that what Weber viewed as the most efficient form of social organization also threatened to become an 'iron cage' of rationalization and rules.

Scientific advancement and *technological innovation* are also viewed as a key driver of social modernization by many of these writers. Even in the eighteenth century Condorcet argued that technological advancement would give people greater control over their environment and stimulate social progress. Some technological utopians argue that 'new' technology will 'galvanize' a 'second Renaissance', just as an explosion of literacy catalysed the first:

We are on the verge of creating new tools which, like the press, will empower individuals, unlock worlds of knowledge and forge a new community of ideas...And when these technologies are fully integrated with each other, they will fuel a 21st century Renaissance outpouring of new learning and achievement. (Sculley 1991: 58)

One of the most popularly influential of such writers was Alvin Toffler (1970, 1980, 1990), who announced in *Future Shock* (1970) a revolutionary change to a 'super-industrial' society and in *Third Wave* (1980) a new civilization with greater flexibility and diversity, with the electronics revolution at its base, peopled by 'information workers' in 'intelligent buildings', organized in networks rather than formal hierarchies. Castells (1996) and Wellman (1979) claimed that networks powered by information technology were the defining organizational structure of the modern age, leading to the rise of the *Network Society* (Castells 1996) and the 'Network City' (Craven and Wellman 1973; Wellman 1979). For all these writers, the rise of information-based networks using digital technologies means a shift away from centralization towards the disintegration of bureaucracy and hierarchy. For Castells, networks become the basic units of modern society, while Wellman focuses on individualized networks and 'networked individualism'. For these writers, the internet put their wilder predictions within reach, leading to the *Internet Galaxy* (Castells 2001) and *Communication Power* (Castells 2009).

For some writers, the crucial driver of social modernization is not technology; it is human ingenuity in the form of *specialized expertise*, which in turn creates the technology and bureaucratic management that organizes it, not the other way round (Perkin 1996). Under this view, modernization is characterized by specialization and professionalization, a key theme of Durkheim's work and typified by Perkin (1989) in the *Rise of Professional Society*, which he identified as made up of 'career hierarchies of specialized occupations, selected by merit and based on trained expertise', based on human capital created by education and enhanced by strategies of closure, 'that is the exclusion of the unqualified and cutting across the horizontal solidarities of class' (Perkin 1989: 2). Daniel Bell (1976*a*) placed the rise of new technical elites and stratification at the heart of the next stage of modernization, *The Coming of Post-Industrial Society*, characterized by service and science-based industries and the rise of new technologies.

In general, earlier writings on social modernization view it as a desirable development. Huntington, for example, argued that countries with a high level of social mobilization and economic development appear the most stable, while economic and social 'backwardness' lead to instability (Huntington 1968, drawing on Gerschenkron 1962). But at the same time, he saw the dangers of social modernization without the accompanying development of appropriate political institutions; 'modernity breeds stability, but modernization breeds instability'. Democratization has been strongly associated with modernization (Lipset 1959, 1981) and some argue that democratization may be viewed as the final stage in the process; 'The specific causal chains consist of sequences of industrialization, urbanization, education, communication, mobilization, and political incorporation . . . a progressive accumulation of social changes that ready a society to proceed to its culmination, democratization' (see Przeworski and Limongi 1997: 158). Black (1966) even suggested that modernity 'could be defined as democracy', in which case 'modernization would be a movement towards democracy'.[7] In contrast, Barrington Moore (1966) argued that there were 'three routes to the

---

[7] Later research argues against this view, finding that 'democracy is or is not established by political actors pursuing their goals, and it can be initiated at any level of development' (Przeworski and Limongi 1997: 177), although the chances of the survival of democracy are greater when the country is richer and, in the early days of economic development, 'political participation must be held down, at least temporarily, in order to promote economic development' (Huntington and Nelson 1976: 23).

modern world'; the way that states transformed from pre-industrial agrarian society would determine what, if any, sort of democratization would emerge.

Many commentators have also emphasised the risks, dangers, and even 'crises' of social modernization, particularly Durkheim, Simmel, and Weber, who saw the risk of the 'iron cage' as central to his whole system of thought. Ulrich Beck writes of a crisis of modernization where consequences of scientific and industrial development are a set of risks and hazards 'the likes of which we have never previously faced' at the society and even global level (rather than the individual risks faced by new developments in the pre-industrial period), affecting even future generations through environmental damage (Beck 1992: 2). Bell (1976b) argues that the trends that created modernity have reached their (negative) limit, in which the Protestant work ethic has been abandoned for egoism, nihilism, and consumerism. Likewise, proponents of postmodernization would argue that historically the concept of modernization has exhausted itself, that we have entered a new epoch, and that the evolution of society in a modernist direction has come to an end.

State-Centred Modernization

State-centred modernization suggests modernization of society driven by the state, rather than the state responding to societal trends. Here, although writers identify and analyse historical and sociological trends, the emphasis is more prescriptive.

In all accounts of and arguments for state-centred modernization, economic change is emphasized as a key driver of perceived developments and proposals for modernization tend to include the search for *economic efficiency*. Gerschenkron (1962) argued that economic development proceeds in determined stages, although backward countries could skip some stages by adopting the advanced technology of more developed countries. The arguments of Karl Marx and his followers might be viewed as the epitome of state-centred modernization, with economic change as the driving impulse behind social change in the modern era. According to their doctrine of historical materialism, human societies move violently through successive transformations according to changes in the mode of production and exchange: 'in every society that has appeared in history, the manner in which wealth is distributed and society divided into classes or orders is dependent upon what is produced, how it is produced and how the products are exchanged' (Engels 1880: ch. 3). Modern societies are 'capitalist' and capitalism will drive towards constant economic transformation, because of the constant pressure for competition, leading to relentless expansion (as firms seek out new markets, raw materials, and cheap labour power).

Economic development is also the key impetus for change in non-Marxist accounts of state-centred modernization, the argument being that social change will bring (or is critical to) economic development; 'Modernization is widely attractive because it enables a society to move from being poor, to being rich' (Inglehart 1997: 5). This leads some modernization theorists to view elements of 'traditional' societies as a block to economic growth, which should in some way be overcome by the state. Modernization theory has been most often applied to development, resulting in an argument that economic development can be achieved by following the processes used by currently developed countries. Talcott Parsons defined the qualities that distinguished 'modern' from 'traditional' (primitive and archaic) societies, arguing that 'the modern system of society has emerged in a single evolutionary arena, the West' (Parsons 1971: 1). Rostow (1960) argued that traditional cultural values and social institutions of low-income countries impede economic effectiveness and prevent progression through the stages of economic growth: a traditional stage, characterized by fatalistic value system, followed by 'take off' to economic growth, followed by a drive to technological maturity, followed by 'the age of high-mass consumption'. Huntington (1968) also determined development to be a linear process which every country must go through, as did Gerschenkron (1962).

Integration in state-centred accounts comes in part from the growth of the state, both as an empirical development and a prescription, discussed (for example) by Colomer (2009), Service (1975), Tilly (1975), Finer (1997), van Creveld (1999), and Alesina and Spollaore (2003). Marxist accounts led indirectly to a massive integration and consolidation of the state. According to Engels's original treatise, the state would eventually die out once it had taken possession of the means of production in the name of society, which would be the last independent act in the name of the state, after which the proletarian movement would be able to achieve universal emancipation. But in Russia, Marxists turned to the idea of the scientific state to deal with the huge mass of peasants and 'the persistence of absolutist and quasi-feudal rule' (Dunleavy and O'Leary 1987: 213) and Stalin's leadership of the Bolshevik party brought a huge extension of bureaucratic control of the economy, forced industrialization, and collectivization.

More recent state-centred theories of modernization have brought an increasing emphasis on the role of state policy in promoting economic growth. In the USA in the 1930s, Roosevelt's New Deal led to major state-centred development. The World Bank (a long-time proponent of free market theories of development) concluded in a 1997 report *The State in a Changing World*, without an effective state, 'sustainable development, both economic and social, is impossible', citing for example economic growth in East Asian NICs during the 1980s and 1990s. Eastern states themselves point to post-developmental models; Utam (2006) claims that the Korean developmental state is evolving into a new 'techno-scientific state', arguing that minimalist or neo-liberal models would ignore the strategic role of the state in creating a distinct 'techno-scientific' ethos.

State-centred accounts of modernization also emphasize the importance of *specialization and technology*, particularly in terms of military technology and expertise. As Charles Tilly argued, 'States made war and war made the state' and military technology is often portrayed as a crucial intervening variable between warfare and the socio-economic effects of war. For example, White (1968) put forward the thesis (by now widely regarded as at least exaggerated) that the introduction of the stirrup in early eighth-century Europe brought the notion of cavalry, because for the first time it was possible for men to fight from horseback (very difficult without a saddle and stirrups), leading indirectly to feudalism, with the rise of a dominant 'aristocracy of warriors endowed with land so that they might fight in a new and highly specialized way' (White 1968: 38). In later accounts of military technology, 'the end of the Cold War led to feverish technological effort to apply information technology to military purposes, known as the Revolution in Military Affairs' (Kaldor 2001), with the development of a 'system of systems' with the interaction between various systems for information collection, analysis, and transmission and weapons systems playing a role akin to the stirrup in White's terms. Military technologies also drive professionalization and specialization; cavalry, for example, required highly specialized training, as do the more technologically sophisticated elements of twenty-first-century warfare.

More generally, technological innovation is claimed as a key driver of state-centred modernization. Technological innovation as a way for firms to beat their rivals was viewed as the driving force of capitalism in Marxist analyses: 'the ever-increasing perfectibility of modern machinery is... turned into a compulsory law that forces the individual industrial capitalist always to improve his machinery, always to increase its productive force' (Engels 1880: ch. 3). Many writers focusing on the power of technology to modernize society also turn their attention to the state's use of technology:

'exactly like businesses, governments are also beginning to bypass their hierarchies — further subverting bureaucratic power' (Toffler 1990: 255).

As might be expected, the normative arguments of modernization theory have been much criticized for the assumptions that development is a 'good thing' and that developing countries should follow the same paths as developed (usually Western) countries. Talcott Parsons, for example, viewed Western civilization as the pinnacle of modern societies and the USA as the most developed of all. 'Post-development' theorists have undermined this 'romantic and uniform' view with a representation of development as vulgar modernization controlled by elites, being concerned exclusively with economic growth and leading to the creation of under-development, (e.g. Corbridge 1990, 1986; Escobar 1995). Huntington (1968) argued that factors such as urbanization, increased literacy, social mobilization, and economic growth cannot automatically be associated with political development, and his argument that 'the primary problem of politics is the lag in the development of political institutions behind social and economic change' (Huntington, 1968: 266) was used against the mod-ernization theory which drove much US policy in the developing world.

Among the strongest critics of state-centred modernization with particu-lar relevance for public policy reform is the political anthropologist James C. Scott (1998) in his book *Seeing like a State*. Here Scott describes a number of state-led modernization projects which have failed, including high-modernist city planning, Soviet collectivization, compulsory villagization in Africa, and scientific forestry. In all these projects he argues that central government bureaucrats have imposed standardization on society from the centre, seeking legibility and simplification, but ignored socially, ecologi-cally, and economically complex polycultures and ultimately failing for this reason. He identifies two key elements of such projects: standardization in the name of legibility and a 'high-modernist' ideology conceived as

a strong, one might even say muscle-bound, version of the self-confidence about scientific and technical progress, the expansion of production, the growing satis-faction of human needs, the mastery of nature (including human nature), and above all, the rational design of social order commensurate with the scientific understanding of natural laws. (Scott 1998: 4)

He argues that when these two elements are accompanied by 'an authoritar-ian state willing and able to use the full weight of its coercive power to bring high-modernist designs into being', and a 'prostrate civil society that lacks the capacity to resist these plans' then these projects will ultimately fail.

Scott's core claim is that there is too much emphasis on the scientific rationality of modernism, which he labelled *techne* at the expense of more localized rationality or local knowledge which he calls *mētis*, which relies on practical knowledge, informal processes, and improvisation in the face of unpredictability (Scott 1998: 6). To conclude, he makes a number of recommendations for incremental development planning and the creation of 'Mētis-Friendly Institutions' which are 'multi-functional, plastic, diverse and adaptable' (Scott 1998: 353), allowing for diversity and certain forms of complexity. Scott's argument has been taken up by other critics of state-centred modernization, particularly Moran (2003) who argues that Scott's principles of high modernism are shaping an epoch of 'hyper-innovation' by the 'new regulatory' British state, whose 'ambitions are ensnared in the problems of high modernity: in the problems of achieving a central synoptic vision, and of converting that vision into control' (Moran, 2003: 181), with policy fiascos reflecting the 'limits of the modernist enterprise'.

Modernization of the State (State to State)

Modernization has long been applied to the apparatus of the state itself, involving many of the same features of modernization observed in society in the preceding sections. Administrative historians and sociologists have charted the history of 'experts' in the state, as traditional forms of authority and principles of governance such as royal privilege, kinship networks, and religious authority gave way to professional bureaucrats and politicians. The Napoleonic reform of the French administrative state, and Pitt's reform of the British Treasury creating a machinery for financial governance of the state in the eighteenth century, are examples of early and highly influential long-term state modernization programmes. Modernization of the state is epitomized for many by Weber's development of bureaucracy as an 'ideal type'; 'agreement exists that bureaucratization is one of the identifying characteristics of the emergence and development of the modern state' (Silberman 1993: 1). As noted above, for Weber, the main dynamic of modern development was the bureaucratic organization of social and economic life according to principles of efficiency on the basis of technical knowledge, in contrast with traditional methods of organization, such as kinship organizations and royal prerogative. Weber's ideas about bureaucracy fed strongly into what Hood (1994) has termed 'progressive era' public administration, ideas about public management which came into favour in the 'progressive era' of the late nineteenth and early twentieth centuries, including lifetime career service, fixed pay rather than pay related to performance, and a stress on procedure rules.

The search for *economic efficiency* has emerged at various points in prescriptions for the modernization of the state. In particular, the utilitarian doctrines of public management developed by Jeremy Bentham emphasized the 'principles of contestability, transparency, consumer-centrism and incentivization' (Hood 1994; cf. Hume 1981). In the early 1980s, a cohort of changes badged as 'New Public Management' (NPM) emerged in Western public administration, representing a shift away from the Weberian and progressive era administration, but with equal claims made for its modernizing effect. The doctrine is that methods of doing business in public organization need to be shifted away from heavy emphasis on general rules of procedure and be focused more on getting results (Hood 1994: 129). NPM has been extensively described and analysed (see, for example, Hood 1994, 2004; Barzelay 2000; Pollitt *et al.* 2007), but a key theme of the reforms was that of incentivization, the idea being to make incentives for public officials more like those for private personnel, with pay by performance schemes and a number of surrogates for private-sector profit motive. Hood (1994) has shown how the basic doctrines of NPM in fact added little of substance to the Benthamite principles noted above. Empirically, in those countries where the reforms were pursued most enthusiastically (such as New Zealand and the UK) NPM led to high degrees of disaggregation and fragmentation (through agencification of large-scale departments, for example) which could be argued to work against modernization (Dunleavy *et al.* 2006), particularly the 'pillar' of integration and interconnectedness.

Technological development within the state has long been claimed as modernization; the use of statistical data collection as a technology for transforming governmental executive capabilities is an early example. From the 1950s onwards, the widespread introduction of information technology into government administration has been claimed as a particularly important and widespread thrust towards modernization of the state (Margetts 1999). At first glance, information technologies would appear to facilitate the modernization process that Weber envisaged to an ever greater extent: to 'out-Weber Weber' (Hood 1994: 140). Such technologies allow the formalization of rules and procedures and enhance scope for increasing standardization of decision-making. Indeed, information technology is often perceived as facilitating, almost by definition, a more modern public administration: 'Informatization in public administration is a process of continued modernization' (Frissen 1995: 8). Such claims have taken on a new twist with increasingly widespread use of the internet. Earlier information technologies were internal to public organizations, with few implications for citizen–government interactions, while the internet has turned into a major societal innovation (discussed elsewhere in this book) and suggests the possibility of a more decisive break with the past. Some commentators have argued that digital-era technologies bring a new 'ideal type' for public organizations — digital-era governance (DEG) — that has become the dominant paradigm for public management reform, meaning that 'NPM is dead' (Dunleavy *et al.* 2006). DEG involves a range of information technology-centred changes which can lead to the reintegration of governmental processes and organizations and a more holistic approach to treating citizens.

Specialization is also a defining feature of modern administration, again underpinned by Weber's view that 'the specialist rules'. Ward and Rustow (1964: 6–7) included 'A highly differentiated and functionally specific system of governmental organization' and 'The allocation of political roles by achievement rather than ascription' in their definition of a modern polity. In fact, Silberman (1993) has argued that rather different models of bureaucratic organization have emerged in terms of specialization, with a professional orientation emerging in the USA and Great Britain and an organizational orientation (where the main criterion is organizational seniority) in France and Japan. But certainly the growth of the modern state from the 1940s has been accompanied by a huge increase in professionalized administration — lawyers, accountants, architects, engineers, scientists, teachers, social workers, public health experts, doctors, and town planners — with a concurrent emphasis on the importance of scientific knowledge (Dunleavy and O'Leary 1987: 302).

Weberian ideas underpin a commitment to *integration* (through centralization) and *standardization* in modern administration, with the emphasis on law and formal rules. The spread of bureaucratic organization implies unification of the state; Weber clearly felt that the administration of all nation-states was proceeding towards a generally similar institutional structure (Silberman 1998: p. ix), although the same author observed that this expectation of convergence of bureaucratic structure has not materialized, particularly in the USA. Ward and Rustow (1964: 6–7) defined a 'modern polity' in part on the basis of a 'high degree of integration'. Certainly, economic growth and developed economies have been historically closely linked to centralized states with a hierarchical ordering and the creation of large-scale integrated central government departments, although these organizational structures were to some extent challenged by NPM reforms in some countries. More recently, from the late 1990s onwards, administrative reforms conducted in the name of 'joining-up' (Pollitt 2003) and 'holistic government' (6 1997; 6 *et al.* 2002) have promoted integration and inter-connectedness as key elements of modernization, in some cases as a counterbalance to years of NPM-induced fragmentation (Dunleavy *et al.* 2006).

Critics of modernization of the state come from two distinct schools of thought. 'Anti-modernists' see modernization as an empirical development, but are deeply concerned about the implications in terms of state control. Weber himself feared unbridled bureaucratic domination and argued for the importance of charismatic political leadership as a counterbalance, just as Huntington argued for political development to counterbalance societal modernization. Likewise, Kafka's *The Trial* (1925), Orwell's *1984* (1949), and Huxley's *Brave New World* (1932) all painted sinister portraits of a future dominated by the rise of impersonal officialdom. Other writers particularly associate the technological elements of modernization with state control. They claim that malign governments holding technological reins will lead to the 'control state' where the 'progressive convergence of information processing and communication technologies in a single infrastructure of control' is sustaining the 'Control Revolution' (Beniger 1991: 288) or the rise of the 'Computer State' (Burnham 1983) or, more recently, the 'Surveillance State', enabled by a host of technologies such as databases, data matching, wire tapping, automatic number plate recognition, and DNA testing (Lyon 2001). Other writers predict that computers are leading to a 'cyborg world' (Levidow and Robins 1989) in which 'infotech systems promote new models of rationality, cognition and intelligence' or a 'military revolution' (Goure 1993). Some of these writers have veered off into claims that the state is heading in a postmodern direction; 'current US Defense policy is creating a postmodern army of war machines, war managers and robotized warriors' (Gray 1989: 44). More optimistically, Frissen argued that in a postmodernized public administration 'fragmentation will lead to an emancipation of the bureaucratic organization — beyond central control' (Frissen 1995: 9). According to his account, 'time and space have become less significant as organizational factors', which 'relativizes progress, so characteristic a concept of modernization'.

Conclusions: Defining Modernization Reform

The charm of the 'new' and the 'modern' as a way of fulfilling dreams and escaping nightmares has been evident in the rhetoric of policy-makers of developed countries, particularly (but not exclusively) in the late nineteenth and early twentieth centuries, the 1960s–1970s, and the 1990s–2000s. The attractions of modernization in the speeches of politicians appear as a glossy finish for whatever plans are being laid, but these visions of modernization are often linked to the work of modernization scholars of the time. Partly for this reason, to identify the key characteristics of modernization it seemed worthwhile to turn to the huge literature on the subject. In doing so, I have endeavoured to develop a characterization of modernization that derives from the work of the earliest modernization theorists, but that is dislocated from the time periods in which, and of which, they wrote. Only in this way can such a characterization be of use in considering current and future reforms.

All three of the 'pillars' of modernization introduced in the first section, economic rationalism, integration, and specialization, appear as recurrent themes in the bewildering variety of literature, evidence, and prescription presented in the name of modernization. These themes have emerged in writing on all three of the 'types' of modernization (state–state, state–society, and society–state) and appear in the labelling of both empirical developments and reforms and in normative prescriptions for modernization. When applied to modernization reforms, as opposed to macro-level social change, they may be viewed as strategies for reform, or at least clusters of strategies. I do not argue that any of them are unique to what I am labelling modernization. Pharaonic society in ancient Egypt could be described as both integrated and centralized, and their development of large-scale technology is still famous. In ancient Rome there were standardized weights and measures and also currency. Commitment to economies of scale was evident in Carthaginian and Roman agriculture, water management, civil engineering, and road building. However, the aim to dislocate modernization from its temporal origins means that these examples represent less of a problem for us than for the early modernization theorists.

An emphasis on economic efficiency and individualism emerges from both social modernization and state-centred modernization accounts of the primacy of economic development, particularly industrialization. Many modernization reforms are justified on economic grounds and based on the idea of incentivization, and the attempt to align the incentives of actors with policy objectives. Prevalence of economic rationalist ideas in modernization of the state peaked in the New Public Management reforms in the 1980s and 1990s.

Integration and interconnectedness have been a feature of modernization accounts of social change, state-centred accounts (in terms of state growth, for example) and the development of the 'modern' state, accompanied by standardization through the formalization of rules and centralisation through consolidation of previous governing arrangements. These characteristics are associated with Weberian bureaucracy but also have origins in industrialization, for example through mass production and economies of scale. Formalization comes from modernity's break with pre-bureaucratic governing principles and forms of authority, such as sovereignty or kinship. In later developments, technological development played a key role in facilitating interconnectedness and social and geographical mobility have aided moves towards globalization, for some the ultimate stage of modernization, while within the state more recent administrative reform proposals have centred on the idea of 'joining up' and 'reintegration'.

An emphasis on expert knowledge and specialization, driving and driven by technological and scientific innovation, has been clear in all three types of modernization. Technological development, scientific knowledge, and specialization have been at the centre of ideas about social modernization and state modernization; the belief that scientific advancement and technology-centred change has been a vital component of economic development and will somehow inexorably lead to progress and improvement, furthering modernization aims. Closely linked to technological development is the increasing specialization identified by Weber, Perkin, and Scott's 'techne', the scientific rationality of high modernism.

To fall into the category of a 'modernization project', a project or reform would have to rest on at least one of these three 'pillars' of modernization: a move justified on economic grounds involving some kind of incentivization; a change which involves greater specialization of tasks or professionalism based on scientific knowledge or the introduction of some system or technological development, accompanied by a belief in the power of these characteristics alone to have an improving effect; or a plan which involves some kind of formalization of rules, standardization, and quantification across the state, or from state to society.

This characterization of modernization leads to a hypothesis. It may be that to achieve the intended effects, a reform needs a balanced distribution across more than one of these 'pillars' of modernization. An overweening emphasis on specialization or technological innovation for its own sake, without the introduction of standardization and formalization and some thought about the incentives of actors is possibly likely to lead to the concentration of power in the wrong hands and technological disappointment. Likewise, an emphasis on standardization and formalization without technological and specialist expertise or attention to economic incentives may lead to a 'deadening' effect, to Weber's 'ruthlessly' pessimistic view of modernity, producing a 'gloomy bureaucratic state where administered uniformity severely limited freedom' (Kolb 1986: 12) and can kill innovation and flexibility. Likewise, unbounded economic rationalism and rampant individualism without attention to specialization or integration and interconnectedness might explain the failures of the worst excesses of New Public Management reforms, characterized by de-professionalization, fragmentation, increased complexity, and lowered levels of trust in government.

As well as allowing us to characterize a modernization reform, the pillars or clusters of strategies may allow us to distinguish different types of modernization. For example, if the internal market and aggregation of General Practitioners' surgeries into fund-holding practices introduced by the Conservative government to the UK National Health Service in the 1980s were clearly modernizing, then was the removal of such mechanisms by the Labour government of 1997 non-modernizing? It may be that rather than being a direct reversal this was actually another type of modernization, relying more heavily on the pillar of integration and interconnectedness and with less emphasis on economic efficiency and incentivization.

Importantly, if this characterization is to have any use, not all reforms would be described as modernization under these criteria. The elements of modernization identified here do not cover all the cultural types identified in the cultural theory of Mary Douglas (Douglas 1970, 1992; Douglas and Wildavsky 1982); hierarchalism, individualism, egalitarianism, and fatalism. Centralization, integration, standardization, specialization, economic efficiency, and incentivization are associated with hierarchalism and individualism but less with egalitarianism or fatalism. So for example, a move towards multidisciplinary teamworking, as introduced in UK mental health services this century (6 *et al.* 2006) and associated with 'enclaves' and 'isolates' by these authors, would not be described as a modernization reform under these criteria. It may be that to succeed, modernization reforms need some kind of counterbalance from these other cultural types, just as Scott identified 'mētis' as an antidote to high-modernism, but only by excluding them from the definition will we be able to identify such a possibility. In Chapter 12 we argue that this further balance may be needed for robustness.

Both the introduction and this chapter have shown that modernization is a concept riddled with confusion and contradiction, evidenced by the conspicuous failures and disappointments of many schemes that have been justified on the grounds of modernization and highlighted by the longstanding arguments and lack of definition that pervade the huge well of thought, scholarship, and rhetoric devoted to the subject. The definition of modernization proposed here does not entirely escape from such contradictions. Indeed we can expect reforms which contain moves towards both hierarchalism and individualism to be prone to well-known tensions between competing worldviews, which will be drawn out in some modernization designs. For example, as noted above, the New Public Management reforms of the 1980s were dominated by one cluster of modernization strategies (economic efficiency, individualism, and incentivization) involving the disaggregation of large departments into multiple agencies, which obviously worked against integration and interconnectedness, another of the clusters. The importance of networks emphasized by Castells and Wellman, also noted above, leads to interconnectedness but works against integration, within the same cluster. But the identification of tensions like these may help to identify and even rectify some of the sources of instability in modernization reform.

The definition of modernization provided here is reminiscent of Scott's characterization of 'high-modernism', but provides a more nuanced breakdown of modernization, perhaps because it is based on a more sympathetic reading. Scott saw modernization as coherent, but a project that would always lead to pathological consequences and the opposite result to that hoped for or predicted by policy-makers. In contrast, the view of modernization presented here is one that is perhaps inherently contradictory, but where we do not assume that modernization will inevitably lead to disaster. Integration, interconnectedness, and standardization have not as yet brought about the dire predictions of Weber, Orwell, Kafka, or Huxley, at least when counterbalanced with the types of political institutionalization which many modernization theorists identified as essential. Neither have technical development, scientific advancement, and specialization necessarily led to the worst excesses of the 'Control State' feared by anti-modernists; indeed, some totalitarian regimes managed very well without these features. Economic rationalism may have much to answer for in terms of inequality both within and between states, but it would be hard to argue that all modernization reforms based on this principle have led to a net loss of quality of life in those states over the many years during which it has been promoted. Nor is the combination of these characteristics necessarily lethal, as Scott argued with regard to the combination of administrative ordering and high-modernist ideology; the introduction of public transport, health, and education systems could all be characterized as modernization reforms, on the basis of these three pillars of modernization.

3

When Forethought and Outturn Part

Types of Unanticipated and Unintended Consequences

Perri 6

Introduction

To expect to find a theory to explain the causes of all and only unintended or unanticipated consequences is no more reasonable than hoping for a general theory of misfortunes. Yet something useful of a general character can be achieved by developing clear conceptual frameworks of definition, classification, and typology. For such frameworks can enable structured comparison, better measurement, and clearer questions with which to distinguish the different kinds of puzzles for which theories and explanations are required. This chapter offers only part of such a general framework, leaving for more detailed examination elsewhere the tasks of more finely grained analysis and specification of theories.

First, some key strands of research of unintended and unanticipated consequences in the social sciences are considered, and some limitations in these bodies of work identified. Then the key terms of surprise, anticipation, intention, and welcome are examined, that go to make up an initial, coarse-grained typology. This tool is used to consider similarities and differences between the cases examined in other chapters in this volume. The chapter concludes by identifying a key conceptual and theoretical issue for further work in the next generation of research in this field.

Literature

Throughout history, political thinkers, historians, and, more recently, social scientists have devoted major works to the effort to understand unanticipated and unintended consequences of political decisions.

Many of the ancient Greek and Roman writers on politics emphasized limited human capacity to foresee consequences of action. In Renaissance times, Machiavelli gave particular attention to the role of fortune and chance in determining outcomes. From the Renaissance to the Enlightenment, a debate continued between those — like Machiavelli in the fifteenth century — who argued that under conditions of uncertainty, political action should be bold and audacious, and those — such as Burke in the eighteenth century — who concluded that uncertainty called for caution. It was the great nineteenth-century analyst of the French Revolution and of American democracy, De Tocqueville, who first developed detailed accounts of particular causal mechanisms by which deliberate political action could unleash large-scale unintended and unanticipated social change (Elster 2009). In the later nineteenth century, though, interest shifted from the objective causal processes by which actions, once committed to, lead to surprising outcomes, to concentrate instead more on the subjective processes that shape the ways in which people anticipate and intend consequences. The great sociologists of knowledge, Marx, Weber (e.g. Cherkaoui 2007), Durkheim, Simmel, and Mannheim each offered explanations, showing how institutions such as religious practices or class situation would influence people's anticipations and intentions in ways that would lead to unforeseen outcomes.

Merton's (1936) article on unanticipated consequences is conventionally regarded as the piece that focused and defined the scope for recent debates in the social sciences. Merton was working in the sociology of knowledge tradition, seeking to specify causal mechanisms that would lead to subjective anticipations being blinkered and intentions skewed. By contrast, he took it to be an altogether less problematic issue to determine just what were the consequences of an action, defining them confidently as those things that would not have occurred had the action not been taken. He distinguished four principal causes of unanticipated consequences: these were ignorance of facts (a much more extreme condition than mere uncertainty), error in appraisal of facts, interest blinding people to risks, and self-defeating prophecy in which a warning leads to action that avoids the very thing foreseen. Unlike the more pessimistic European thinkers on whom he drew, Merton however regarded at least the first three of these as deviations from what he took to be a normal or benchmark condition of rational action. By using social science to enhance understanding and explanation, he hoped that these four processes might prove amenable to efforts to minimize them. This would require policy-making to reduce ignorance and error, better to guide interest and to manipulate the mechanisms and probabilities of self-defeating prophecy. His four categories of causes were neither mutually exclusive nor jointly exhaustive. Much subsequent work has extended and refined his list (see especially Boudon 1982; Cherkaoui 2007). For many, the optimism of Merton's piece may seem rather quaint, as surely it must have seemed to many readers in the grim years of the mid-1930s when it was published.

A major recent contribution was Hirschman's (1991) trichotomy of types of both unintended and unanticipated welcome and unwelcome consequences. He distinguished *futility*, where the policy has little or no effect, from *perversity*, where the policy has an unwelcome effect on the very thing it was both intended and anticipated to affect for the good (cf. Hadari 1989 on boomerang effects), from *jeopardy*, where it had an unwelcome consequence for some other factor which was not its original target. The opposite of jeopardy, where the policy has a benign effect on some untargeted factor, he called *mutual support*. Originally developed to analyse critiques of policy reforms, Hirschman's categories have been widely used in analysing policy consequences (e.g. cf. Klitgaard 1997).

Subsequent research in the social sciences using the notions of unintended, unanticipated, and unexpected consequences of policy decisions is too vast for any one individual systematically to collect, review, and analyse it systematically in anything less than a lifetime. However, searches were run on the main academic journal article databases (Academic search elite, ASSIA, IBSS, Ingentaconnect, Intute (social sciences), JSTOR, Science Direct, Web of Knowledge, Social Science Citation Index), using combinations of 'unanticipated' or 'unexpected' or 'unforeseen' or 'unintended' or 'unexpected' together with either 'consequences', 'effects', 'outcomes', or 'results', and always with 'policy'. The series of searches on policy-oriented studies yielded several thousand articles. From the results, a number of distinct strands of literature and trends in argument can usefully be distinguished.

Restricting the search to those studies which related to 'policy' has the effect of excluding a wide range of sociological work. Much mid-twentieth-century sociological theorizing on unintended consequences was conducted in the course of debating the structure, character, and conditions for validity of functional explanations or the concept of a latent function (see e.g. Merton 1968; Giddens 1977; Stinchcombe 1986); more recent sociological work tends simply to emphasize the ubiquity of unintended consequences (see e.g. Sztompka 1993). This is still a matter of some concern in contemporary methodological debates, and of some methodological discussion about just how unintended they need be to count as functional or institutional explanations (see e.g. Parsons 2007: 73). A major sociological study was that by Boudon (1982), which carefully distinguished and documented mechanisms bringing about unintended consequences from processes of aggregation of individual decisions made in pursuit of private objectives, by emergence (see also Vernon 1979; Opp 2002). Studies of social and political causation in the long run often emphasize processes of reaction and counter-reaction, or chains of alternating error–correction that, by definition, outrun what can be intended (Schneider 1971; Tilly 1996; Fine 2006).

A huge economic literature concerned with unanticipated inflation and monetary policy is not considered here, because its concern workers', consumers', and investors' anticipations, rather than those of policy-makers.

A preliminary distinction can be drawn between studies that frame the issue as one about vulnerability to 'surprises', meaning outcomes to which the causal contribution made by the policy-makers who are surprised may be absent or at least is not of concern for the study, and that work which frames the issue in more evaluative terms, devoted to arguing for claims that particular decisions led to outcomes variously described as unintended, unexpected, unforeseen, unanticipated.

In international relations, there is a body of work on 'strategic surprises' including sudden military attacks but also sudden diplomatic demarches and *volte-faces* in policy that affect other states: this work is interested almost exclusively in unwelcome surprises (e.g. Wohlstetter 1962; Bar-Joseph and Sheaffer 1998; Byman 2005; Wirtz 2006; Zegart 2007; Betts 1982, 1989; Levite 1987, 1989). The 'orthodox' school explains vulnerability to strategic surprises as due to lack of preparedness rather than absence of warning information (Betts 1982), whereas 'revisionists' argue that information of a sufficient quality to serve as an effective warning is often unavailable to states, but that where it does happen to be, states can and do respond by preparing at least to some degree (anticipation), setting aside resources (resilience) or acting to prevent the attack in the first place (e.g. by negotiation) (Levite 1987, 1989). Much of the debate between these schools turns on the question of what thresholds are held to be methodologically appropriate before declaring information 'available' and clearly indicating likelihood and direction of attack or appropriate action. More akin to the evaluative study of unintended consequences in other fields is international relations research on 'blowback', a term first introduced after the CIA-assisted overthrow of the

Mossadegh regime in Iran in 1953 produced consequences that were adverse to American interests. More recently, the word has come to be used for many kinds of contrary reaction to a policy: for example, Capling and Nossal (2006) describe as 'blowback', political lobbying for changes to future treaties in response to unwanted litigation against states resulting from opportunities created by treaties signed.

A growing body of work in environmental research is concerned with surprises administered by biological systems in response to human intervention. This field has developed a series of typologies of surprise (Streets and Glantz 2000), by type of causality, scale (Brooks 1986; Gunderson *et al.* 1997), speed of surprising process (Cunha *et al.* 2006), degree of lack of anticipation (Schneider *et al.* 1998; Smithson 1988), stance of those who are surprised towards the event (Smithson 1998; Hassol and Katzenberger 1995; Faber *et al.* 1992; Schneider *et al.* 1998; Thompson *et al.* 1990: 69–75; Holling 1986), severity of effect (Timmerman 1986), and so on. The literature has yet to develop plausible hypotheses that values of surprises on any of these dimensions are systematically associated with other values on other dimensions: hitherto, they have been treated as largely independent of each other, but useful for descriptive comparison.

Research on surprises in organization and business studies (e.g. Pullen 1993; Weick and Sutcliffe 2001) shares with the environmental and international relations literatures a central concern with the dilemmas of choice identified in risk management, between greater investment in anticipation and reliance upon resilience (Wildavsky 1988; Hood and Jones 1996), but is also interested in the sense-making strategies by which people (Louis 1980) and organizations (Weick 1995, 2001) handle surprising events.

Evaluative studies on unanticipated and unintended consequences are scattered extremely widely across the disciplines of social science and the fields of public policy, and show little integration of framework or cumulation of theory and knowledge. Apart from Merton's (1936) article and perhaps two or three other general works, most cite only work in their own empirical field.

Articles in public health, environmental and development policy often seemed to be written in a manner that suggested that unintended or unanticipated consequences could be reduced or avoided ('minimized' is a term used quite often in these fields) by the adoption of more or less readily learned skills and procedures, whereas those in foreign policy and social policy tended to be written in a much less optimistic vein (e.g. Casalino 1999; Binder 2002; Willis *et al.* 2000; Wolfson and Hourigan 1997; Klitgaard 1997).

Of particular interest are two special issues of journals devoted to the topic of unintended consequences of policy: *Population and Environment*, 25(4), March 2004, edited by B. S. Low, and *American Behavioral Scientist*, 47(11), July 2004. The *Population and Environment* collection includes some more generally reflective articles on causation. The editorial line of argument in *American Behavioral Scientist* issue (see e.g. Preston and Roots 2004) leans clearly towards a general claim that government is peculiarly vulnerable to these kinds of consequences, although none of the articles in the collection offers comparative empirical evidence on the private or voluntary sectors or on informal individual or household action.

The evaluative literature exhibits a number of weaknesses. A vast number of articles simply pointed to outcomes which were simply asserted to be unanticipated or unintended or both. As long ago as 1977 Giddens (pp. 107–8) criticized the tendency, even in the major writers such as Merton and Stinchcombe, wrongly to use the terms 'unanticipated consequence' and 'unintended consequence' largely synonymously: the same error is still being made today, although some analysts of the policy process such as Rao (2002) are careful to distinguish them.

Indeed, most argue from the character of the 'downstream' outcomes to their putatively unanticipated and/or unintended status, without offering empirical evidence about 'upstream' policy formulation in any detail beyond occasional quotations from public statements. Hagan and Bickerton's (2007: 14) book on unintended consequences of US wars specifically states that they considered no other evidence about intentions than presidential public statements. Of course, policy-makers very often have good reasons to disguise their true intentions in their public statements. Few used policy-makers' diaries, memoirs, or declassified documents to determine who might have anticipated or intended just what (Newberry 2002). Refreshingly, for example, Wolfson and Hourigan (1997) cite material on the debates at state level in the USA about the restrictions adopted on access to alcohol and tobacco by those under 21 years, to support their claims that the consequences were not fully thought through, and to identify some risks that were recognized at the time of adoption. Unfortunately, their data do not really enable them to determine what was anticipated but unintended from that which might have been unanticipated.

Very few articles devoted much space to the question of the thresholds, standards, or methodological measures of intention or anticipation to be used, before a consequence might be deemed to be unintended, unanticipated, or unexpected. None of the articles identified considered in any detail how far it would have been possible for policy-makers to have anticipated the consequences described. In a great many cases, the fact that the policy in question was the principal causally contributory factor to the outcomes considered was asserted but not evidenced in any detail.

Many articles assume that a policy using a particular instrument could only have been taken with one kind of intention. Often, policy-makers' explicitly avowed intentions are taken at face value. For example, Ratanawijitrasin *et al.* (2001), reviewing the effects of national policies on medical drug availability on use, presume that the goals of such policies are the palpable ones of improving 'availability, affordability, quality and rational use' of the drugs. Yet it is hardly difficult to imagine quite other goals for such policies, including cost containment, electoral advantage, or even corrupted goals reflecting the influence of pharmaceutical companies on governments.

Some draw inferences about intentions from data about the manner of a policy's announcement and implementation, and the prevailing ideas being debated at the time that might have supported the policy. For example, Blomberg *et al.* (1998) examine penal policy in the USA. Relying on information about the general ideological stances of the governing parties, the academic debates, and sometimes the avowed claims made by politicians, they attribute implicit theories of goals and causal means to the principal approaches relied upon in penal policy for some of the main periods of US history. Without data from declassified policy documents, memoirs or diaries of policy-makers, transcripts of meetings, etc., this does not enable us to rule out the possibilities that policy-makers might have had other intentions or indeed have been engaging in symbolic politics.

Most articles identified were concerned with unwelcome consequences. With respect to anticipation, studies often presume without evidence that unwelcome consequences must not have been anticipated. For example, Branston's (2002) study of the policy in England and Wales to encourage new entrants into electricity generation identifies a series of outcomes in pricing and consumer inertia that are taken to be unwelcome to policy-makers and which Branston concludes must have been 'unforeseen'. Yet there is nothing in his analysis to suggest that policy-makers might have foreseen these, at least as possibilities, and perhaps been prepared to accept the risks. In the same way, Rodriguez *et al.* (2006) assert that in urban policy, the unwelcome effects of some growth containment policies such as reduced affordability of housing and increased miles travelled and additional congestion are 'unanticipated', yet they provide no evidence about the policy process of decision-making for any of the twenty-five US cities in their sample, offering instead data only on outcomes. The study already mentioned by Blomberg *et al.* (1998) shows a willingness to make quite large claims about absence of anticipation. For example, writing of the 1980s, they write 'With little forethought given to the impact of purely retributive and incapacitative policies in the absence of a dedicated funding source, the U.S. penal system literally [sic] collapsed' (1998: 277). The assertion of 'little forethought' could be true, but the kinds of data offered in the study do not suffice to warrant it.

Definitions and Thresholds

How might we tell whether a policy outcome might be unanticipated, unexpected, unforeseen, unintended?

An unanticipated outcome of a policy decision is one that transpires, but which was not conceived in advance by the policy-maker. Likewise, an unintended one is produced by a decision where the outcome falls outwith the desire that is at least commonly (and in the governmental case, nearly always, although in the individual case not necessarily) reasoned — in other words, the motive — to bring about the preferred outcome, combined with a commitment of action to fulfil that desire, or a volition of sufficient strength to yield action, if it might compete with other desires. An unwelcome one falls outside the scope of outcomes regarded by policy-makers as desired, or as goals of their original decision.

Typically, though, we are interested in cases where the outcome was either specifically contrary to, diametrically opposed to, or at least surprising given what was in fact conceived or intended or wanted in advance.

Surprises might be defined as events that are unanticipated, whether or not they are in any significant degree causally influenced by prior decisions of those policy-makers who have not anticipated them. Although economists use the word 'shock' with particular attention to asymmetry between economic regions or units, more generally a shock might be defined as a surprising policy outcome that is also sudden.

Important methodological decisions have to be taken in any given study about the thresholds set on such questions as the following. If an outcome is anticipated under one description, but that is a quite different description or framing from that used when the outcome does occur, is it then still unanticipated (intensionality)? Just whose anticipations in the circle of those making a contribution to the decision should count, and how peripheral can those people be who might conceive the possibility (agency)? How vague or implicit does anticipation have to be before it ceases to count (implicitness)? How far should possible consequences have been deliberated upon before they would be relevant (deliberation), and what degree of consensus among the policy-makers deemed relevant should be required? How low a probability should policy-makers attach to an outcome they have conceived before we can regard it as effectively unanticipated at all, unforeseen, or unexpected (likelihood)? For example, is it fair to say that if policy-makers conceive the possibility of an outcome but regard it as more likely than not that it will not transpire, then it was anticipated but not expected? How far do we require policy-makers to anticipate the detail of an outcome, in respect of its distribution, scale, severity, impact, timing, duration, or linkages (Weick and Sutcliffe 2001: 36–9) (detail)? How remote in time and causal chain can an outcome be from a decision before we should say that policy-makers could not reasonably have been expected to have anticipated it (remoteness)? How great a causal contribution to the outcome should the policy decision have to make before it is appropriate to classify it as relevantly a consequence of that decision (causality)?

Very similar threshold decisions are required before we might deem an outcome unintended or unwelcome. In the same way, researchers need to determine thresholds for intensionality, agency, implicitness, deliberation, likelihood, detail, remoteness, and causality for intentions. But intention brings with it some additional complications because it is often even more critical in determining blame and exculpation than is intention.

Preferences about what policy-makers will welcome may change after a decision is made, and before the surprising outcome transpires; the policy-makers making the decision may well have left office by the time the surprise arrives. Normally, it would be more rigorous to determine whether the outcome is unwelcome by reference to the preferences of the original decision-makers, although many studies in the literature appear to relax this threshold.

The particular thresholds we might set will differ, depending on the research question. Political biographers might reasonably set low thresholds for anticipation, given their interest in reconstructing the whole thought style of their subject politician. By contrast, evaluators might want to set rather higher standards of deliberation and consensus.

Broad Types of Cases

If we can, at least for any given study, settle upon a set of thresholds for each of these things, then the combination of the scores on anticipation, intention, and welcome for a policy outcome, this yields a simple, jointly exhaustive, and mutually exclusive typology, shown in Table 3.1.

Table 3.1. Types of consequences of reform by anticipation, intent, and welcome

Type	Anticipation	Intention	Welcome
1. Bad surprise	Unanticipated	Unintended	Unwelcome
2. Happy surprise	Unanticipated	Unintended	Welcome
3. Unconscious intention; or despairing hope	Unanticipated	Intended	Welcome
4. Unconscious self-destructive intention	Unanticipated	Intended	Unwelcome
5. Benign side-effect	Anticipated	Unintended	Welcome
6. Risks knowingly run	Anticipated	Unintended	Unwelcome
7. [Regret? Be careful what you wish for?] OR [logically empty, because even regret requires bad surprise]	Anticipated	Intended	Unwelcome
8. Success	Anticipated	Intended	Welcome

In this chapter, success is of lesser interest, although another chapter in the present volume (Boyne) is concerned with a case where people who were not the policy-makers themselves but researchers, observers, and critics did not anticipate the outcome.

Most of the literature that is presented as being about either unanticipated or about unintended consequences concerns what the authors take, with varying of degrees of evidence about the state of policy-makers' minds at the time of policy formulation, to be cases of bad surprise.

Happy surprises are rather more rarely studied by evaluative policy analysts. Identification of happy surprises is subject to the difficulty that policy-makers have powerful incentives retrospectively to claim that happy surprises were in fact cases of success, denying that the benign results were either unintended or unanticipated. It also presents the methodological issue raised by Norman Lamont singing in his bath after the failure of his own government's monetary policy after the pound's ejection from the European exchange rate mechanism, that the coding of the outcome as welcome should — if the argument above is accepted — follow the values of the decision-makers at the time of the policy formulation, rather than any changes of mind.

Benign side-effects are relatively common. Not infrequently, governments — or at least, lucky ones — undertake a policy for one reason and find that its implementation turns out to be useful for other goals. The principal reasons, for example, insofar as we can fathom them, for which Harold Wilson in the 1960s refused President Lyndon Baines Johnson's requests for military assistance in the war in Vietnam were to do with foreign policy. However, the benefits for the fiscally hard-pressed Labour's public expenditure plans, which included the scaling back of military commitments 'east of Suez' as the phrase of the time had it, are fairly clear.

Cases of risks knowingly run are especially important for methodological reasons, and examples abound. Too often, cases may be coded as unanticipated consequences of a policy, when it is quite likely that either a more careful coding of agreed facts or discovery of a modest number of new facts about the policy process would suggest that they may be examples of risks knowingly run.

The phrase 'knowingly run' has been chosen with some care to describe the situation where policy-makers have to some degree anticipated that an unwelcome outcome may flow from their policies, and where they do not intend that outcome and may fear it, but proceed to take the action anyway. 'Knowing' here describes the policy-makers' state of being in possession of information that indicates a significant possibility, a probability that may well lie below (say) a 50 per cent threshold of being 'as likely as not', but is still greater than (say) a 2 or 3 per cent chance that might be regarded as merely 'a remote possibility'. That is to say, the 'knowledge' implied by the claim that the policy-makers knowingly ran the risk is not one of certainty but of probability to the level required for expectation.

Where a policy-maker runs a risk, expecting (>50 per cent probability) that the risk will transpire, we may be faced with a problem that might more accurately be classified as one of despairing hope.

In some cases, these risks may perhaps also be willingly run. But this may well not be the case. For policy-makers may feel compelled or at least constrained to bear those risks, whether by threat of *force majeure* or the bonds of honour or duty to allies. During the Second World War, there were several occasions on which Churchill had to make decisions about whether or not to pursue military action based on intelligence gleaned from the work of the code-breaking team at Bletchley Park, where taking that military action would likely reveal to the German armed forces that the British had broken their codes, yet where failing to act would very probably lead to the loss of lives on the Allied side. In such tragic dilemmas, it would be entirely unjust to the policy-makers to describe their running of risks as done 'willingly', but fair to recognize their knowledge.

Churchill's dilemmas were faced deliberately, but there are many cases where we cannot be confident that it would be accurate to speak of risks being 'consciously' run when policy-makers are in possession of information indicating risk. For there is a wide range of causal processes in individuals and in groups that can lead people to make decisions bearing risks about which they do possess information, but where that knowledge is not at the forefront of their minds when making decisions. Temporarily forgetting something important is the simplest case, but the presence of advisers, colleagues, and papers in decision-making are designed to reduce that risk. Deeper and more complex psychological processes can be at work in individuals and in groups that lead to the under-appreciation of the significance of information possessed. Whatever really went on, for example, in the mind of Adolf Hitler when he made his fateful decision to attack the Soviet Union will surely be debated endlessly by historians (see e.g. Kershaw 2007: 54–90). Certainly, he possessed enough information from German history about the dangers to the state of war on two fronts, enough information from the present condition of the state's resources to indicate the current risks of overstretch. Whether he really felt constrained by his sense of German historical destiny, whether wild individual hubris provides any very satisfying causal mechanism for explanation, whether rather simpler group dynamics of optimism bias within his immediate circle had anything to do with it, whether he really under-estimated the true scale of the risks, will perhaps never be settled with any confidence, given the limited evidence that has survived the wreckage of his regime.

President Johnson certainly regretted the outcomes of his Vietnam policy, for they forced him to abandon his hopes of running for re-election. The persistent advice of such sceptics within his administration as George Ball and indeed warning papers going back to the Eisenhower years provided him with enough information that his government can be said to have anticipated the outcomes, but the President decided to run the risks anyway (see e.g. Welch 2005: 129–47; Tuchman 1984; Khong 1992; Dallek 1999). One at least plausible explanation suggested or implied by some writers (e.g. Welch 2005; Preston 2006) is that Johnson felt constrained to pursue his policy of escalation of the war by considerations of both his own domestic credibility and of America's credibility internationally, should he withdraw or scale back his commitment: the same consideration was probably in the mind of President Kennedy in his decisions to introduce a blockade of Cuba in response to the discovery of the Soviet nuclear missile installations in October 1962 (as emphasized by e.g. Weldes 1999). Further consideration of causal mechanisms in such cases will be given in Chapter 4 below.

Another example might be one already given above in relation to the healthcare financing policies of the new Labour government in Britain in the mid-2000s. Whether or not one would want to call the risks of gaming arising from the activity-based finance scheme, 'carefully calculated' or 'reckless' depends on one's view of the prior assessment of scale of the political damage done to the government by the perceived deficits and of the relative scale of fiscal losses and opportunity costs for healthcare from gaming and deficits when offset against the modest overall improvements in output and perhaps some aspects of productivity associated with the scheme. Nevertheless, the evidence does suggest that this should be coded as a risk knowingly run rather than a bad surprise.

Methodologically, however, the boundary between bad surprises and risks knowingly run will often fall at somewhat different points, depending on just which thresholds for likelihood, centrality, detail, causal chain, and temporality are selected for the threshold for the outcome being anticipated. That sensitivity should be reflected in some kind of qualitative sensitivity analysis in case-based research on unanticipated outcomes, although it is rarely undertaken.

The situation where an outcome is anticipated and intended yet unwelcome is a problematic one. In simple taxonomic terms, it is the inverse of the happy surprise. If the argument above is followed, that the coding of outcomes should follow the evaluations of decision-makers at the time of the original decision, then it should be the only logically empty cell, because an outcome intended at a given time must, by the definition of intention, be regarded by the actor as welcome at that time. If, however, that argument is rejected — for example, for the purpose of a biographical historical study that addresses changes of mind — then it could be used for cases of regret.

Unconscious intentions may be much more interesting theoretically than they are in fact routinely important in public policy settings. These code the situations in which people do not anticipate to some threshold of likelihood that which they intend.

The simplest but liminal case of a situation where an outcome is not anticipated, yet intended and welcome, is one in which policy-makers commit to a course of action that they feel they either must take, might as well take, or ought to be seen to take, in the not very confident hope that it might have the results they would ideally expect and must say publicly that they expect from it. In the table, this is called 'despairing hope'. The reason that this is a liminal case, is that hoping against one's belief in the adverse probabilities that the action one takes just might turn out well in the way that one proclaims publicly it is meant to, is problematically located at the margins both of intention and of anticipation. A despairing hope would be said by many either only just or hardly to count as an intention, while a belief that an outcome is a low probability but still one that the actor has considered might be said to border upon anticipation, at least if we are using a low or bare threshold, as well we might. Alternatively, despairing hope of this kind might be said to be a case of conflicting intentions between the proclaimed one and those of being seen to do something or of simply complying with constraint.

An equally interesting but more paradoxical case of a despairing hope arises from the definition of an intention with which at least this book and scholars more generally have worked. This requires us to downgrade our claim to intend a thing to a claim merely to hope for it or desire it or try to bring it about if we can, when we cannot anticipate that our actions could bring it about, with a likelihood greater than some threshold. In individual behaviour, there are examples with which psychopathology is familiar of unconscious intentions that in fact guide a person's action, even though they are not consciously pursuing those aims. How far such things are possible in contemporary governments is a moot point. One possibility might be the operation of something like groupthink dynamics (Janis 1982). Certainly, there are cases where political leaders seem to show an unconscious self-destructive impulse in their decisions that is not apparent to them at the time.

Again, though, the coding of cases on the boundaries between unconscious self-destructive impulses and risks knowingly run will be sensitive to thresholds adopted for a policy-maker's consciousness of the possibilities of failure. Although he never discussed it with his aides and never acknowledged that he had not thought through what to do if and when it occurred, Khrushchev probably did recognize the possibility that his missiles in Cuba would be discovered by the Americans before he would be able to announce them as a *fait accompli*. He gambled everything on not being discovered, and apparently showed great confidence until very late in the summer and autumn of 1962 that he could avoid discovery prior to being able to make an announcement himself: perhaps this could be a case of a despairing hope too. Clearly, the outcome in the form President Kennedy's decision to blockade announced on 22 October was neither unintended by nor welcome to Khrushchev, but whether this was an unconscious self-destructive impulse or a risk knowingly run is very sensitive to the thresholds we set for anticipation.

Classifying Cases Studied in this Volume

The chapters in this volume illustrate several common types of case identified in Table 3.1, but do not cover the waterfront of possibilities. We do not present cases of unconscious intentions, nor do we explore the conceptually problematic possibilities of regret.

Some are more or less unambiguously bad surprises for those policy-makers who devised and undertook the interventions. This is the case for Sridhar's account of the World Bank's Tamil Nadu Integrated Nutrition Project and for Keen's tale of large-scale information systems programme in Britain's National Health Service.

Other chapters present outcomes that appear to be bad surprises for some people who contributed to the developments, but may well have been risks knowingly run for others. Just who anticipated or intended what is critical. Hofmann's study of the internet's early years shows that the emergence of cybercrime beyond that which could be contained by the initial communities of users disappointed their utopian hopes. On the other hand, some developers, governments, and regulators did anticipate the risks of outright criminality and of unscrupulous commerce.

Boyne *et al.* find that performance management in English local government was an unambiguous success. Only the anticipations of researchers, whose work suggested that such schemes typically fail, were happily dashed. But their intentions are of no consequence (therefore, it cannot be a case of a happy surprise). If policy-makers were surprised at all, then presumably it would have been by councils' greater than anticipated responsiveness to their scheme or by the speed with which their performance improved.

Wilks presents a case where anticipated and unanticipated consequences compounded each other. He also argues that Berners-Lee's original intention or at least hope was to produce, not the rather simple system of linkages that was the first-generation World Wide Web, but something much more like the semantic web that was only finally achieved many years later. If Berners-Lee anticipated the semantic web, he did not anticipate the causal path by which it was finally achieved, almost as a benign side-effect; conversely, bringing forth the World Wide Web while hoping to build the semantic web was a happy surprise.

Marsden's study of performance-related pay in British public services reports people learning from an initial disappointment to produce a happy outcome by an unanticipated path. Improvements in performance arose, not from the direct incentive effects of the performance-related pay schemes, but from the refocusing of managerial effort and attention on objectives. Some of the early committee reports advocating the system had indeed foreseen some of the risks, thus making this a case where risks were knowingly run.

British Rail's investment programme, in Leunig's treatment, was driven by goals defined in engineering terms — principally, the deployment of advanced, large-scale technology rather than consumer satisfaction, efficiency in delivering workers from residential areas to places of work, or even the maximization of votes. Under-achievement on these other, arguably more important measures may have been a risk knowingly run by the company or by governments in the later decades of the company's existence, even if it was a bad surprise prior to the Beeching review of the early 1960s.

There are interesting contrasts in the causal pathways bringing about outcomes. Two bad surprises appear to be the result of blinkering (itself an unintended process achieved by institutions) that produced the rejection of certain types of information (Thompson and Wildavsky 1986; 6 2004; 6 *et al.* 2007). Sridhar argues that hierarchical ordering in the World Bank sustained a commitment to the use of theories from medicine and economics that were insensitive to local context and especially to social structure and the vagaries of implementation. Likewise, Keen argues that, in the case of NHS IT systems, individualistic institutions sustaining ministers' hubris, and more hierarchical ones enabling capture of government by the IT industry sustained institutional blinkering against early signs of failure. Similarly, in Hofman's chapter, enclaved small communities supported the utopian thought styles of some early user communities of the internet.

Wilks's study of the semantic web and Marsden's examination of performance-related pay both show the opposite dynamic: in these cases, institutional positive feedback was not so extreme as to prevent people from learning from their early results.

The happy surprise in performance management of English local government seems to have result from overdetermination: several powerful incentive effects were at work. First the scheme informed a segment of the local electorate that was willing to vote on the basis of performance, even putting aside initial preference for a party. Second, the scheme mobilized senior managers' career aspirations. Third, the enclaved local government world was tightly enough networked for reputations to be circulated quickly. Finally it drew upon local civic pride. These mechanisms were sufficiently strong, the authors argue, to overcome what might otherwise have been the dismal series of processes of distraction, distortion, gaming, instrumentalization, and capture that led public administration scholars to expect failure.

In several of the case studies, then, we observe the chaining (or concatenation: Gambetta 1998) of types, running from bad to worse surprises (IT in the NHS), from bad to happy surprise (performance-related pay), from

59

mixed bad and happy to happy (the emergence of the semantic web from the World Wide Web).

Finally, pathways of causation producing outcomes from interventions, to the extent that they are independent of those which shape anticipations and intentions, are in no way distinct from those known to the social sciences generally. The role of opportunities created by technologies for the malign and benign alike (cybercrime and commerce on the internet), the importance of overdetermination and positive feedback in alignment of incentives (performance management for local government), or the tendency of systems designed to concentrate on technological advance not to achieve more consumer- or voter-friendly outcomes (investment in British Rail), are entirely familiar processes, not ones that are particular to unanticipated or unintended consequences.

Conclusion

There are still some fields in social science where the application of fairly simple and coarse conceptual frameworks, falling short of theories that can be tested, can furnish progress in understanding. This chapter offers just such a simple scheme of categories in order to try to resolve some muddles and confusions that have too long vitiated the study of unintended and unanticipated consequences. The scheme does no more, but also no less than distinguish carefully between anticipation, intention, and welcome, set thresholds of probability before we should call an anticipation a true expectation, require clarity about whose anticipations and intentions are of interest, and contrast the value of welcome for an outcome as it affects the intended goal with the manner in which it meets other goals (Hirschman 1991). Yet even such a simple piece of machinery serves to help us to understand the nature of what is paradoxical about such cases. Moreover, even the simple distinction between causal mechanisms which principally affect anticipation and intention, and those which mainly govern the results of action, however the actors themselves anticipate or intend its results, helps us both to search for and to classify some of the principal pathways by which paradoxes can arise.

II

Societal Innovations

4

Ranking US Public Affairs Educational Programmes

Searching for Quality, Finding Equilibrium?

H. George Frederickson and Edmund C. Stazyk

Editors' Overview

In this chapter, George Frederickson and Edmund Stazyk analyse the effects of ranking systems, a form of quantitative performance indicator that has been much to the fore in governance and public management in recent decades. While the authors see such performance measures as 'modernist' in a sense, reflecting Weber's view that quantification is an aspect of modernity, they also suggest that many rankings can also be seen as 'a postmodern wedding of simplified social science and popular entertainment'. The case they examine is that of the ranking of public affairs programmes in US universities, which was initiated in the mid-1990s not by any government or NGO body but by a newspaper, US News and World Report. *The rankings, conducted every three years, were introduced by James Fallows, former editor of that newspaper, apparently for a mixture of commercial reasons (to sell extra copies of the newspaper) and a more high-minded mission to give better information to student consumers and their parents making choices about colleges or programmes.*

As the authors show, some of the effects of that newspaper initiative were precisely as anticipated and intended by the originators. The rankings did indeed attract a great deal of attention and sold millions of extra copies of US News and World Report. *Further, they came to be widely accepted by universities and colleges after initial hiccups and were soon being taken very seriously by colleges in their marketing and positioning in spite of predictable criticisms by social-*

science methodologists about their validity and reliability. Moreover, there is at least strong circumstantial evidence that college students used them in large numbers as part of their selection decisions. But other effects of these rankings could hardly have been intended even if they were anticipated — such as marketing, hiring, and gaming on the part of organizations trying to shore up or boost their ranking scores, and the fact that much of the movement in the rankings from one period to another is statistical noise rather than 'news you can use' in any more substantive sense. Some other effects, notably the tendency of ranking positions to stabilize over time (which the authors see as part of a 'general theory' of ranking behaviour), seem not to have been anticipated, whether or not they were intended by those introducing or advocating such rankings. And in some cases it is not entirely clear just what was anticipated or intended, particularly over the tendency of rankings to work against adventurous but risky changes to their programmes by top-ranked institutions — producing institutional isomorphism and dampening creativity and innovation by creating a defensive arms race.

Introduction

Approximately every three years *US News and World Report* (hereafter *US News*) publishes its rankings of master's degree programmes in public affairs. As part of its 'America's best graduate schools' series, the most recent *US News* rankings of public affairs programmes appeared in 2008. Earlier rankings were published in 2004, 2001, 1998, and 1995. What were the intentions of those introducing these rankings, what form did the rankings take and what intended or unintended effects did they have? Our study begins with a consideration of the background, rationale, scope, and methodology of the *US News* ranking programme, and what those who introduced it intended and anticipated the rankings would do. We then describe a 'general theory' of academic rankings, set out our findings in the context of that theory, and consider those findings in the light of what effects were anticipated or intended by those who introduced the rankings.

Background of the *US News* Ranking Programme

James Fallows, who served as editor of *US News* from 1995 to 1998, was a strong advocate for 'news you can use', and argued that university rankings are just such news. His intentions in introducing a ranking of US Public Affairs graduate programmes seem to have been a mixture of market exploitation and the development of consumer information. As for the former, publishing university rankings is very good business at a time when the print media are struggling. *US News* 'estimates that it sells over 2.2 million copies of the college ranking issue, reaching an end audience of 11 million people, and an additional 1 million copies of the related college guidebook. Taken together, the *U.S News* ranking publications account for nearly half of the total market of 6.7 million copies of newsmagazine college rankings and guides' (Dichev 2001: 237; McDonough *et al.* 1998). Fallows said that the annual issue ranking schools and colleges is to *US News* what the annual swimsuit issue is to *Sports Illustrated.*

Linked to the intention to sell more copies of *US News* was the anticipation and intention that such a ranking would help consumers. *US News* and other ranking outfits, following the long-standing success of *Consumer Reports*, argue that they bring objective third-party evaluation to the marketplace of goods and services, thereby increasing consumer information and reducing consumer risk. Indeed, school and college rankings generally fit the modern world of performance measurement and evaluation, organizational metrics, and measures of social and economic outcomes. Like the promise to tell readers about the best cities, the best hospitals, the best airline on-time record, and the best place to retire, school and college rankings promise to tell magazine readers where to study. On a more serious side, the 'failing school' category in the application of the US 'No Child Left Behind' policy introduced under the Bush presidency in 2001 is a test-based ranking regime. So too are the US Office of Management and Budget's President's Management Agenda system of giving green, red, or yellow lights to agency performance, and their Program Assessment Rating Tool (PART) and its 'percent accountable' measure. Report cards are a close cousin to ranking and essentially the same thing (Gormley and Weimer 1999). Ranking is the fashion of the day. Rankings are everywhere. Rankings are powerful. All goods and services can be ranked, including graduate programmes in public affairs.

US News' first ranking of graduate programmes in public affairs in 1995 produced several effects that were unanticipated by Fallows and his staff. The survey instrument had been distributed in 1994 using a mailing list acquired from the National Association of School of Public Affairs and Administration (NASPAA), assuming the list was the universe of graduate programmes. Wrong. When the first ranking appeared in 1995, the public policy programmes at the University of California at Berkeley and the University of Michigan at Ann Arbor, among others, were simply not ranked (Frederickson 2001*b*). After a loud protest from the universities that had been left out and from the Association for Public Policy Analysis and Management (APPAM), the survey instrument for the second *US News* ranking, mailed in 1997, was distributed to an integrated mailing list of NASPAA and APPAM member institutions.

When the first *US News* ranking of public affairs graduate programmes appeared in 1995, it purported to rank master's degrees in the field. However, neither the instructions nor the survey instrument mentioned master's degrees, and asked only for a comparative evaluation of graduate programmes in public affairs, evidently assuming that master's degrees and graduate programmes in public affairs are the same thing. We will never know how many survey respondents compared doctoral programmes or compared both master's and doctoral programmes. Again, after a protest, the *US News* survey mailed in 1997 corrected that mistake (Frederickson 2001a).

Easily the loudest protest to the 1995 rankings, however, had to do with a basic assumption on the part of *US News* that master's degree programmes in public administration (the MPA) could be reasonably grouped with master's degree programmes in public policy (MPP) or policy analysis under the broader rubric of public affairs. After all, the protesters pointed out, public affairs graduate education is not like the study of law or the study of business administration. Almost all law schools give the *juris doctor* (JD) degree and almost all business schools award the master's degree in business administration (MBA). However, although most graduate public affairs programmes award the MPA degree, a small but significant and prestigious group of universities award the MPP or its equivalent. In the late 1960s the Ford Foundation assisted eight universities (Berkeley, Carnegie-Mellon, Duke, Harvard, Michigan, Texas, Stanford, and RAND) in the establishment of graduate programmes in public policy analysis (Ellwood 2008). At the time, and still today, this was thought to be an important break with the traditional study of public administration. By the mid-1990s, at the time of the first *US News* rankings, several more prestigious universities had developed public policy graduate programmes and several other universities long associated with the traditional study of public administration were transforming their courses into public policy programmes. The collective claim of the public policy schools that it was unreasonable to group them with public administration programmes in an overall public affairs graduate education ranking was somewhat successful.[1] For their 1998

---

[1] Distinctions between policy schools and public administration schools are not always clear. Several top schools offer both the MPA and the MPP degrees. Some schools, such as Syracuse and U.S.C., have deep roots in public administration but give no quarter with respect to their policy *bond fides*.

ranking and all subsequent public affairs rankings, *US News* did general public affairs rankings as well as separate rankings in established fields or specializations. Four of the nine specializations — environmental policy and management, health policy and management, public policy analysis, and social policy — are best described as policy fields. Having responded to some extent to the protests of the policy schools, *US News* stuck with its overall public affairs master's degree ranking, mixing together degree programmes with somewhat different emphases.

Not long after the publication of the first public affairs rankings in 1995, critical articles began to appear (Perry 1995; Teasley 1995; Ventriss 1995) — something Fallows might well have anticipated, since criticisms of rankings of this kind are commonly made. The strongest criticisms were methodological, questioning the design of the survey instrument, the aggregation of data, and the interpretation of those data. There were also strong arguments that the *US News* rankings were entirely reputational, lacking any objective measures of quality, such as indices of peer reviewed publication. Not only are the surveys reputational, they are limited to the opinions of deans, directors, and faculty members and not the opinions of students or clients. Critics pointed out that reputational surveys present aggregate opinions about programme quality rather than actual measures of quality. Furthermore, it is very difficult to uncouple the reputation of public affairs master's degree programmes from the overall reputations of the universities of which they are a part. This, critics claimed, privileged graduate programmes at prestigious universities. Critics claimed that this form of ranking was essentially a popularity contest. Critics also pointed out that the distinctions or spaces between the first, second, and third ranked programmes were so slight as to have little meaning. Indeed, there are many ties in the rankings, in some cases ties involving several degree programmes. Finally, critics pointed out that the rankings were made by deans, directors, and faculty members, almost all with doctorates. It was claimed, therefore, that the ranking regime privileged master's degree programmes associated with schools that also grant doctoral degrees.

The second round of *US News* ranking of master's degrees in public affairs, published in 1998, was better received. Not only was the world of public affairs education more accustomed to the idea, the addition of rankings in nine separate fields or specializations allowed more programmes to win. This time, for example, a university could note in its promotional literature that it was ranked high in information technology or environmental policy. Dozens of master's degree programmes could point to their specialized standing and gain at least some bragging rights (Frederickson 2001*b*). Top overall rankings were somewhat reordered with the inclusion of Berkeley, tied for fifth, and Michigan, tied for eighth. By the time of the publication of the third round of ranking in 2001, the primary patterns were established and there were few big surprises. In both the overall ranking and the specialized rankings a programme might move up or down two or three or even four positions, but there were few examples of dramatic advances or retreats. About the same has held for both the fourth round in 2005 and the recently published fifth round.

The thirteen-year history of *US News* ranking of public affairs master's degree programmes reveals other important developments, some that James Fallows probably intended and anticipated and others less likely to be in either category. First, as Fallows intended and anticipated, rankings attract a lot of attention both inside and outside the small world of education for public service. We may agree that rankings are reputational popularity contests and casual social science but they are also exciting and fun. In fact, while as noted above the ranking business has some of the features often associated with modernism (particularly quantitative measurement on the basis of performance in some sense), it can be most usefully thought of as a postmodern wedding of simplified social science and popular entertainment. Complicated matters are distilled to simple one, two, three categories and are put into sound bites that busy people can easily digest without being conceptually overburdened. Image has become reality (Frederickson 2001*a*).

Second, most of what we know about the importance of ranking comes from the study of general university and college ranking. In separate studies, C. J. Fombrun (1996) and P. M. McDonough *et al.* (1998) found that prospective students who use rankings tend to have higher grades and are in general better prepared for college. In addition, in 1998 McDonough *et al.* found that more than 400,000 perspective students considered college rankings as an important factor in making their college application choices. Ilia Dichev (2001: 238) concludes that 'albeit grudgingly, most top university administrations have accepted the importance of rankings'. We have no comparable data on the salience of the *US News* rankings to the application decisions of prospective master's degree students in public affairs. Reason suggests, however, that student's public affairs graduate school choices are not that different from the choices made by students (and their parents) regarding undergraduate education. Indeed, there is the possibility that rankings are more important to students making graduate school choices. An extensive survey of studies of the responses to rankings of law schools indicates that reactions to rankings are rather pronounced. 'Even small differences in rank affect the number and quality of applications a school receives and its yield....Shifts in applications and yield change the selectivity score used by *USN* to compute its ranking and in this way reinforce the original differences which were often largely a product of measurement noise' (Espeland and Sauder 2007: 12).

Third, albeit reputational, the *US News* ranking regime is fairly democratic. Each of the 114 schools ranked is in the peerage, and the rankings provided by those who do the scoring at Portland State have the same status as those who do the scoring at Harvard. The one school/one vote system (actually each school has two votes) takes the opinions of deans, directors, and faculty in all schools equally into account.

Fourth — and beginning to move into developments less likely to have been anticipated or intended by James Fallows — the addition of rankings in nine public policy and administration specializations in the 1998 ranking and subsequent rankings has caused *US News* to develop a particularly complex survey instrument. After completing their overall ranking using the list of master's degree programmes in the instrument, respondents are asked, specialization by specialization, to list the top ten programmes in descending rank. In the public policy analysis specialization, for example, respondents are asked to parse between Harvard, Berkeley, Michigan, Carnegie Mellon, Duke, Chicago, and many others as to which is best, second best, and so forth. And this is to be done in nine specializations. Critics argue that such a process assumes, on the part of respondents, an unlikely level of knowledge and expects a sublime level of precision. Nevertheless, the specializations feature of the *US News* public affairs master's degree rankings has, over time, come to be at least as important as the overall rankings.

Fifth, between the second ranking in 1998 and the third ranking in 2001 a form of programme marketing appeared. Using the NASPAA and APPAM mailing lists and other lists, graduate programmes started sending their annual reports, programme materials primarily designed for potential students, locally published journals, and other promotional materials to all member institutions. This relatively subtle form of marketing has continued and has flourished. Some promotions have been less subtle. There have been, for example, letters and emails from particular institutions to all deans and directors saying, in effect, 'You will soon receive the *US News & World Report* ranking instrument for master's degrees in public affairs. As you fill them out, please keep our programme in mind. The attached materials will tell you about the qualifications of our faculty, the incoming average test scores of our students, etc., etc.' Visibility in the peerage is important in the era of rankings.

Sixth, there is evidence of positioning, which takes many forms including attracting the editorship of a leading journal, hiring a well-known scholar, serving as a conference host, or organizing a doctoral programme. To be sure, positioning has always been with us. We do not know the extent to which rankings have stimulated positioning but we can be sure that ranking has done nothing to hold it back. Further, there is evidence that rankings are affecting certain programmes' searches for and selection of deans and directors. Search committees are not shy about asking candidates what they know about ranking and, if they were dean, what they would do to retain or improve a school's position. In the case of law schools, evidence indicates that such institutions respond by more nearly conforming to the ranking criteria used by *US News* and tend to abandon unique missions not measured in rankings. We have no direct evidence of reactions of this type to the ranking of master's degrees in public affairs, although we do have indications of marketing, hiring, and gaming (Frederickson 2001a, 2001b).

Finally, as ranking is a factor in public affairs education, so too is strategic planning. It is no surprise that the two have found each other. The language of ranking seems ideally suited to the logic and language of strategic planning. The University of Kentucky is well known for its Top 20 Business Plan. The University of California at Santa Cruz advertises for a leader who can implement its plan to improve its national standing. There is evidence that schools of law, business, engineering, and, yes, public affairs also have combined strategic planning and rankings. This is indeed strategic as the case of the University of Kentucky illustrates: 'Perhaps Dr. Todd's (the president) most significant accomplishment came last year (2006) when he persuaded the Legislature to appropriate an additional $21 million a year for the plan, much of it for raises among faculty members and the hiring of 110 professors' (Finder 2001: A19). Time will tell whether this investment will improve the Kentucky ranking.

Outcomes: A General Theory of Academic Rankings

The observed outcomes of the *US News* public affairs rankings can be argued to be a particular case that fits with a broader general theory of academic rankings, which we describe in the following pages before turning to what was intended or anticipated about these outcomes.

Principle One: Under ranking regimes universities and colleges may in the short run move up or down the ranks, but in the long run university ranking will be stable. Although rankings tend towards stability, equilibrium, or path dependence, there may from time to time be examples of dramatic change that require explanation.

Ilia Dichev's study of the *US News* rankings of the top twenty-five national universities and the top twenty-five national liberal arts colleges found that

changes in the *USN* rankings have a strong tendency to revert in the next two rankings. The reversibility in rankings is strong not only in statistical terms but seems to account for a strikingly large part of the total variation in rankings changes. Using a simple model of two-period reversibility, it appears that between 70 and 80 percent of the variation in rankings change is due to 'noise,' to transitory effects, which quickly disappear in later rankings. Thus, most of the 'news' in *USN* annual college ranking is essentially meaningless noise. (Dichev 2001; see also the Morgeson and Nahrgang 2008, study of MBA rankings for a similar result)

With this empirical claim we turn to Table 4.1, the *US News* rankings of master's degrees in public affairs and a summary of five ranking periods over a thirteen-year period.

The 2008 rankings of master's degrees in public affairs are in the left-hand column and the earlier rankings and their year are indicated in the other columns. First, the anomaly or noise between the 1995 rankings, which left out several leading schools, and the 1998 rankings indicates a reallocation of several of the top twenty-five positions. Even with that, however, the pattern of equilibrium is strong. Positions 1 to 6 have been ultra-stable. Kansas, at number 7 (tied) in 2008 was at number 6 (tied) in 1995 and bounced around in the intervening years. However, the University of North Carolina at Chapel Hill, which was also tied for the sixth position in 1995, has ranged between tenth and fourteenth ever since. Among the top twenty-five, there are only two that appear to be exceptions to the equilibrium rule. The University of Texas at Austin was at position four in 1995 and has gone gradually but steadily down to being tied for position fourteen in 2008. New York University, left out of the 1995 rankings, first appeared in 1998 and has climbed from position twenty-six to position ten. Whether UNC at Chapel Hill, Texas at Austin, or NYU will become examples of dramatic change, requiring explanation, or will revert to their original positions or stay at or near their 2008 rankings when the rankings are done again in 2011 remains to be seen.

The second group, positions 25 to 50, also exhibits strong patterns of equilibrium, although the data prior to the 2002 rankings are not as

Table 4.1. *U.S. News* ranking of master's degrees in public affairs

2008	2004	2001	1998	1995
1. Syracuse University	1	1	1	1
2. Harvard University	2	1	2	2
2. Indiana University-Bloomington	3	3	3	4
4. Princeton University	5	4	3	2
4. University of Georgia	3	6	5	6
6. University of California-Berkeley	5	4	5	—
7. University of Kansas	10	12	14	6
7. University of Michigan-Ann Arbor	8	7	8	—
7. University of Southern California	7	7	8	6
10. Carnegie Mellon University	8	7	8	10
10. Duke University	10	19	11	18
10. New York University	17	19	26	—
10. University of Chicago	17	12	14	13
14. American University	10	12	14	13
14. Columbia University	21	12	18	13
14. George Washington University	10	19	20	13
14. Georgetown University	17	29	30	—
14. SUNY-Albany	10	12	11	—
14. University of Califomia-Los Angeles	21	24	26	—
14. University of Minnesota-Twin Cities	21	12	18	18
14. University of North Carolina-Chapel Hill	10	12	14	6
14. University of Texas-Austin	10	7	5	4
14. University of Washington	26	24	20	24
14. University of Wisconsin-Madison	17	11	11	10
25. Arizona State University	26	24	30	24
25. University of Maryland-College Park	21	19	20	—
27. Florida State University	26	24	—	18
27. Georgia State University	26	31	—	—
27. University of Nebraska-Omaha	26	31	—	—
27. University of Pittsburgh	21	19	20	13
27. Virginia Tech	26	24	20	18
32. Johns Hopkins University	26	29	30	—
32. Rutgers State University-Newark	26	46	—	—
32. University of Colorado-Denver	35	35	—	—
32. University of Kentucky	34	31	—	—
36. Cornell University	35	35	26	24
36. Ohio State University	42	35	30	18
36. Texas A&M University-College Station	35	46	—	—
36. University of Arizona	46	31	30	—
36. University of Missouri-Columbia	35	35	—	—
41. Northern Illinois University	35	41	—	—
41. University of Delaware	35	41	—	—
41. University of Illinois-Chicago	46	—	—	—
41. University of Pennsylvania	42	35	—	—
45. Cleveland State University	42	35	—	—
45. George Mason University	46	46	—	—
45. Indiana University-Indianapolis	—	—	—	—
45. Naval Postgraduate School	42	46	—	—
49. Portland State University	—	46	—	—
49. University of Connecticut	—	—	—	—

complete. Therefore, claims of equilibrium among the second group are based on three ranking cycles rather than five.

It appears that the overall ranking of master's degrees in public affairs fits the pattern of equilibrium over time set out in the general theory of ranking. This suggests that Dichev is right, that much of the 'news' associated with the publication of the results of new *US News* ranking of master's degrees in public affairs every three years is mostly 'noise.' Dichev also found that methodological changes and glitches explain some of the variation in overall *US News* rankings, and we see evidence of this in the public affairs rankings, particularly the faulty mailing list used in 1995.

The ranking of specialties in master's degrees in public affairs by *US News* also conforms to the first principle of the general theory of university and college ranking. Analysing the rankings of the nine specialties (city management/public policy, environmental policy and management, health policy and management, information technology and management, nonprofit management, public finance and budgeting, public management/administration, public policy analysis, and social policy), six of the nine specializations turn out to exhibit equilibrium from the first specialty rankings in 1997, and the other three — public finance and budgeting, nonprofit administration, and health policy and administration — are at equilibrium for the past two ranking cycles. There may be examples of dramatic change that will, in time, require explanation. For example, in 2008 Arizona State tied for the sixth position in city management and urban policy, never having been in the top ten before. Columbia and Wisconsin-Madison are eighth and tenth respectively in the 2008 environmental policy specialization. There are a few other short-term exceptions to principle one of the general theory. Nevertheless, it is likely that in the long-term the specialty rankings will regress to the mean.[2]

If stability and equilibrium are the default condition in higher education ranking regimes, how are patterns of innovation and change explained?

Principle Two: Significant and lasting change to equilibrium in university and college ranking regimes follow the S curve of the diffusion of innovation.

In the theory of the diffusion of innovation, the benefits of innovation are greater to early adopters than to intermediate and late adopters (Rogers 1995). One explanation for the staying power of the top fifteen master's degree programmes in public affairs is this: almost all the schools now in

---

[2] Readers may visit http://ecstazyk.com/SupplementalMaterial.aspx to view a table of *US News* specialty rankings of master's degrees from 1998 to 2008.

the upper ranks have a long history of association with the field of public administration, either as schools of public administration (the Maxwell School of Citizenship and Public Affairs of Syracuse University, the School of Public Administration and Citizenship at USC and, later, the Littauer School of Government at Harvard University); as a strong and distinct field and faculty within political science (Chicago, Berkeley, Michigan, Minnesota, Wisconsin, Indiana); or as strong and well-financed institutes of government (Georgia, Berkeley, North Carolina). Between the late 1920s and the mid-1950s, the field of public administration was an innovation and the schools most particularly associated with that innovation are even today among the most highly ranked. Several of the top fifteen schools were also part of a later innovation, the development of the policy schools starting in the 1970s. It is no surprise that of the original eight universities supported by the Ford Foundation, six (Harvard, Berkeley, Michigan, Carnegie-Mellon, Duke, Texas) are included in the top ranks (Ellwood 2008). So several universities were early adopters of public administration as an innovation and also early adopters of public policy as an innovation.

Intermediate and late adopters may borrow the templates of early adopters and may even do it better than early adopters. But in the world of rankings, so long as early adopters remain competitive, it is difficult for intermediate and late adopters to displace them. The second twenty-five in the *US News* rankings of master's degrees in public affairs is filled with solid programmes in public administration and/or policy. Nevertheless, it is difficult for them to move into the top twenty-five.

This argument is about both equilibrium and change. Patterns of university and college equilibrium are epochs, not changed quickly. The emergence of public administration reordered the equilibrium, and the emergence of public policy study reordered the equilibrium again. At present there does not appear to be a movement, an event, or a collective academic jailbreak strong enough to challenge the present equilibrium.

Principle Three: Specialization matters.

Indiana University, beginning in the 1940s, built a strong public administration programme in their political science department, including many of the leading scholars of the day — York Wilburn, Gaylon Keith Caldwell, Alfred Diamont, John Ryan, and, later, Elinor and Vincent Ostrom. In the 1970s, like many other public administration programmes in political science departments, the administration and faculty at Indiana University decided to establish a separate school and chose to call it the School of Public and Environmental Affairs. Two points are notable in this nomenclature. First, there is the brilliant linking of the field of public administration to the environmental policy field. Second, there is the use of the broader and ambiguous phrase 'public affairs' rather than the narrower and somewhat out-of-fashion phrase 'public administration'. Together, these choices were the foundation for an Indiana programme that is now consistently ranked second or third overall and always ranked first in environmental policy and nonprofit management. Additionally, Indiana is ranked sixth in information and technology management, third in public finance and budgeting and third in public management/administration.

The point is this: to be thought of as generally good, it helps to be thought of as specifically good. Five of the top ten master's degrees ranked best overall are also ranked best in a least one specialization. The others in the top 10 are ranked at least second or third in a specialization. Princeton is the only outlier, and only because for some mysterious reason US News does not rank a specialization in international affairs, a specialization in which Princeton would almost certainly be first.

We ran some simple statistical correlations and found the closest association between overall ranking and specialty ranking to be between the top policy schools and the four policy specializations.[3]

Rankings in the specializations can be very important to public affairs master's degree programmes at universities that are not highly ranked overall. Cleveland State, Northern Illinois, North Texas, and Delaware are, for example, in the top ten for the city management and urban policy specialization. Georgia Tech is highly ranked in information and technology management. Indiana University and Purdue University at Indianapolis is third in nonprofit management, with Washington (Seattle) fifth, Minnesota sixth, Johns Hopkins eighth, and New York University ninth. Georgia State, Connecticut, SUNY Albany, and Nebraska-Omaha are in the top ten in public finance and budgeting.

---

[3] Using Spearman's Rho, we examined correlations between collapsed groupings of the 2008 overall ranking and each specialty ranking. Although crude, the results provide support for Principle Three. None of the public administration specialties, including city management (Rho = -0.042; $p = 0.766$), information technology (Rho = -0.174; $p = 0.214$), nonprofit management (Rho = -0.204; $p = 0.143$), public budgeting (Rho = -0.252; $p = 0.068$), and public management/administration (Rho = -0.405; $p = 0.003$), correlated with the overall rankings. However, each of the public policy specialties were negatively correlated with the general rankings — environmental policy (Rho = -0.533; $p = 0.000$), health policy (Rho = -0.511; $p = 0.000$), public policy analysis (Rho = -0.537; $p = 0.000$), and social policy (Rho = -0.608; $p = 0.000$). These findings suggest public administration programmes with high general rankings are no more likely to have a specialty ranking than programmes lower in the overall rankings. In comparison, public policy programmes were more likely to be positioned poorly in the overall rankings and highly in policy specialties.

Principle Four: Under ranking regimes, universities and colleges in the top ranks will strengthen their assets to retain their ranks. Universities in the intermediate ranks will also strengthen their assets as they attempt to improve their ranks.

Assuming limited resources (the phrase 'scarce resources' does not seem appropriate in the context of billion dollar endowments), universities will invest in their strengths. Rankings, however flimsy they may be, constitute visible marks of strength or measures of reputational capital. Under conditions of limited resources, arguments for across-the-board allocations will almost always lose to arguments for allocations to retain the strengths of 'known' or ranked programmes. Elite universities with many top ten ranked disciplines and schools may have more grants and larger endowments, but the competition for university resources is fierce nevertheless. Highly ranked programmes will have an edge in this competition.

The counter argument is that universities take highly ranked programmes for granted and will be spare in their allocation to such programmes so as to allocate more to programmes with potential. This is an argument made by the deans of highly ranked programmes that are seeking greater university allocations. It is our observation that the evidence generally runs in the opposite direction.

Less elite universities, say universities not in the overall top twenty-five, but with a top ten specialization, will almost certainly allocate in favour of that specialization and that programme.

The idea that under ranking regimes universities in the upper and intermediate ranks will attempt to strengthen their assets suggests a kind of reverse tragedy of the commons, a state in which multiple competing institutions in a field have unique allocation advantages with which they can compete. Higher education, it turns out, is not the same thing as fishing villages or irrigation systems because every institution in the upper and intermediate ranks is strengthening its assets. It may be that, like accreditation, the ranking of universities generally and public affairs programmes specifically has an overall salutary effect on programme quality.

Principle Five: If equilibrium is the default condition under university and college ranking regimes, universities and colleges privileged by the rankings will not risk change. Rankings are, therefore, an enemy of college and university creativity and innovation and a form of institutional isomorphism.

Taken together, principles one to four of the general theory of the effects of rankings on colleges and universities account for ranking equilibrium over time, the salience of specialization, a consequent general improvement of ranked programmes over time for high and intermediate ranked institutions, and an occasional or epochal diffusion of innovation that settles into a new equilibrium. Principle five suggests that rankings, like accreditation, increase the isomorphic tendencies of highly ranked universities and colleges, making innovation less likely.

It was Max Weber (1968) who warned that the rationalist order, and particularly bureaucratization, is a force so powerful as to constitute an iron cage of order, reliability, and resistance to change. In their adaptation of Weber's iron cage thesis, Paul J. DiMaggio and Walter W. Powell (1983) set out a theory of institutional isomorphism that is particularly suited to explaining the influence of the ranking on universities and colleges, including master's degrees in public affairs. Modern universities are bureaucracies subject to the forces of homogenization. But, as DiMaggio and Powell (1983: 147) contend, 'bureaucratization and other forms of organizational change occur as the result of processes that make organizations more similar without necessarily making them more efficient'. The predictors of this kind of isomorphism include uncertain relationships between institutional means and ends, high reliance on academic credentials, high levels of professionalization, dependence on a single (or limited) source of support for vital resources, a limited number of visible alternative organizational models in a field, high levels of interaction between organizations in a field, and visible orders of status. All these predictors are in evidence in American universities and colleges, including master's degree programmes in public affairs. There are three mechanisms of institutional isomorphism. Coercive isomorphism results from imposed rules and policies, a common legal environment, regulatory regimes, licensing and accreditation, and other exogenous forces. Under conditions of mimetic isomorphism 'organizations tend to model themselves after similar organizations in their field that they perceive to be more legitimate or successful' (DiMaggio and Powell 1983: 152). In the case of higher education one must add the word prestigious to the words legitimate and successful. The logic of institutional benchmarking, essentially a form of copying, comes to mind. Finally, isomorphism is a result of normative pressures, including the filtering processes of formal education and credentialing; professional organizations as carriers of norms, standards, and culture; and, especially in recent decades, the professionalization of managers.

The evidence from law school rankings shows widespread institutional isomorphism (Espeland and Sauder 2007). Although there is no such direct evidence of an isomorphic effect in public affairs rankings, the law school findings are a caution.

Making the institutional isomorphism point, there is no doubt that NASPAA accreditation standards have been a powerful homogenizing force, particularly among the public administration schools. Established patterns of similarity in curriculum and pedagogy are also evident among the policy schools (Ellwood 2008).

The argument in principle five is not good news to those interested in institutional creativity and innovation. All the characteristics of institutional isomorphism are abundant in graduate public affairs education. To be sure, there are two primary models, the public administration model and the public policy model. Nevertheless, the deans and faculties of public affairs schools tend to conform to one or the other model or to squabble about which model they wish to conform to. There is precious little consideration of other models. Rankings, we argue, are powerful coercive, mimetic, and normative isomorphic forces that militate against the risks of exploring other models, particularly by schools privileged by the rankings.

Conclusions and Implications

What has been the outcome of public affairs rankings? For those like James Fallows who originated and support rankings, *US News* serves several valuable purposes. Commercially, *US News* sells millions of copies of its rankings issues, bringing the magazine a great deal of income, prestige, and attention. Furthermore, there seems to be strong evidence college students often rely on rankings to select between universities. For this reason, the rankings have come to be taken seriously by colleges and universities — in spite of strong criticism from statisticians and methodologists. In fact, universities are increasingly involved in marketing campaigns and other efforts that might increase their position in the rankings. Finally, supporters argue rankings provide students with useful information — Fallow's *news you can use* — that can aid students and families in the decision between schools. On whole, these factors would suggest rankings serve the purposes intended by Fallows. Yet, at a more basic level, as the general theory described above shows, rankings have brought about numerous, unintended consequences that have serious implications for universities.

In the most basic sense, rankings influence university behaviour in important, and potentially harmful, ways. Because rankings are largely reputational (rather than objective), universities increasingly seek to manipulate criteria linked to reputation by, in part, mimicking other prestigious schools. These universities also engage in marketing, hiring, and gaming to shore up their rank. Consequently, it appears rankings create powerful homogenizing, or isomorphic, forces that may diminish institutional innovation and creativity. Given that rankings tend towards equilibrium, the trend towards isomorphism is problematic.

The overriding significance of ranking equilibrium over time suggests that an attempt on the part of a particular dean or a particular faculty to improve their overall rank is a fool's errand. That is particularly the case for programmes ranked in the second twenty-five or lower. However, as principle four of the general theory asserts, schools and programmes advantaged by ranking, say those ranked in the top twenty-five, not only enjoy reputational capital, they almost certainly have an advantage in campus competition for resources. While the dynamics of ranking competition between programmes at or near the top may tend to equilibrium, those same dynamics compel top programmes to strengthen their assets just to hold their positions.

Although there is also equilibrium in the public affairs specialty rankings, it does not appear to be as pronounced as the overall ranking equilibrium. Some evidence shows movement in some of the specialty rankings, particularly in the positions between ranks five and ten. This suggests tactical possibilities for ambitious programmes. For example, in the past four or five years Arizona State University has forged a partnership with the International City/County Management Association and added a high-profile senior scholar in city management and urban policy. Between the 2005 and 2008 rankings ASU moved from the second ten in the city management and urban policy specialization to sixth. Will the forces of equilibrium pull ASU back to the second ten in the 2011 rankings? Or will ASU hold its sixth position and come to be at least a small example of meaningful change or evolution? Time, and ASU tactics, will tell.

Whether James Fallows intended the *US News* ranking of public affairs graduate programmes to be a monopoly is not clear, and the fact that it has become so must be counted either as a happy surprise for Fallows or as the intended result of his business strategy. But the *US News* ranking displays a feature often found in other rankings, when an established ranking continues to be dominant even when superior alternatives are or could be available. For example, Gormley and Weimer (1999) call for greater objectivity in ranking and are generally critical of reputational measures. Indeed, they unfavourably compare the *US News* and *Business Week* reputational rankings of MBA programmes with much more sophisticated and objective rankings by Tracy and Waldfogel (1997) that are based primarily on citation density analysis. Their research is buttressed by a study by Trieshmann *et al.*

(2000). The reputational and citation density approaches yield starkly different results, dropping several elite MBA programmes and replacing them with less prestigious programmes. The National Research Council's (1995) rankings of doctoral programmes are also more objective (citation density and awards) than the *US News* reputational methodology, again with somewhat different results. In a most interesting comparison of the two approaches, Diamond and Graham (1997, 2000) found that, in most fields, and overall, the top ten positions using either method are rather similar. However, below the top ten the differences were often great. The application of citation density ranking in public affairs education might similarly show a group of 'rising institutions' whose achievements are masked by reputational surveys, and the development of one or two credible ranking alternatives of public affairs graduate programmes, particularly if they were at least somewhat objective, would blunt the monopoly *US News* now enjoys. The problem is that, in line with the general theory described earlier, the institutions now privileged by the *US News* reputational model might have little incentive to push such a project.

5

Et in Arcadia Ego

From Techno-Utopia to Cybercrime

Jeanette Hofmann

Editors' Overview

In this chapter, Jeanette Hofmann investigates the origins of cybercrime, the darker consequence of the development of the internet and World Wide Web. Early users of the internet developed a utopian vision of the internet as an anarchic space, free from government intervention, which could act as a vehicle for radical social change, which might be labelled postmodernization. Hofmann shows how this 'cyberspace' community found analogies between their vision of social organization and the original network design of the internet. She delves into the technical history of the internet, showing how its original architects (largely government and academic computer scientists) envisaged a network for 'themselves', technological pioneers with the relatively modest aim of modernizing part of the state by interconnecting academic and military networks. In line with this aim, they designed a 'stupid' network, oblivious to applications and content, in contrast to the telephone carriers who aimed at publicly controlled national data networks. The internet engineering community won out and it was their technological vision that allowed the socially utopian vision of the cyberspace community to flourish.

However, as use of the internet became widespread, cybercrime also flourished. From the end of the 1990s, there was a steady and rapid increase of spam, viruses, and malware, but it was largely an amateur business. From 2003, cybercrime became more organized and indeed modernized, developing into a highly profitable global industry, with new virus-based spamming techniques and 'botnets', causing some to claim an 'online criminal revolution'. Although many new technologies have at some point been taken over by criminal activity, for different reasons, none of the original actors in the story of the internet appear to have anticipated this development. The internet engineering community hardly envisaged usage outside their own narrow (and to them, inherently trustworthy) community. In turn, the utopian early users also envisaged a 'cyberspace community' of people like themselves and saw only the charms of their new world, which with the advent of more organized cybercrime began to look more like the old one. Meanwhile, the growing proportion of individuals and firms who now rely on the internet battle with an increasingly sophisticated barrage of threats to on-line business and social life. Some commentators now predict that cybercrime may bring regulation to what was regarded as the ultimate 'ungovernable' space. Such a development would not be paradoxical in the strictest sense, but certainly an unwelcome surprise for the architects of the internet and especially the techno-utopians.

Introduction

The early history of the internet was characterized by a David and Goliath battle between modernizers and traditionalists. In the 1980s, when the organization of data communication was a much debated question, a new generation of engineers came forward with a vision of network design that challenged the hegemonic concept of the telephone carriers. Ten years later, in the 1990s, a first generation of non-technical users translated the technical properties of the internet into a political language and portrayed its architecture as a cosmopolitan and libertarian counter-project to prevailing forms of modernity. These early, mostly academic, users saw the internet as a new means for realizing democratic goals such as emancipation and social equality, and they often used a liberal vocabulary to promote a non-territorial, post-national and anti-hierarchical form of social organization.

Cybercrime is interpreted as one of the many unforeseen consequences enabled by the unprecedented extent of freedom the internet offers, shaped by the stress of both the internet developers and the 'techno-utopian' group of early users on autonomy and freedom. Neither of these groups, however, paid much attention to the question of mastery or 'how to govern life in common' (Wagner 2008: 2).

One might argue that there is nothing new about such unforeseen consequences arising from the development of large technical systems. At the outset, new technologies such as the train system or nuclear power typically evoke utopian dreams while their weaknesses and vulnerabilities remain largely underestimated or ignored. Furthermore, it is not uncommon for a technology that its use becomes increasingly regulated throughout its life cycle. What might set the internet apart from other technologies is the extent to which it permeates the private and social dimension of modern societies, more than most other technologies. The design of the internet minimizes central control to a degree that prevents any discrimination between socially desired and undesired, legal and illegal forms of use. Sooner or later, the internet might be as ubiquitous as electricity — yet, with an unprecedented potential for abuse. As a consequence of cybercrime, the internet could undergo changes that affect not only the freedom of use and innovation that made it so attractive as a social space, but also the technical architecture that enabled them in the first place.

In retrospect, one may also ask if such mischief could not have been foreseen in the early stages of internet development. This chapter tackles this question by exploring the dominant orientations of two groups who significantly contributed to the understanding of the internet. The first section explores the technological history of the internet, focusing on the engineering community that developed the internet in the 1970s and 1980s and the 'revolutionary' design philosophy that inspired its architecture. The second section describes the ways in which the early users of the internet in the 1990s used the characteristics of the technological network to inspire a utopian vision of the internet, their belief in the internet as an ungovernable and anarchic space, and their response to pending government regulation. The subsequent growth of the internet and the diversification of users and usages were clearly beyond the imagination of both the developers and the early academic users. Both groups argued in a context of conflicting visions. They defended their concept of autonomy against more traditional understandings of organizing and regulating data communication. The third section of this chapter describes cybercrime as an unforeseen, yet increasingly dangerous way of making use of the internet.

Technical Origins of the Utopian Vision: Conflicting Visions of Communication Networks

Turning to the 1970s, it is possible to trace the technical origins of the utopian vision of the internet. The emerging landscape of data communication in the 1970s lacked general standards for data transmission that would facilitate communication across different computer networks, or 'internetworking', and the 'internet' was an attempt to provide that bridge.

Among the various attempts to develop computer network architectures, two standard developing initiatives stood out that aimed at open, vendor-independent solutions that would enable universal data communication: the 'Internet protocol suite',[1] which originated in the US defence research environment, and 'X.25', a set of technical recommendations jointly developed by intergovernmental standardization bodies for telecommunication networks[2] (Salus 1995: 124). Both engineering communities pursued the same goal; a single network architecture that would enable digital communication across networks, organizations and countries. Yet, 'for those watching the development of network standards, X.25 and TCP/IP became symbols of the carriers' and the Internet community's opposing approaches to networking' (Abbate 1999: 155).

The telephone companies envisioned data exchange as a public service that would basically follow the same organizational model as telephone networks. The heterogeneous landscape of network architectures of the 1970s appeared as a mere interim stage soon to be replaced by a single public network. Like voice transmission, data communication would be organized and controlled by national carriers which would connect their networks to those of other national carriers. As Abbate (1999: 156) notes, to the developers of X.25, 'it seemed self-evident that the best service to customers would result from a system where a few large telecommunications providers controlled network operations'.

The engineers who developed the TCP/IP network architecture started from a different set of assumptions. While they also identified the incompatibility of existing network architectures as a problem, they did not expect the diversity of networks to disappear. Instead, the research community aimed for a network architecture that would acknowledge and tolerate heterogeneity. As Hafner and Lyon (1996: 225) put it, the challenge was to 'devise protocols that would cope with autonomous networks operating under their own rules, while still establishing standards that would allow hosts on the different networks to talk to each other'. An experiment carried out in 1977 that managed to connect a radio network on a moving van, a satellite network, and the ARPANET, the forerunner of the internet,

---

[1] The internet protocol suite consists of the Transmission Control Protocol (TCP) and the Internet Protocol (IP) and is usually referred to as TCP/IP; see http://en.wikipedia.org/wiki/TCP/IP.
[2] The International Telecommunication Union (ITU) and the International Organization for Standardization (ISO).

meant to demonstrate just that: the possibility of connecting autonomous network architectures through a simple type of meta-network, an *Internet*.

The different assumptions about the future organization of data communications — in simplified terms, centrally operated homogeneous networks versus autonomously operated heterogeneous networks — had crucial implications for the technical design of network architectures. The paradigmatic fight that broke out between the telephone community and the nascent internet community revolved around these implications. One of them concerned the division of labour between the network and its end points, the devices or applications attached to the network (Blumenthal and Clark 2001: 80). While telephone networks traditionally achieved reliable performance by placing control functions in the network, the developers of the internet chose to depart from this principle of central control and opted for the 'stupid network' approach (Isenberg 1997), which minimizes the functions in the network and maximizes the responsibility of the network's end points. Because the stupid network delegates the control over data transmission to the applications, the network itself neither knows if the data reach their destination, nor what kind of data it transmits; it is 'oblivious' to the content it transports (Aboba and Davies 2007).[3]

The internet engineering community offered several reasons for this stupid network approach, which some years later became summarized as the 'end-to-end argument', a now famous architectural principle that is still often quoted (Saltzer *et al.* 1984; Blumenthal and Clark 2001; Kempf and Austein 2004; Russell 2006).[4] Placing the control at the end points of the network had the advantage that the network itself could be more easily changed and, more importantly, new applications could be added without changing the network. As the 'end-to-end' aficionados reminded the community,

building complex function into a network implicitly optimizes the network for one set of uses while substantially increasing the cost of a set of potentially valuable uses that may be unknown or unpredictable at design time. A case in point: had the original Internet design been optimized for telephony-style virtual circuits..., it would never have enabled the experimentation that led to protocols that could support the World-Wide Web...(Reed *et al.* 1998)

---

[3] The 'guaranteed service approach' of the centralized telephone network was replaced by a 'best effort delivery' model that shifts the responsibility for error control to the end points.

[4] Given the military research environment, the original motivation for shifting control out of the actual network had to do with considerations of reliability and resilience: a network was assumed to survive hostile attacks more easily if the end points could re-establish communication after network failures (Clark 1988).

Thanks to the end-to-end principle, new services and applications could be introduced without changing the core of the network and, hence, without asking anybody's permission (Kempf and Austein 2004). Thus, the core architectural principle of the internet enabled a global communication space free of barriers to access or use that allowed any user to run any type of application. In light of the tight operational controls that are typical for most public infrastructures, this refraining from central management functions looked like an unprecedented, if not revolutionary approach. It reflected both military considerations of resilience and the orientations of those who developed the architecture. These researchers 'had little interest in exercising control over the network or its users' behavior...Keeping options open for growth and future development was seen as sensible, and abuse of the network was of little worry because the people using it were the very people designing it' (Zittrain 2006: 1989).

From the point of view of the telephone carriers and the major vendors, the TCP/IP architecture looked like an 'academic toy', a 'research thing' (Hafner and Lyon 1996: 247–8; Malamud 1992) soon to be replaced by proper public networks with a guaranteed high-quality service delivered by public carriers. The 'David versus Goliath' constellation between the small internet engineering community and the powerful telecommunication carriers notwithstanding, the 'end-to-end' principle became subject to a heated technical argument and power struggle between the two engineering communities. At first glance, this controversy seemed to revolve around technical issues of performance, reliability, and cost. However, the contested design options had social implications which were later framed in the more political terms described below.

The obvious example is the end-to-end principle, a true 'boundary object' (Star and Griesemer 1989) with technical (reliability) as well as political (freedom of innovation) connotations. But the differing visions of the future networking landscape present another example. The liberal model of a network connecting autonomous local networks emerged in contrast to the paternalistic model of data communication as a public service controlled by a state-run carrier. While the latter vision centralized authority at the expense of freedom of use, the first maximized autonomy at the expense of central control. The internet engineers framed these different design philosophies in the form of endless jokes: 'Many web generations ago, the ARPA knights started a revolution against the telco circuit-switching empire and determined to destroy the death stars and their twisted pairs'.[5] Both models of data networking have advantages and disadvantages some of which were not fully visible before the internet advanced as a mass medium.

The fundamental design criteria that shaped the architecture of the internet reflected military priorities such as resilience and tolerance for heterogeneous networks (Clark 1988; Abbate 1999). As Clark *et al.* (2005: 93) recalls, 'the Internet was designed in simpler times, when the user community was smaller. It was reasonable to trust most of the users, and it was possible to track down and deal with misbehavior.'

The Utopian Moment: Framing the Internet Architecture in Modernity's Terms

Until the privatization of its backbones in the mid-1990s, the internet constituted a public research network whose access was more or less restricted to academic institutions (Shah and Kesan 2003). Universities and research institutions were the first organizations that provided access to the internet in the early 1990s and 'as a form of life, its birth was tied to university life' (Lessig 2006: 33). Not surprisingly, the early academic users experienced the internet as a homogeneous social space populated by like-minded people. As a student put it, 'it feels like walking into a room full of friends' (Harasim 1994: 15). In retrospect, authors such as Lessig (2006) and Zittrain (2006) have stressed the extent to which the academic user context of the 1990s shaped the optimistic expectations on the internet's future.

To the early generation of academic users, referred to here as the 'techno-utopians', the internet appeared as a radically different social space that challenged or even broke with the familiar structures and principles of modern society that had enabled the internet. In the 'Coming of Cyberspacetime and the End of the Polity', for example, Nguyen and Alexander (1996: 107) observed the 'breakdown of modernity' underpinned by examples for the transformation or erosion of conventional forms of power. Proponents of such views were encouraged by the distributed character of the internet; in other words, the lack of an agency in charge of the communication services and data flows. This lack of 'change control' has been

---

[5] Bob Metcalfe (Ethernet inventor, 3Com founder, now VP at IDG) at the MIT Enterprise Forum satellite broadcast from MIT's Kresge Auditorium, 26 June 1997. Quoted from: http://cyber.law.harvard.edu/archived_content/people/reagle/inet-quotations-19990709.html.

regarded as one of the unique features of the internet: 'the result is a grid that is nearly completely open to the creation and rapid distribution of... innovations' (Zittrain 2006: 1980).

The architecture of the internet, as outlined above, operates according to an 'end-to-end' principle, which means that users, not the network operator, determine the choice of applications. More by accident than design, the internet became the first 'many-to-many' mass medium (Walker 2003): 'Individuals, all over the globe, were empowered to create and exchange information of all kinds, spontaneously form virtual communities, and do so in a totally decentralized manner, free of any kind of restrictions' (Walker 2003). One particularly enthusiastic observer expressed the experience of liberty and communality by characterizing the internet as 'the best and most original American contribution to the world since jazz. Like really, really good jazz, the Internet is individualistic, inventive, thoughtful, rebellious, stunning, and even humorous. Like jazz, it appeals to the anarchist in us all' (Valauskas 1996). The allusion to anarchism was not just coincidence. To Valauskas and others, the lack of governmental control made the internet 'the closest approximation of perfect anarchy', that is 'a utopian society of individuals, individuals who enjoy complete and utter freedom of government' (ibid.).

Until the mid-1990s, the internet was more or less left to its own devices (Handley 2006). As Goldsmith and Wu observe (2006: 32), 'from the 1970s through much of the 1990s, the U.S. government was passive, happy to let the engineers do their thing' and act as an 'absentee custodian'. The political zeitgeist in the USA at the time suggested deregulation. From the perspective of European governments, the internet appeared as an interim phenomenon sooner or later to be replaced by a proper data network architecture, which therefore didn't merit much political attention (Werle 2002: 146; Christou and Simpson 2007: 153).[6] The question of state regulation appeared on the political agenda only after 1995 when it became obvious that the internet was turning into a mass medium. The US 1996 Communications Decency Act, which was later ruled as unconstitutional for violating the First Amendment, presented an early attempt to regulate the internet.[7] Cybercrime was just about to move into the public eye at that time.

---

[6] According to Genschel (1995: 138), the EU Commission excluded TCP/IP products from public procurement until the early 1990s. Yet, governments kept funding the networks that connected universities and the US government also funded administrative functions such as the 'Internet Assigned Numbers Authority'. However, no attempts were made to regulate the internet.

[7] For details see http://en.wikipedia.org/wiki/Telecommunications_Act_of_1996.

However, the mere possibility of bringing the internet under public control and subjecting it to the rules of the 'real world' evoked a passionate academic debate about the feasibility and implications of state control over the internet. The specific attributes of the network architecture featured prominently in this debate. As many contributors confidently argued, the internet would prove immune to attempts of hierarchical control. As Walker (2003) put it, 'the very design of the Internet seemed technologically proof against attempts to put the genie back in the bottle'. Among academia, it was commonplace to argue that 'the Internet could not be regulated' (Lessig 2006: 27) and, hence, the grassroots revolution not be stopped. The internet's characteristic resilience against technical failure would protect it also from any form of political control. John Gilmore's claim that 'the Net interprets censorship as damage and routes around it' (*Time* magazine, 6 December 1993) became a popular slogan that reflected both the military heritage of the internet architecture and confidence in its ungovernability.

In a famous article on law in cyberspace, Post and Johnson (1996) argued that the decentralized, cross-border architecture of the internet prevented it from coming under public control. According to them (ibid. 3, 6), national laws can only be effective within a system of territorial states and geographical borders:

Global computer-based communications cut across territorial borders, creating a new realm of human activity and undermining the feasibility — and legitimacy — of applying laws based on geographic boundaries... The Net thus radically subverts a system of rule-making based on borders between physical spaces, at least with respect to the claim that cyberspace should naturally be governed by territorially defined rules.

This view that state sovereignty could not be effectively exercised on the internet was very common throughout the 1990s (for a critical review, see Drezner 2004: 479–81). The internet would not only route around regulatory impediments; by virtue of its global architecture it would also delegitimize attempts to enforce regulation on cyberspace. Laws are valid only within clearly defined geopolitical boundaries, Post and Johnson argued, and the internet basically negates such boundaries. Public authority in the form of territorial control would therefore be replaced by the 'law of the Internet', an aggregate of choices made by engineers and individual users (Post 1998: 539).

In the context of the debate on internet regulation, academic observers such as Johnson, Post, and Lessig and political advocates such as Kapor and

Weitzner (1993) interpreted the TCP/IP architecture as a political expression of a new form of social organization constituted partly by technical, partly by social norms. Technical and social rules were thought to reflect each other. Well-known expressions of this idea are Reidenberg's (1998) 'Lex informatica' and Larry Lessig's (2006) 'Code is law', the latter of which suggests first that technical code, namely the TCP/IP architecture, is the actual regulator of cyberspace and second that its regulatory effects are intentional:

The Internet is built on a simple suite of protocols — the TCP/IP suite.... Like a dreaming postal worker, the network simply moves the data and leaves its interpretation to the applications at either end. This minimalism in design is intentional. It reflects both a political decision about disabling control and a technological decision about the optimal network design. (Lessig 2006: 32)

The first generation of academic users thus reframed specific technical features of the internet, particularly the end-to-end principle, into a political language of regulation and held that, within this frame of reference, the internet and its users are capable of setting their own rules. Some of these rules did already exist; and so did its 'governors', humans and code who 'impose values on the space' (Lessig 1998). In more general terms, the argument was that laws are not the only means of rulemaking and that, on the internet, technical standards fulfil a similar role. As Reidenberg (1998) saw it, technical norms form a 'lex informatica' much like the 'lex mercatoria', which evolved in the Middle Ages in response to the practice of cross-border trading. The internet architecture was believed to protect cyberspace against governmental intervention and, at the same time, provide its community with values and (minimal) rules to govern their interaction. In short, as Mitchell Kapor put it in 1991: 'architecture is politics!'[8]

The political interpretation of the network architecture as a set of constitutional rules for cyberspace formed a central part of the utopia that distinguished the early academic writing about the internet. Another, perhaps more vague, element consisted of the 'we', an imaginary global community of internet users or 'netizens' who identified with the new virtual world and claimed to live a social life significantly different from that of *real*-world society. As Lessig (1995: 1746) put it, 'People meet, and talk, and live in cyberspace in ways not possible in real space. They build and define

[8] See http://cyber.law.harvard.edu/archived_content/people/reagle/inet-quotations-19990709.html.

themselves in cyberspace in ways not possible in real space.' The iconic expression of this claim of 'otherness' and 'elsewhereness' is John Perry Barlow's often-cited 'Declaration of the Independence of Cyberspace'. Barlow modelled his manifesto after the American Constitution and wrote it in response to the adoption of the US government's 1996 Communication Decency Act, which intended to regulate content on the internet. It opens with a direct attack of modern society — on behalf of 'liberty itself':

Governments of the Industrial World, you weary giants of flesh and steel, I come from Cyberspace, the new home of Mind. On behalf of the future, I ask you of the past to leave us alone. You are not welcome among us. You have no sovereignty where we gather. We have no elected government, nor are we likely to have one, so I address you with no greater authority than that with which liberty itself always speaks. I declare the global social space we are building to be naturally independent of the tyrannies you seek to impose on us. You have no moral right to rule us nor do you possess any methods of enforcement we have true reason to fear. (Barlow 1996)

Even if Barlow's declaration of independence may sound somewhat histrionic from today's perspective (see Morrison 2009), its rhetoric dichotomies between the past 'giants of flesh and steel' and the new space of the 'Mind', between the tyranny of democratically legitimate laws and the great promises of liberty, did indeed echo the sentiments of many internet users in the 1990s. As Geist (2003: 325) recalls, it 'served as a clarion call for a new regulatory approach to the Internet and gave a voice to thousands of "netizens"'. One can assume that many internet users in the mid-1990s shared the feeling of superiority that Barlow's declaration conveyed. The early generation of internet users held strong reservations about the hierarchical structures of the real world's society and at the same time believed that, thanks to the internet, radically different ways of social self-organization were possible.

The anti-government attitude, bolstered with references to the social-scientific swan songs of the nation-state, formed another important element of the 1990s cyberspace culture. Academic observers portrayed democratic forms of political organization as territorial institutions of the pre-digital past and assumed the 'death of the nation-state' and the end of 'geographical tyranny' to be in close reach. They associated governmental regulation with central control and inflexibility, bureaucratic tardiness and outdated business models (Spar 1999), an attitude echoed by some parts of the US government.[9] Governments epitomized the antithesis of the

---

[9] As the US Department of Commerce (1998) stated in the White Paper that preceded the founding of ICANN: 'Certain management functions require coordination. In these cases, responsible, private-sector action is preferable to government control. A private coordinating

unbridled, dynamic internet. As Lessig (1998) summarized the zeitgeist of cyberspace, 'so, while we believe that there is a role for collective judgments, we are repulsed by the idea of placing the design of something as important as the internet into the hands of governments'. In other words, governmental regulation of the internet was regarded as a bad thing while ungovernability and powerlessness were regarded as good things. Ungovernability would ensure that, to use the terminology of Santos (2001: 253), the project of social emancipation wouldn't be cannibalized by the project of social regulation. The 'epistemic community of elite citizens' (Morrison 2009: 55) was intent on building a virtual world for people like themselves, people who believed in similar values and principles such as autonomy and self-determination, freedom, equality, and openness.

One of the few concrete models for this utopia of self-governance was the Internet Engineering Task Force (IETF) and its standard setting process. The IETF has been frequently cited as proof that the internet enabled new, and superior, forms of collaboration and decision-making. In contrast to the ITU, its intergovernmental equivalent, the IETF is an informal association without legal status, organizational boundaries, or formal membership rules. Standards were, and still are, developed by open working groups, which keep public archives of their discussions. There is neither representation nor voting in the IETF but institutions such as 'rough consensus' among working group members and 'running code', i.e. working implementations of proposed standards. The explicit rejection of governmental standard-setting procedures became a defining slogan of the IETF that has adorned many t-shirts, drawing on the words of one of the internet architects, David Clark: 'We reject: kings, presidents and voting. We believe in: rough consensus and running code.'[10] Self-regulatory structures committed to openness, inclusiveness, and bottom–up decision-making such as those developed by the IETF were believed to work also in other contexts and therefore provide an ideal for the future management of the internet.

On the whole, the utopian project of self-determination in cyberspace in the 1990s oscillated between overconfidence and fear of external interference (Drezner 2004). The latter referred to one specific threat, the regulatory power of governments. Governmental regulation constituted the

process is likely to be more flexible than government and to move rapidly enough to meet the changing needs of the Internet and of Internet users.'

[10] David Clark coined the phrase in 'A Cloudy Crystal Ball: Visions of the Future', a plenary presentation at the 24th meeting of the Internet Engineering Task Force, Cambridge, Mass., 13–17 July 1992.

single danger unanimously recognized by the epistemic community in cyberspace. Because unlimited freedom was deemed an absolute positive thing, nearly any form of restriction seemed condemnable. This Manichaean worldview, which contrasted emancipation with regulation, freedom with tyranny, and 'internet natives' with 'internet immigrants' (Barlow 1996), did not allow for concerns about dangers or evils emanating from cyberspace itself. The belief in self-regulation implied a great trust in the composition of this 'self', the individual users on the internet. The on-line community, the imaginary 'we', was thought to consist of enlightened human beings who would make good use of the freedom the internet offered. Users trusted each other because they shared a similar university-based cultural background. The internet community's concept of the enemy was remarkably narrow; it focused on governments and their intention to apply 'real space regulations' to the internet. Such intentions were countered with freedom of expression arguments (Wall 2005). However, the defence of unconditioned freedom on the internet didn't take into account the explosive growth and diversification of users brought about by the stunning success of the open network architecture. Moreover, it didn't prepare for the 'people with a wider range of motivations for using the Internet', as Blumenthal and Clark (2001: 72) elegantly paraphrased the emerging group of new 'immigrants' who violated the unwritten ethical code on the internet.

Disenchantment of the Internet: The Emergence of Cybercrime

Throughout the internet's first decade as a research network, social interaction in cyberspace was regulated by conventions collected under the term 'netiquette'.[11] Netiquette prescribed acceptable social behaviour in the various public fora on digital networks. Notwithstanding the libertarian culture in cyberspace, the netiquette rules were quite explicit about what constituted an abuse of the common communication resources:

Never send chain letters via electronic mail. Chain letters are forbidden on the Internet.
Your network privileges will be revoked...
— Don't send large amounts of unsolicited information to people....

---

[11] Most forms of netiquette emerged on the USENET, originally a communication network independent of the internet, but there were also collections of rules designed for internet applications.

Unsolicited advertising that is completely off-topic will most certainly guarantee that you get a lot of hate mail. (Hambridge 1995)

The first striking violation of netiquette in the form of mass postings[12] on the internet occurred in 1994. The 'green card spam', which offered (superfluous, as many observers pointed out) support for enrolling in the American 'green card lottery', became notorious as a turning point in the history of the internet. Canter and Siegel, the authors of the advertisement, were retrospectively described as 'innovators with a penchant for technology' (Everett-Church 1999). The first commercial spammers on the internet had commissioned a 'script', a little program developed specifically for mass-posting, which sent their advertisement to roughly 6,000 USENET discussion groups. As a response to what was deemed an outrageous violation of netiquette, angry users intent on making a public example flooded the spammers' email account and phone lines. While Canter and Siegel lost their email account as a result of their spamming activity, they apparently won more than 1,000 clients and thus made a big profit (Specter 2007). As the article on Wikipedia about Canter and Siegel notes, the green card spam, 'coming not long after the National Science Foundation lifted its unofficial ban on commercial speech on the Internet, marks the end of the Net's early period, when the original Netiquette could still be enforced'.[13] Spam was perceived as 'the first really bad thing that people started doing on the internet, in terms of letting the small town rules break down and start abusing people' (Templeton cited in Kleiner 2008).

Over the following years, 'malware' (malicious software) became a regular occurrence on the internet and the netiquette rules fell into complete oblivion. In 1998, four years after the 'green card' advertisement, the new meaning of the term spam made it into the *Oxford English Dictionary*.[14] The growing public awareness of spam, viruses, and other misdoings on the internet made it obvious that a new type of user had discovered the amazing openness, innovativeness, and ungovernability of the internet and set out to explore ways of making use of it.

---

[12] For details about the history of spam, see Templeton. For a timeline, see http://keithlynch. net/spamline.html.

[13] http://en.wikipedia.org/wiki/Canter_&_Siegel

[14] The *OED* first definition for 'spam' was: 'trademark, a tinned meat product made mainly from ham'. The second definition was: 'irrelevant or inappropriate messages sent on the Internet to a large number of newsgroups or users'. http://news.cnet.com/2100-1023-214535. html.

The first decade of cybercrime was characterized by a steady and rapid increase of, often fraudulent, spam, viruses and other types of malware. Yet, the cybercrime profession itself appeared to be rather scattered and heterogeneous, a mixture of professionals and amateurs, most of them working on their own. Viruses and self-replicating worms, for example, used to be simple programs that emerged as part of a reputation-driven sport. The authors tended to be 'kiddies writing scripts in their bedrooms' (Specter 2007) who wanted 'to become famous and gain the admiration of their peers...demonstrated most famously by the "ILOVEYOU" worm of May 2000, created by a disaffected student in the Philippines' (Select Committee, House of Lords 2007: 13). 'Sasser', a rather harmless worm which just stalled the networks of a news agency, an airline, a coastguard, an investment bank and the European Commission, was released in spring 2004 — on the 18th birthday of its author. The fact that viruses could create so much damage is probably more indicative of the vulnerability of the internet and the computers' operating systems than it is of the skills of 'script kiddies'.

Sending out messages from their 'throw-away' dial-up accounts (Steward 2003), early spammers imitated traditional mass-market mail practices. Sanford Wallace, one of the first 'spam kings', had started his career with junk fax marketing. Spammers like Wallace benefited from the trans-border structure of the internet that allowed millions of emails to be globally distributed at very low cost and, thanks to the unclear jurisdiction over cyberspace, also at almost no risk of prosecution. As Specter (2007) notes about early spamming practices, 'it wasn't hard to find out who the e-mail came from, and almost nobody lied about his identity'. Email addresses, automatically collected by 'bots' (short for robots) crawling through the internet, could be bought on CD together with simple spamming tool kits, the trade of which evolved into a lucrative side business of spamming: '2 Million Email Addresses for $19.95' (Anderson 2004).

As a cheap alternative to the dial-up account, spammers discovered so-called 'open mail relays' to send out spam. 'Open relay' refers to the original default configuration of mail servers, the program responsible for sending emails. Open mail relays allowed anyone, including unknown users, to send their email through them.[15] The increasing abuse of open mail relays for spamming transformed the convenient feature into a vulnerability of

---

[15] For details: http://en.wikipedia.org/wiki/Open_mail_relay.

the internet. As a result, open relays became controversial[16] and eventually blacklisted[17] as important sources of spam and other forms of malware. Sadly, the closing down of open relays had more impact on the internet's receding openness than on the amount of spam. Their originators quickly figured out new ways of spreading spam (see also van Eeten *et al.* 2008: 10), for example by using free email accounts. In 2008, spammers managed to break the security system that prevented the automatic registration of free email accounts. CAPTCHA (Completely Automated Public Turing test to Tell Computers and Humans Apart) usually consists of a number of characters that a user needs to decipher and copy in order to prove that a human and not a 'bot' is trying to set up a new account. Automatically created email accounts or websites have been used to a growing extent for hosting and circulating spam (MessageLabs 2008).

Anderson's (2004) satire about a fictitious 'spammer-in-training', an amateur who quickly succeeds in creating his own 'spam empire', illustrates the dynamic arms race that has emerged between spammers and the anti-spam groups or companies. Stan, the spamming trainee, escapes anti-spam legislation by operating his business via 'bulletproof hosting services'[18] in China. However, the highest amount of spam still originates from the United States, a country with anti-spam legislation.[19] It is well known that legal efforts to combat cybercrime haven't had a noticeable effect on the amount of spam on the internet. The actual arms race takes place between the cybercrime and the security industry, both of which have evolved into highly interrelated markets. The higher the level of cybercrime (measured by the security industry, see Anderson *et al.* 2008), the larger the market for security services (van Eeten *et al.* 2008: 18). As some observers note, the arms race does not only transform the internet, it also drives the inventiveness of the cybercrime industry. Anti-spam techniques have been compared to pesticides 'that do nothing more than create a new, resistant strain of bugs'.[20] Each generation of spam or virus detection and blocking techniques is counteracted by new methods of evading those filters. The

[16] Controversial because some cyber-libertarians regarded open mail relay as a matter of free speech and refused to close them down. Ironically, John Gilmore's open mail relay was used in 2006 to spread a virus.

[17] Blacklisting refers to the practice of filtering incoming traffic according to blacklists (DNSBL), see van Eeeten *et al.* 2008: 28.

[18] Bulletproof hosting companies help their customers evade content regulation, see: http://en.wikipedia.org/wiki/Bulletproof_hosting.

[19] Daily updates about the top ten worst 'spam origin countries' can be found on the spamhouse website: http://www.spamhaus.org/statistics/countries.lasso.

[20] Paul Graham, Aug. 2002, http://www.paulgraham.com/spam.html.

more spam gets successfully blocked, the greater the volume of spam that has to be sent out to keep up the profit. 'If you used to have to send fifty thousand pieces of spam to get a response, now you have to send a million' (Sorrow, quoted in Specter 2007). Like every year before, '2008 set a new record for overall spam volume' and 'the average unprotected user would have received 45,000 spam messages in 2008 (up from 36,000 in 2007). All indicators suggest that this trend will continue' (Google 2009).

Until 2003, cybercrime used to be an annoying but ultimately harmless business (van Eeten *et al.* 2008: 6). In 2003, spamming techniques began to change and cybercrime underwent reorganization. The forerunner of this transformation was a virus called Sobig,[21] first noticed 'in the wild' in early 2003. Sobig combined elements of a self-replicating worm and a 'metamorphic Trojan horse'.[22] It was designed to modify itself by autonomously downloading additional files from various websites and over several stages. In its final stage, the original virus had completely disappeared and was replaced by a hidden Trojan that had been configured to function as an open mail relay to send out spam. Computers infected by Sobig turned into 'zombies' that were no longer controlled by their owners but by third parties who ran networks of zombies known as 'botnets'.

A few years after open mail relays had more or less disappeared from the internet, spammers had figured out a way to create them anew by turning individual computers into open relays. Sobig became the fastest spreading virus ever in 2003 with one million copies reported to be caught within twenty-four hours by one security company. Botnets have made it possible to send out spam anonymously and in ever growing quantities. Due to the new virus-based spamming technique, two-thirds of all spam circulating on the internet in 2003 originated from infected zombie computers and, for the first time, spam at times exceeded the volume of legitimate mail. Recent data suggest that between 5 and 20 per cent of all computers may be infected with malware that can turn them into zombies (Select Committee, House of Lords 2007: 14; van Eeten *et al.* 2008: 6). Whereas Sobig infected computers by conventional means in the form of email attachments, more recent versions of malware programs have been propagated through malicious websites, thereby exploiting the weak protection of web browsers. About 10 per cent of all websites were found to be malicious in a 2007 study

[21] A good explanation of the 'sobig family' can be found in Steward (2003): http://www.secureworks.com/research/threats/sobig/?threat=sobig.
[22] Trojans are pieces of malware that appear like a legitimate program, e.g. a screensaver, but are designed to do something malicious such as creating a backdoor on a computer that can be used by spammers.

(Provos *et al.* 2007). Visiting a compromised website causes 'drive-by downloads', an automatic, unnoticeable installation of malware that implants a 'ghost' in the browser, henceforth recording every key stroke of the user and spying on passwords and other forms of sensitive information (Provos *et al.* 2007; Thomas and Martin 2006). A current example of this sophisticated technique is a botnet called Torpig, which is coordinated, 'harvested', and hidden through regularly changing internet addresses and domain names.[23]

The trading of illicit digital goods on the internet takes place with the help of one of its oldest communications services called Internet Relay Chat (IRC). This communication service provides the exchange of messages in real-time through dedicated virtual channels, which function in the underground economy as open markets for goods and services. The trading of illicit products is a rather fast and very lucrative business. Thomas and Martin (2006) calculated that within twenty-four hours and in just one of many IRC channels operating in parallel, access information to accounts worth at least US$1.5 million changed hands (see also Franklin *et al.* 2007 for more empirical data).

The year 2003, when the first botnets appeared on the internet, has been recognized as a turning point in the organization of cybercrime. Anderson *et al.* (2008: 10) portray this change as an 'online criminal revolution' and liken it to the 'rapid specialization by artisans' in the eighteenth century that led to the Industrial Revolution. Cybercrime has evolved from a 'reputation economy (i.e., receiving 'street cred' for defacing Web sites or authoring viruses)' into a 'bustling underground economy… that actively flaunts the laws of nations and the rights of individuals' (Franklin *et al.* 2007). Characteristic of this new underground economy are specialized networks of skills and functions. There is the new profession of the 'botnet herder' or 'botnet master' who manages the networks of computer zombies and rents them out as a service (see Stone-Gross *et al.* 2009: 8) to spammers or to 'phishermen',[24] another new profession which specializes in operating bogus websites of banks or shops to obtain access to credit cards, passwords, and other personal information (Anderson *et al.* 2008: 10). Other relevant professions are the 'malware writers' who produce malicious software on commission, the brokers who manage the trading of tools, credit cards, or

---

[23] Torpig has been hijacked for 10 days by a group of researchers who monitored about 180,000 infections and the collection of 70 GB of data (Stone-Gross *et al.* 2009).

[24] According to the report of the House of Lords (2007: 14), the cost of renting a botnet for spamming amounts to 3–7 US cents per zombie per week.

social security numbers and the 'mules' and 'drops' which facilitate the money laundering (see Thomas and Martin 2006). The underground networks now also 'invest in the proper research, development, quality control and customer service' (Anderson *et al.* 2008: 11). Even statistics are collected to measure performance and 'to make sure their revenue stream is maintained' (Evron 2008). Cybercrime thus has evolved from an amateur business into a highly profitable global industry, which is getting more and more sophisticated.

Conclusion: Regulation and the End of the Utopian Dream?

The advent of spam, fraud, and theft has lasting technical and political implications for the internet, its tradition of ungovernability, and its spirit of openness. The explosive growth of cybercrime has shown that the internet does indeed empower all users and usages. As Cerf put it, it is 'open to the exploration by virtually anyone'. The fact that the end-to-end architecture of the internet is unable to discriminate against innovations, let alone tell apart desirable and undesirable ones, used to be a reason to cheer. In the mean time, however, the internet has come to be regarded by more and more users as a dangerous place and the networks' end points, once the privileged locus of control and innovation, have disappeared behind walled gardens and firewalls. Since firewalls are designed to treat everything new and unknown as a potential threat, they create barriers against malicious as well as desirable innovations (Handley 2006: 124). Cybercrime also affects the general attitude towards self-regulation on the internet. Lessig (2006: 27) certainly reflects the zeitgeist with his observation that, notwithstanding the old belief in the internet's unregulability:

in a world drowning in spam, computer viruses, identity theft, copyright 'piracy', and the sexual exploitation of children, the resolve against regulation has weakened. We all love the Net. But if some government could really deliver on the promise to erase all the bads of this space, most of us would gladly sign up.

Zittrain (2006: 1977) predicts a shift in consumer demand for more security that could lead to 'an outright elimination' of what he calls the 'generativity' of the internet. Unless we, the users, accept a revision of the end-to-end principle, Zittrain (2006: 1978) warns, 'our PCs may be replaced by information appliances or may undergo a transformation from open platforms to gated communities to prisons, creating a consumer information environment that betrays the very principles that animate end-to-end theory'.

The imminent death of the internet has been predicted many times and for various reasons. In this case, however, the danger does not emanate from the outside world; its source is inherent to the internet architecture itself. The end-to-end principle has enabled an impressive flow of innovations but it also allows for a growing amount of destructive and malicious activities. In retrospect, the development of the internet seemed to have brought about its specific paradox of modernity. The emancipatory drive towards a truly liberal cyberspace that would, to new extents, privilege social autonomy over political authority, may end up in a regime that largely undermines the freedom it once enabled. Lessig (2006: 32) gloomily predicts that 'cyberspace will be the most regulable space humans have ever known. The "nature" of the Net might once have been its unregulability; that "nature" is about to flip'.

When the engineering community chose to delegate control over the network to its end points, it was assumed that users could be trusted and regulation was unnecessary. In the 1990s, the idea of public regulation even evoked a counter movement. However, internet users turned out to be far more diverse than expected, and so were the ways they made use of the freedom the internet provided. The advent of cybercrime in the 1990s indicated that cyberspace would after all be not that different from the social world that brought forward the internet in the first place.

6

Happy Surprises?

The Development of the World Wide Web and the Semantic Web

Yorick Wilks

Editors' Overview

In this chapter, Yorick Wilks discusses the unintended and unexpected benefits that have arisen from the development of computing technologies and most specifically the World Wide Web and the Semantic Web. He shows how the World Wide Web, developed within the state by the physicist Tim Berners-Lee, has turned the internet, developed by academic and military computer scientists, into a major social innovation. In turn the internet, developed by computer science 'geeks' as a restricted network for military and research purposes, has turned via the World Wide Web and the development of search engines, into a major social innovation. In this respect, the internet looks like the archetypal 'state-centred' modernization project. Yet Wilks argues that the architect of the World Wide Web, the physicist Tim Berners-Lee, never really anticipated the free untrammelled use of the WWW by citizens, but rather was always planning something along the lines of what is now called the Semantic Web (SW) — a more restricted and organized network of data.

Some have argued that the SW is an Artificial Intelligence project, an attempt to create a 'smart' web that organizes data itself, a project independent of the WWW. In contrast, Wilks argues that rather the SW rests on 'Natural Language Processing' technologies, that annotate 'natural language' text from WWW documents to create a higher level of formality. Meanwhile, Tim Berners-Lee it seemed always had this formality in mind, using the 'Web of documents' to form a 'Web of things'. In this sense the Semantic Web was an even more modernizing project, of which the World Wide Web is a less modernizing spin-off. The World

Wide Web and the thousands of applications that rest upon it, used by billions of people for an ever increasing array of social, economic, and political purposes, is perhaps the happiest 'unintended consequence' to arise from a technologically based government modernization project.

Introduction

This chapter starts by setting out what different kinds of unintended consequences have been exemplified in modern computer technology generally; and more specifically, in the development of the internet, the World Wide Web (WWW) and the Semantic Web (SW). The second section looks at the story of the early days of the internet and the WWW, while the third looks at the SW and its relation to various developments in computer science. The fourth section examines the intentions of Tim Berners-Lee in developing the WWW and the SW, examining the hypothesis that we may have 'piggy-backing' levels of the unintended: first the internet itself, as it has become, may be regarded as unintended through the development of the WWW. If the WWW is, as I hint, itself unintended, there is now a myriad of popular and totally unforeseen consequences piggy-backed upon it, many of them of socially profound and transformative. The good news at the end of the chapter is that, if the WWW as we have it now is, in any way, unintended, it is also a thoroughly Good Thing, as Sellar and Yeatman (1930) divided up British history long ago.

Paradoxes and Unintended Consequences in the Development of Computer Technology

The notion of *serendipity* is very close to that of things being *designed for one purpose but actually found to work for another*. On the good side, that description covers the classic case of post-it notes, where weak glue was perfect for the notes but little good as the real glue it was designed to be. Again, the claim goes back to Gregory (1967) that the brain was an engine designed largely for seeing, but which had its 'seeing mechanisms' diverted to the (much) later development of the language faculty. If one turns to the bad, or at least dubious, consequences under the same heading one might refer to the French MINITEL system, an early online service accessible through telephone lines launched in 1982 by the French Post and Telecommunications agency. The system was designed to allow users in their homes to make on-line purchases, make train reservations, access information services, and search the French telephone directory for free, but it became largely a tool for the sex industry, with Paris Metro trains full of adverts with obscene MINITEL call signatures.

It is now a familiar observation that the French suffered the disadvantage of early innovators, and the widespread penetration of MINITEL made the later advance of the WWW slower there because they already had a popular system with some of its features and, moreover, one that was believed to be French, even though, in fact, MINITEL was a transplant of the British PRESTEL system that failed to find backing in the UK.

The paradoxes with which this chaper is concerned relate to the internet and the World Wide Web. Although these names are often used inter-changeably and indeed the way they have evolved means that they are inextricably linked, there is a distinction that is important to some people. Basically, the internet is the network which allows physically separate networks to communicate with each other in a 'logical network'. The WWW is a software program which works on top of the internet, making it possible for people to find and organize information.

Some of the most striking developments on the internet and WWW in recent years are simple surprises, in that no one even at the beginning of the WWW era (in the early 1990s) could possibly have predicted them. Examples include:

- the sheer scale of media sharing via sites such as Flikr (for photos) and YouTube (for video clips);
- the massive use of autobiographical social networks, such as MySpace and Facebook;
- the reduction ad absurdum of instant communication as exemplified by Twitter;
- the return of mass texting for communication represented by SMS, and the new abbreviated telegraphese it has created.

The last is most extraordinary, given that texting was originally merely a maintenance facility on phones for engineers. In the early phases of successful speech research (ASR) it was simply taken for granted that speech recognition would oust all written forms: as US military funders used to put it 'Generals don't type'.

Satellite navigation systems (Satnav) and 'mashups' of data based on internet map representations are less surprising, and could have been pre-dicted: Kuipers's Stanford thesis (1977) was the first internal computer representation of a map. It was developed at the Stanford AI Lab from which so much of the modern age developed, the extraordinary thing being that he made nothing commercial from the crucial development he started.

Further unforeseen novelties created on top of the WWW include:

- the Web takeover of the cell phone system (initially Skype);
- the Web takeover of all personal data, and the return to the timeshared mainframe model (alias the Cloud);
- peer-to-peer file sharing, which was totally unforeseen (and occupies the WWW all night, like dreaming in humans!);
- the concept of Web 2.0, applications on the WWW which allow users to generate content or provide real-time feedback, so that a significant proportion of internet users become 'producers' as well as consumers of web-based material. Examples of Web 2.0 applications include blogs (on-line diaries), social networking sites (such as Facebook or Myspace), social commenting sites (such as Twitter) and applications which allow users to provide real-time feedback on goods and services (such as Amazon reviews or Trip Advisor). Web 2.0 technologies have facilitated the new paradigm of 'crowd science' such as Wikipedia (the user-generated encyclopedia) and wikiproteins (a dictionary of biomedical concepts, developed by scientists).

The Story of the Internet and the WWW

The internet therefore, has clearly led to a succession of unanticipated 'happy surprises' (and some unhappy surprises as well, for which see the conclusion and Chapter 5). Unlike the many huge public-sector failed IT projects that litter the history of government computer technologies, particularly in the UK and USA, the internet may be regarded as a vast (US) government success, in the sense of having had positive social benefits. This section investigates the extent to which they were intended. Much has been written about the history of the internet and the World Wide Web (see Cerf 2001; Zittrain, 2008; Gillies and Cailliau 2000), but some points are particularly pertinent to the theme of this book and the central paradox of this chapter.

The internet was originally developed in the US Defense Department's Advanced Research Projects Agency (then known as ARPA). Its precursor, the ARPAnet was developed initially by computer scientists (for example, J. C. R. Licklider) as an attempt to create a way of connecting physically separate networks (specifically, three separate networks that ARPA was using located in Santa Monica, the University of California, Berkeley, and MIT) in a single logical network. Once the basic technology (known as packet switching) had been developed, various universities were added through the 1960s and 1970s across the USA. This government-funded network was restricted to research at military sites and universities; commercial use was strictly forbidden. Later in the 1980s the military portion of the ARPAnet was broken off as a separate network.

The first paradox evidenced by the development of the internet is that this tool, developed by and for the technological elite, has become a democratic leisure aid and marketplace. The internet was developed first for ARPA-fundees, then for academics in computer science and later for universities more widely and none of its original architects had any notion that it would become a major social innovation. Indeed, David Clarke, a senior research scientist at MIT who served as chief protocol architect for the government's internet development initiative in the 1980s, has argued that the design of the internet around the purposes for which it was originally intended is stifling further growth and is himself working on an NSF-funded project to create a whole new infrastructure to replace the internet, Internet 2 (*Wired*, 29 June 2005). Clark points out that the goals of the original internet structure were rigorously prioritized and that 'an entirely different network architecture would result if the order were changed' (Clark 1988: 2). For example, he argues, 'since this network was designed to operate in a military context, which implied the possibility of a hostile environment, survivability was put as a first goal, and accountability as a last goal.' 'While the architects of the Internet were mindful of accountability, the problem received very little attention during the early stages of the design and is only now being considered. An architecture primarily for commercial deployment would clearly place these goals at the opposite end of the list.' Observing that 'in the context of its priorities, the Internet architecture has been very successful', he claims that 'its success has made clear that in certain situations, the priorities of the designers do not match the needs of the actual users'.

The second major paradox relates to the World Wide Web (WWW). The internet would never have reached widespread usage without a method of finding and organizing files and information. Various projects were developed aiming to create ways to organizing data using 'hypertext' developed by Ted Nelson's Project Xanadu. Such projects included 'Gopher' and the 'World Wide Web', invented by Tim Berners-Lee, a physicist working at CERN. This latter invention was released for public use and gradually became the preferred interface for accessing the internet in the 1990s, see below.

It is not now always appreciated that many of the features we associate with the WWW were available on the earlier forms of the internet that carried email, but which was still dominated by its origins as a military-academic communication system. There was already the ability to shift large files round the internet from site to site: the protocol was not the current web protocol http but ftp, the 'file transfer protocol'. I can remember Minsky, the MIT AI guru, sending out the whole of his draft book on frames to *everyone* on the internet in 1972. Another application, Usenet was a system of peer-to-peer file transfer with no central administration. Usenet supported a huge range of user groups open to anyone, and sent images as well as text: all interests were catered for right down to alt.sex.com. And it is important to remember that until 1986, when the first general commercial or 'civilian' email became available, all subscribers would have been part of the (mostly US) academic community, which rapidly swamped the internet's military originators. Blogging certainly started there, rather than on the later WWW, and many people set up file sites designed to lure users into reading their personal diaries.

However, the advent of the WWW in 1992 made a considerable difference, in part because it stimulated the creation of algorithms to search the names of web-servers and their files, none of which were part of the WWW design itself, and even these were a carryover from a system that searched the names of the (pre-WWW) ftp files. Berners-Lee initially constructed simply a list of WWW servers until that number became too large to be useful. But he did not develop a search engine able to search for site names nor for text within documents.

The Semantic Web

The paradox exemplified by the WWW can only be understood by examining the original WWW and its relationship to the Semantic Web (Berners-Lee *et al.* 2001), or what one might call Berners-Lee's second great idea, one that has aroused considerable controversy (e.g. Wilks 2008) and is not yet fully in being. The question this chapter raises is whether the conventional view is correct — that the SW is a later development, riding as it were on the back of the WWW of documents — or whether in fact the SW was what Berners-Lee wanted all the time, in which case the WWW was serendipitous because it did not have the key property that he was looking for. So the

WWW, the application that has brought the internet into so many aspects of social and economic life, was in itself unintended by its architect. To explain this I shall first have to give a brief description of what the SW is.

The Semantic Web (SW) is no longer simply an aspiration in a magazine article (Berners-Lee *et al.* 2001) but a serious research subject on both sides of the Atlantic, with its own conferences and journal. So, even though it may not exist in a demonstrable form, in the way the WWW itself plainly does exist, it is a topic for research and about which fundamental questions can be asked, as to its representations, their meanings, and their groundings, if any.

In Berners-Lee *et al.* (2001) the authors describe a system of internet services, such as one that would fix up a doctor's appointment for an elderly relative, a task that would require planning and access to both the databases of the doctor's and relative's diaries and synchronizing them. This kind of planning behaviour was at the heart of Good Old Fashioned AI (GOFAI), a much older discipline and program. Artificial intelligence is a branch of computer science dedicated to describing and codifying human intelligence so precisely that it can be simulated by a machine. The assumptions of GOFAI have certainly been apparent in both the original SW paper and some of what has flowed from it, but there have been at least two other traditions of input to what we now call work on the SW and I shall discuss one in some detail: namely, the way in which the SW concept has grown from the traditions of document annotation. Indeed, many have assumed that there must be some direct transition from Berners-Lee's WWW — a web of documents — to his SW concept; one version of this is that the SW will be a web of documents, along with their meanings, so that a computer could read and understand the documents on the web in the way that people now understand what is in the WWW (but computers, of course, do not).

Annotation and the Lower End of the Semantic Web

If one looks at the classic SW diagram from the original *Scientific American* paper (see Figure 6.1), the tendency is always to look at the upper levels: rules, logic framework and proof, and it is these that have caused both critics and admirers of the SW to say that it is the GOFAI project by another name. But if one looks at the lower levels of the diagram the words describe products (such as Namespaces and XML) of what we may broadly call information extraction. Information extraction is based on different assumptions and techniques from AI; that is, Natural Language Processing (NLP) technologies are used to obtain annotations of texts by a range of

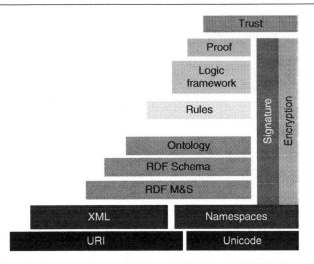

Figure 6.1. Levels of annotation and objects in the Semantic Web (from Berners-Lee *et al.* 2001)

NLP technologies, basically working up from the language of the text to create information.

Methods of information extraction that can turn text into data are important because available information for science, business, and everyday life still exists overwhelmingly as text; 85 per cent of business data still exists as unstructured data (i.e. text). So, too, of course does the WWW itself, though the proportion of it that is text (as opposed to diagrams, photos, videos, and tables) is almost certainly falling.

And how could the WWW become the SW, one might ask, except by information being extracted from natural text and stored in some other form? The standard candidates are provided by information extraction (e.g. Cunningham *et al.* 1997) being either a database of facts extracted from text, or annotations on text items stored as metadata either with or separate from the texts themselves. XML, the annotation standard (also used for non-text domains, such as TimeML and VoiceML, etc.), is the latest in a history of annotation languages that attach codings to individual text items so as to indicate information about them, or what should be done with them in some process, such as printing.

Information extraction is now a technology with some twenty-five years of history: it began with Leech's CLAWS4 program (Leech *et al.* 1994) to do automatic part-of-speech tagging in 1966: the first program systematically to add to a text 'what it meant' even at the low level represented by parts-of-speech. Information extraction now reliably locates names in text, their semantic types, and relates them together by (learned) structures called templates into forms of fact, objects virtually identical to the so-called RDF triple stores (Resource Description Format) at the basis of the SW, i.e. things low down in Figure 6.1. These are not quite logic, but very like information extraction output. Information extraction began with automating annotation (from the original hand additions of annotations) but now has what we may call large annotation engines based on machine learning (Brewster *et al.* 2001) which learn to annotate texts in any form and in any domain.

Extensions of this technology have led to effective question-answering systems against text corpora in well-controlled competitions and, more recently, the use of IE patterns to build ontologies directly from texts (Brewster *et al.* 2005). Ontologies can be thought of abstractly as conceptual knowledge structures, which organize facts derived from IE at a higher level. They are very close both to the traditional knowledge representation goal of AI, and they occupy the middle level in the original SW diagram. I only want to draw attention here to the strong case to be made that the SW rests on some technology with the scope of IE, probably IE itself, to annotate raw texts and derive first names, then semantic typing of entities, fact databases, and later ontologies.

On this view of the SW, which is not the only one, as I emphasized at the beginning, but is the one that underlies most work on the SW and web services in Europe (Brewster *et al.* 2001), the SW could be seen as a conversion from the WWW of texts by means of an annotation process of increasing grasp and vision, one that projects notions of meaning up the classic SW diagram (Figure 6.1) from the bottom. Richard Braithwaite (1956) once wrote an influential book on how scientific theories obtain the semantic interpretation of 'high level' abstract entities (like neutrinos or bosons) from low level experimental data; he named the process one of *semantic ascent* up a hierarchically ordered scientific theory. The view of the SW under discussion here, which sees NLP and information extraction as its foundational processes, providing the meanings of entities at the top of the Figure 6.1 pyramid, bears a striking resemblance to that view of scientific theories in general.

Blurring the Text and Program Distinction

The view of the SW sketched above has been that the information extraction technologies at its base, technologies that add 'the meaning of a text' to the text in varying degrees and forms, is a blurring of the distinction between language and knowledge representation because the annotations are themselves forms of language, sometimes very close indeed to language they annotate. This process at the same time blurs the distinction between programs and language itself.

So, one might say that work like Hewitt's (1972) contribution to a book on Natural Language Processing, devoted to how to plan the building of a wall and containing the claim that 'language is essentially a side effect' of programming and knowledge manipulation, is a claim that using a language (like English) is really a way of programming. Longuet-Higgins (1972) also devoted a paper to the claim that English was essentially a high-level programming language. Dijkstra's (1979) view of natural language was in essence that it was really not up to the job it had to do, and would be better replaced by precise programs, which is almost a form of this view.

Over against these views is what one might term the Wittgensteinian opposition, and I will cite my own version (2005), which is the view that natural language is and always must be the primary knowledge representation device, and all other representations, no matter what their purported precision, are in fact parasitic upon language — in the sense that they could not exist if NL did not — and they cannot never be wholly divorced from NL, in terms of their interpretation and use. This chapter is intended as a modest contribution to that tradition: but a great deal more can be found in a dialogue with Nirenburg (Nirenburg and Wilks 2001).

Systematic annotations are just the most recent bridge from language to programs and logic, and it is important to remember that not so long ago it was perfectly acceptable to assume that a knowledge representation must be derivable from an unstructured form, i.e. from a natural language text. Thus Woods in 1975: 'A KR [Knowledge Representation] language must unambiguously represent any interpretation of a sentence (logical adequacy), have a method for translating from natural language to that representation, and must be usable for reasoning.' The emphasis there is on a method of going from one to the other, that is, from the less to the more formal, a process which inevitably imposes a relation of dependency between the two. This gap has opened and closed in different research periods: in the original McCarthy and Hayes (1969) writings on KR in AI, it is clear that NL was thought vague and dispensable. The annotation movement associated with the SW can be seen as closing the gap in the way in which we have discussed it, but it is quite clear that the SW view stated first in this chapter (that the SW is roughly GOFAI) still holds to the old McCarthy–Hayes position on the issue, that language is a dispensable extra.

The separation of the annotations in metadata (versus leaving them within the text as in Latex-style annotations) has strengthened the possibility of the dispensability of the original language from which the representation was derived, whereas the infixing of annotations in a text suggests that the whole (original plus annotations) still forms some kind of linguistic object. Notice here that the 'dispensability of the text' view is not dependent on the type of representation derived — in particular to strongly logical representations. Schank (1972) certainly considered a text dispensable after his Conceptual Dependency representations had been derived from it, because he believed them to contain all the meaning of the text, implicit and explicit. This is the key issue that divides opinion here: how can we know that any representation *whatsoever* contains all and only the meaning content of a text? What could it be like to know that?

The standard philosophical problems may or may not just vanish as we push ahead with annotations to bridge the gap from text to meaning representations, whether or not we then throw away the original text. David Lewis in his (1972) critique of Fodor and Katz, and of any non-formal semantics, would have castigated all annotations as 'markerese': his name for marking up language with markers that are still within language itself, and thus not reaching out to any meaning outside language. The Semantic Web movement, as described in this section of the chapter at least, takes this criticism head on and continues, hoping URNs (Universal Resource Names: see below on these) and 'popping out of the virtual world' (e.g. by giving the web representation your — real world — phone number!) will solve semantic problems.

That is to say, the view under discussion accepts that the SW is based on language via annotations and that these will provide sufficient 'inferential traction' with which to run web-services. But is this plausible? Can all you want to know be put in RDF triples, and can this then support the reasoning you may require? Web agents-based assumptions like these do seem to work in practice, however philosophically untidy they are.

There is another view of the SW, different from both the GOFAI and NLP views that I have contrasted in this chapter. That is, in my view, one close to Berners-Lee's own vision of the SW, as expressed in Berners-Lee (2005), one that emphasizes databases as the core of the SW: namely, in databases, the meanings of features are kept constant and trustworthy by a cadre of guardians of their integrity, a matter quite separate from both logical representations (dear to GOFAI) and to any language-based methodology, of the kind described in this chapter. Berners-Lee's view deserves careful discussion and consideration that cannot be given here, but it will have the difficulty of any view that (like GOFAI) seeks to preserve predicates, features, facets, or whatever from the NLP vagaries of sense change and drift with time. We still 'dial numbers' when we phone but that no longer means the action it did a few decades ago, before push-button phones; so not even number-associated concepts are safe from time.

In some ways Berners-Lee's view has the virtues and defects of Putnam's later theory of meaning (Putnam 1975): one in which scientists became the guardians of meaning, since only they know the true chemical nature of, say, molybdenum and how it differs from aluminum, which looks exactly like it. It was essential to his theory that the scientists did not allow the criteria of meaning to leak out to the general public, lest they become subject to change. Thus, for Putnam only scientists knew the distinguishing criteria for separating water and deuterium dioxide (heavy water) which seem the same to most of the population, but are not. Many observers, including this author, have argued this separation cannot really be made, in principle or in practice.

What did Berners-Lee Intend When he Began All This?

This is the interesting question to which we have been building up. The conventional view is that Berners-Lee first set up the web of documents (the WWW) and then shifted his interests towards what we now call the SW. I believe this is not correct and that there is an element of serendipity about the WWW as we have it. Here is his own account of what he initially did:

... in 1989, while working at the European Particle Physics Laboratory, I proposed that a global hypertext space be created in which any network-accessible information could be referred to by a single 'Universal Document Identifier'...I wrote in 1990 a program called 'Worldwide Web', a point and click hypertext editor which ran on the 'NeXT' machine. This, together with the first Web server, I released to the High Energy Physics community at first, and to the hypertext and NeXT communities in the summer of 1991... After much discussion I decided to form the World Wide Web Consortium in September 1994, with a base at MIT in the USA, INRIA in France, and now also at Keio University in Japan. The Consortium is a neutral open forum where companies and organizations to whom the future of the Web is important come to discuss and to agree on new common computer protocols. It has been a centre for issue raising, design, and decision by consensus... The great need for information about information, to help us categorize, sort, pay for, own information is driving the design of languages for the web designed for processing by machines, rather than people. The web of *human-readable documents is being merged with a web of machine-understandable data.* The potential of the mixture of humans and machines working together and communicating through the web could be immense. (Berners-Lee 1998: 1; emphasis added)

This passage, written ten years after his original proposal to CERN for what became the WWW should be taken in conjunction with the diagram accompanying the original proposal (Figure 6.2).

Berners-Lee's (TBL) key innovation in the WWW — and it is important to remember the key roles of others such as Andreessen's MOSAIC browser and hypertext itself, an idea of Ted Nelson's — was that of the *unique identifier.* And the issue there is: identifier of what? In his recollections, quoted above, TBL uses the phrase 'Unique Document Identifier' (UDI) — a phrase which has disappeared from the lexicon and does not appear

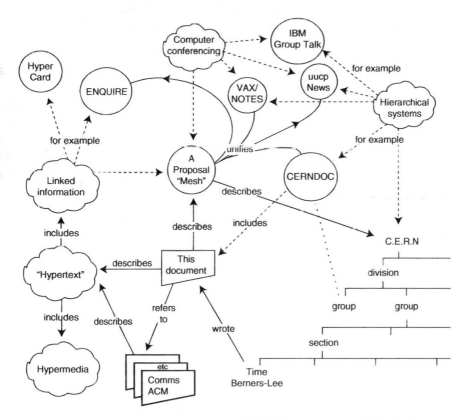

Figure 6.2. Original diagram in Berners-Lee's WWW proposal to CERN (1989)

in Wikipedia, for example. It was soon replaced with the still familiar Universal Resource Locator (URL) which is normally taken as the unique name of a document. All this leads naturally to the WWW as we know it, as a web of documents.

Why is this of importance? Well, the reminiscence above and the diagram can also be read another way. TBL says explicitly: 'The great need for information about information . . . is driving the design of languages for the web designed for processing by machines, rather than people. The web of *human-readable documents is being merged with a web of machine-understandable data*. The potential of the mixture of humans and machines working together and communicating through the web could be immense.'

This is precisely the spirit of the original SW document several years later in the *Scientific American*, and even in the 1989 diagram you can see the lines from documents pointing to objects in the real world, like himself TBL. That is, not a web of documents only but also of *things*; which is to say data, or data standing for things, a matter much closer to TBL's heart, as a database specialist, than language in documents, and it is the evidence for what I called the third view of the SW above: the web of data, but data for machines rather than human readers. Under this view, things mean what they mean because they are in a database (a physicist's view), rather than the AI view of meaning through logic.

The UDI disappeared and became the URL, the core indicator of the 'document web', the WWW, but the URL notion was then redefined as being only one kind of unique resource indicator or URI:

A URL is a URI that, in addition to identifying a resource, provides means of acting upon or obtaining a representation of the resource by describing its primary access mechanism or network 'location'. For example, the URL http://www.wikipedia. org/ identifies a resource (Wikipedia's home page) and implies that a representation of that resource (such as the home page's current HTML code, as encoded characters) is obtainable via HTTP from a network host named www.wikipedia.org. A Uniform Resource Name (URN) is a URI that identifies a resource by name in a particular namespace. A URN can be used to talk about a resource without implying its location or how to access it. For example, the URN urn:isbn:0-395-36341-1 is a URI that specifies the identifier system, i.e. International Standard Book Number (ISBN), as well as the unique reference within that system and allows one to talk about a book, but doesn't suggest where and how to obtain an actual copy of it. (from the Wikipedia entry for 'URI'; Wikipedia is as reliable source as any for Web-related information)

Conclusion

So, Unique Resource Indicators were later divided into two quite different classes of things by the W3C, the World Wide Web Consortium (see above): URLs identify documents, but not what is in them, and so yield the WWW we have. Other URIs are URNs, which yield the unique names of objects (like books, people, and places) and which may be mentioned in documents. These of course are just names, with all the philosophical ambiguity that brings: so a URL for a document that is a book (i.e. a web page where the book's text content is), may correspond precisely to a URN that is the published book with that same document content (and is attached to an ISBN number). Yet that URN does not pick out in the world a unique real object (a 500g book)–in the way 'Tim Berners-Lee' does pick out a unique object — because there may well be thousands of copies of any book, and only the RFID tag the bookseller puts in inside it in a store to stop stealing identifies a *particular* hard copy.

These ambiguities over the names of general classes of things and particular individuals are familiar and not important here, except in so far as it is illusory to think that the SW (of linked data) has solved any two-millennia-old problems about names and how they connect to the world of things.

The conclusion of this chapter is that, in the particular case of modernization represented by the internet, the WWW and SW, we have a series of paradoxes. Technological innovations devised for narrow and technical purposes have had major social spin-offs. In the case of the internet, a network devised for military and research purposes provided a network that a significant proportion of the global population could use for an increasingly wide array of purposes. The WWW provides an interesting case that one could gloss by saying that TBL always wanted a universal web of data and unique data objects, as his early writings and diagrams make clear. But what he actually helped give the world, and which has served us well for nearly twenty years, was the WWW of documents, each picked out uniquely by a URL and without the philosophical ambiguity of the world of real objects. The WWW made the internet far more usable than was ever intended or imagined. That has been a great boon to humanity yet, whatever the future developments of the SW and their ultimate realization of TBL's early dreams, it is clear that the WWW had from its inception a serendipitous element and that, with its inevitable focus on language and meaning, it may not have been what he originally had in mind at all.

Under this analysis, the good things resulting from the internet and the World Wide Web are 'happy surprises', unintended and unanticipated by their architects. Some of the less happy consequences (some of which are discussed in Chapter 5) could perhaps have been anticipated more easily, such as the predominance of sexual content on the web. For example, on the WWW YouPorn is now the size of the whole WWW in 2000, and Vodaphone claims that 80 per cent of phone text messages relate to sex, love, or personal communications. Computer networks have always been prone to takeover by sexual activity, and the pointers were there in the precursors to the internet; email has been used personally ever since the days of ARPA, Usenet Bulletin Boards were often dedicated to sexual topics (alt.sex.fetish.diapers being a notable example); and MINITEL became a primary venue for sexual advertisements.

For the future, the history of computer technologies point to further, less happy consequences. There are other examples of technologies that were designed for the elite and have become democratic leisure aids to the surprise of some at least, such as air travel. But in these cases we have generally seen an elitist fight back; the return to all-business flights and planes with full-length and phenomenally expensive beds, for example. In a similar way, the free internet might already contain the seeds of its own destruction, as we see a rise in demand for new paid information services. The media mogul Rubert Murdoch has already argued publically that iPlayer should be charged for, and others have argued that paying for email would be the only way to reduce spam. The Semantic Web is likely to involve data organization and privacy issues on a scale never seen even in the bewildering array of personal data currently available on-line. We should, it seems, enjoy the untrammelled use of the WWW while we can.

III

State-Centred Reforms

7

Addressing Undernutrition in India

Do 'Rational' Approaches Work?

Devi Sridhar

Editors' Overview

In this chapter, Devi Sridhar shows the unintended limitations of an apparently rational World Bank strategy for tackling undernutrition in developing countries, by reporting on her detailed fieldwork on the Tamil Nadu Integrated Nutrition Project, originally developed in the 1980s. She shows that the World Bank, as an institution whose mission precludes it from 'political' activity, had to construe undernutrition as a curable 'economic' problem rather than an issue of human rights, and thus conceived it as arising from lack of information and knowledge, downplaying other causes. The resulting programme put the emphasis on 'education' by a scheme that linked selective food supplementation to growth monitoring and nutritional education in local nutrition centres. However, fieldwork showed that the way the scheme operated on the ground was very different from the way officially envisaged by the World Bank's staff. Whereas the scheme assumed that the principal barrier to better nutrition was lack of information on the part of women, many of the obstacles turned out to be those of poverty (preventing women from carrying out the practices that were recommended to them) linked to gender inequality (such as men controlling household expenditure, particularly on alcohol) that limited women's ability to feed their children better.

Sridhar shows that — like the eighteenth-century rational foresters James Scott described in his Seeing like a State — *the Bank failed to anticipate these problems, rooted in local culture and power-structures, when it first rolled out the programme. But it also failed to change the programme later as information began to emerge about why the programme did not work as intended, because of career incentives within the Bank to stick with existing blueprints and concentrate on moving money to major recipients. That process of information rejection seems to have been rooted in the Bank's bureaucratic mind-set and method of operation.*

Introduction

The estimated number of undernourished people around the world has increased to nearly 923 million and is projected to rise with increasing food prices (FAO 2008). A large majority of those affected live in India. In India alone, about 200 million are undernourished while the government hoards wheat surpluses, now at about 52 million tonnes, that would stretch to the moon and back at least twice if all the bags were lined up (Waldman 2002). How did a nation that prides itself on its agricultural self-sufficiency and booming economic growth come to have half of its preschool population undernourished? Why have strategies to combat malnutrition failed so badly?

This chapter examines one of the key efforts to address undernutrition in a targeted and rational manner in India. The resulting project, the Tamil Nadu Integrated Nutrition Project (TINP) was rational in that it was based on a combination of two Western-based scientific and modern disciplines, namely biomedical and health economic models. TINP was funded by the World Bank and has often been referred to as one of the most 'successful' nutrition projects in the general nutrition literature, so the way it was designed and implemented are of particular interest. Moreover, since the Bank has used the TINP model as a blueprint to design projects in many different countries, this case reveals much about the Bank's role in nutrition more generally, particularly the policy process within the Bank: how is policy created, how are problems defined and addressed, and what are the local effects of such projects in practice?

The World Bank

At first sight, it might seem surprising that the World Bank is the largest financial contributor to health-related and nutrition projects. Annually, it now commits more than US$1 billion towards the Health, Nutrition, and Population Sector. On top of its role as a lending agency, the Bank has innumerable unofficial functions such as an advisory body, an intellectual research institute, and a training centre for developing country civil servants. Its annual World Development Report and staff working papers have established it as an intellectual powerhouse in the field of development policy and research. Combining intellectual prestige and financial power, the World Bank is the arbiter of development norms and meanings.

The Bank first started its work on nutrition in the 1970s under the Presidency of Robert McNamara (see Sridhar 2008: 20–54 for full history). The Bank's directorate struggled with two key questions: was malnutrition a 'development' problem which impacted productivity and growth, and therefore one that the Bank should address, and if so, were there feasible things that could be done about it, particularly by deploying the Bank's assets? They concluded that the answer to such questions was 'yes' and, at the urging of McNamara, the Bank's Board decided to finance the implementation of nutrition projects in four countries that were already principal recipients of Bank aid: Brazil, Indonesia, Colombia, and India.

Two particular reasons led to the selection of India. First, India has been the World Bank's largest borrower and the recipient of the largest sum of interest-free credits from the International Development Association (IDA), part of the World Bank group. Kamath notes that India has been the World Bank's 'star patient' and almost the 'raison d'être' of its growth (Kamath 1992). Mason and Asher, the Bank's semi-official historians, write, 'No country has been studied more by the World Bank than India ... India has influenced the Bank as much as the Bank has India' (Mason and Asher 1973: 675, 681–2).

So TINP, a project run by the Indian state of Tamil Nadu and funded by the World Bank, was created as a product of a particular configuration of forces at a particular time in history for the World Bank and India. India was looking externally for assistance in addressing malnutrition, and the World Bank had moved towards nutrition-specific lending. Initiated in 1980 (TINP-1), it was extended in 1989 (TINP-2) and subsequently merged with the Indian central government's Integrated Child Development Services in 1997, retaining significant features of the original Bank design despite the change in name (Pyle and Greiner, 2003: 116). The project's main goal throughout was to improve the nutritional and health status of pre-school children, primarily those 6–36 months old, as well as pregnant and nursing women.

The World Bank chose Tamil Nadu as the project site for several reasons. First, the Government of India had requested assistance in reducing malnutrition in the state in 1977. Second, the United States Agency for International Development (USAID) had just completed a survey on malnutrition which showed that over 50 per cent of pre-school children were undernourished, measured as under two standard deviations of weight-for-age. Third, the state government had proved itself committed to social development.

A central tenet of TINP and the World Bank approach was that malnutrition is the result of inappropriate child care practices, and 'not of income, famine or unpreventable health problems' (World Bank, OED 1995: 1). The overarching objective was behavioural change of mothers at the individual level. So TINP was run from community nutrition centres (*anganwadis*) and combined growth monitoring, nutrition education, and food supplementation. Growth monitoring involved the monthly weighing of all children aged 6–36 months, so that the mother of a child whose growth was faltering could be targeted for intensive nutrition counselling. The World Bank's Operations Evaluation Department (OED) saw growth monitoring as an educational tool to provide mothers with 'an objective feedback on how they were caring for their children' (ibid.).

Supplementary feeding was used for relatively brief periods for children experiencing growth faltering, defined as the failure to gain adequate weight for one's age between two serial weighings, as well as for pregnant and lactating women. The feeding programme lasted 90 days, after which children were removed from the programme if their growth was on track again. The Bank described this strategy as an educational tool to show mothers that very small amounts of additional food, 'affordable in almost everyone's household budget' (Heaver 2002: 9), were sufficient to keep a child well-nourished. The feeding part of the programme consisted of a supplement in the form of small balls of a slightly sweetened mix of rice and gram. These services were provided by a community nutrition worker who was selected from the village. In addition, a key 'modernist' aspect of TINP was its elaborate quantitative monitoring and evaluation system: every month over twenty-seven performance indicators were prepared by the TINP Project Coordinating Office using data collected by nutrition workers and collated by their supervisors.

Nutrition Policy Process

During the 1970s when the World Bank started making loans for health-related projects, undernutrition was defined by the nutrition team as 'the pathological condition brought about by inadequacy of one or more of the essential nutrients that the body cannot make but that are necessary for survival, for growth and reproduction, and for the capacity to work, learn and function in society' (Berg 1987: 4). This definition frames malnutrition as a disease located within the body with an organic basis in biochemistry and physiology. It is essentially a biomedical perspective on undernutrition. Thus, the 'cure' advocated by the Bank for the disease of hunger was education to women through the tools of growth monitoring and short-term supplementary feeding.

Once nutrition had been packaged as a 'curable' problem, the Bank, which by the terms of its official mandate is an 'economic' rather than 'political' institution, inserted the construct into a human capital framework. In nutrition projects, the worth of project beneficiaries is based on their contribution to the economic growth and GDP of the borrower country. The Bank thus frames health as an economic asset, a form of capital that should be invested in so that a country can increase its national output. This aspect of productivity is emphasized as the sole characteristic upon which resource allocation and loan decisions can be made. The Bank abjures the use of human rights language in project documents (since that is considered to be 'political') and instead has to justify loan decisions for nutrition projects on the basis of 'sound economic analysis' that assumes the worth of an individual to be determined by his/her contribution to the economy.

The human capital framework for nutrition within the Bank was thus a reflection of the dominance of economics in public health projects. Even within the Bank's Health, Nutrition, and Population sector, operations and activities were dominated by economic paradigms and frameworks. Only by presenting undernutrition as an issue of lost productivity and packaging it as an element of human capital were Bank nutritionists able to convince managers to make stand-alone nutrition loans.

Economists run the 'development apparatus' of the Bank. Within the Bank, the discipline of economics is hegemonic, the only legitimate way of examining problems, defining their essential features, and suggesting solutions. The strength of economic knowledge is seen to lie in its ability to generalize, reduce complexity associated with proper names and particular places, and extract indicators and specific policy goals (Woods 2006). Local knowledge is considered messy, complicated, political, and incomprehensible to the institution. Thus, an economic approach reduces problems, such as nutrition, to their core elements so that the professional expertise can digest them and prescribe solutions.

This is a similar situation to that described by Daniel Moynihan (1969) in his book *Maximum Feasible Misunderstanding* in which he describes the failings of the 'community action' plan in the War on Poverty. He notes

Table 7.1. Biomedicine and economic influence on the World Bank

	Biomedicine	Economics
Main agents are	Medical doctors, Biochemists	Health economists
Agents self-described as	Technicians	Technocrats
Hegemony in realm of	Health	Development
Institution symbolically associated with and mainly composed of	Men	Men
Does this institution fit Mary Douglas's 'Strong grid, Strong group' model?	Yes. Strictly conformist, strongly integrated, and rigid boundaries *vis-à-vis* outsiders	Yes. Strictly conformist, strongly integrated, and rigid boundaries *vis-à-vis* outsiders
Knowledge considered	Scientific, objective, technical, rational	Scientific, objective, technical, rational
Mission is to help	Patients	Beneficiaries
Addresses	Symptoms	Efficient treatment of symptoms
Nutrition framed as	Disease	Element of human capital
Undernutrition framed as	Medical problem (individual)	Educational problem
Institutional home	World Health Organization	World Bank
Constructs	Functional groups	Target groups
Women defined as	Mothers	Mothers
Mothers important for	Children to be healthy	Children to be productive
Reliance on visual	Growth charts, anthropometry	Quantitative analysis, statistics, models
Foucauldian framework	Clinical gaze	Economic gaze

that the programme assumption was that, 'They needed not money, but identity; not jobs, but self-respect; not decent homes, but a sense of community and finally not better schools with more funds to make education effective, but control over their destiny' (1969: p. xxi). Moynihan argues that the relative incapacity of Congress to comprehend complex social science ideas and monitor community action at the local level resulted in 'elite condescension' in which the middle class decided what was good for the lower class. Thus he argues that a certain part of society, driven by social scientist expert knowledge and the private ideology of white middle-class actors, took a personal agenda and converted it into an organizational identity and bureaucratic ideology. The parallels to the Bank approach to malnutrition are notable.

The nutrition approach of the Bank was based on a combination of two eminently rational and modern disciplines, namely biomedical and health economic models (see Table 7.1). As a Bank health economist in New Delhi, said, 'We use the medical model but bring in the cost aspects.' However, this approach was not only based on expert analysis and knowledge. Rather, it was a reflection of the political pressures and institutional constraints operating within the Bank along with self-justifying altruism (see Sridhar 2007). Technical expertise is ultimately moulded by political, institutional, and bureaucratic incentives. The structure and organization of the Bank ultimately shape the way it defines its problems and promotes solutions: 'Each institution fashions its policies to fit the resources available' (Woods 2006).

So the Bank framed nutrition using biomedical and economic inputs because it ultimately had to construct a problem that its own instruments could address. The Bank is in the lending business. It makes time-bound, repayable loans. Any Bank actions have to fit within the overall Bank goal of lending for growth. Thus, loans have to be made for profit-creating projects that have measurable economic returns. To address undernutrition, the Bank has to ensure that it is defined as a 'curable' problem (a disease) that when addressed will have an impact on GDP and economic growth (human capital). The prevailing policy is shaped by 'economic analysis, institutional constraints and bureaucratic organization' (Woods 2006: 56).

Local Impact

What exactly were the effects of TINP? Although official Bank documents stated that the official data collected were of high quality, interviews with key Bank officials revealed that there were significant data problems, especially with the baseline and midterm evaluations. These problems included inadequate matching of controls in the TINP-1 midterm and terminal evaluations, delays in the TINP-1 midterm evaluation and poor quality of the data collected. In addition, evaluations tended not to distinguish the effects of TINP from those of other programmes such as the Mid-Day Meal Scheme or even the secular trend at the time.

The first main evaluation was carried out by the Department of Evaluation and Applied Research of the state Planning Commission; however, this department did not have experience with evaluating nutrition and behavioural change so the resulting report was quite weak. A Bank consultant remarked,

Part of the controversy about TINP has been due to uncertainties about what the program has achieved. They arise because of a variety of flaws in successive evaluations of the program. In the case of some interventions, data to measure impact were not collected, so evaluation was impossible. The reliability of the data collection or processing was questionable and throughout the TINP program, there were issues about the validity or absence of controls which make it difficult to know whether reductions in malnutrition were due to TINP or other factors. (Heaver 2002: 21)

Reflecting on TINP, a Food and Agricultural Organization (FAO) report noted, 'As the evaluation was not systematic [nor] supported by statistical analyses, all conclusions should be interpreted carefully' (Vijayaraghavan 1997).

To address the question of TINP's effectiveness, fieldwork was conducted in four caste communities in Tiruvallur (formerly Chingleput) district in Tamil Nadu: Forward Caste (FC), Other Backward Caste (OBC), Scheduled Caste (SC), and Scheduled Tribe (ST). Several assumptions of the Bank approach to malnutrition were tested, including the assumptions that women were the household decision-makers, that 'poor caring practices are the biggest cause of protein-energy malnutrition' (World Bank 2006: 204), that inappropriate caring practices were due to women's ignorance, and finally that households could change their caring behaviours. Data collection consisted of both structured and semi-structured questionnaires as well as visits to the village *anganwadi*.

Tiruvallur has a population of 2.7 million, about equally divided between rural and urban areas. The district consists of fourteen blocks, six municipalities, and nineteen town panchayats (local councils). The main religion is Hinduism but there are also a number of Christians and Muslims. The villages in which fieldwork was conducted were located in Poondi block near the Andhra Pradesh border. Approximately 39 per cent of the block population was classified as Scheduled Caste/Scheduled Tribe. The block is agricultural with the major crops being rice, ragi (finger millet), green gram (mung beans), black gram (black matpe beans), sugar cane, and groundnut. A summary of the results of the fieldwork is given below (for fuller details see Sridhar 2008: 108–55).

Growth Monitoring

Most women in all caste communities reported that their child was weighed, yet the majority could not recognize a growth chart or correctly explain what it showed. Weighing was seen as merely an obstacle to be overcome before children could receive food and health services. Thus, growth monitoring was not understood in any of the study communities, regardless of income or educational level of the household, indicating a mismatch in the programme at three different levels. The first level was that of basic design: it will be recalled that TINP's objective was to use growth monitoring as an educational tool. The discourse in Washington, DC, Delhi, and Chennai revolved around how growth monitoring could make malnutrition 'visible' to mothers. The second level was that of the front-line workers who believed that growth monitoring occurred for data collection purposes. The health workers routinely collected massive amounts of data, usually not fully understanding why they were doing it or what the information would be used for. Growth monitoring often distracted the health workers from the welfare of children since they were more concerned with collecting data than consulting with mothers and children. One health worker was particularly sceptical of the project. She remarked, 'They do not give services to the women they actually need. They give food that is inappropriate, growth charts to illiterate women, and the room is just too crowded.' The third level of understanding is that of beneficiaries. Mothers mentioned weighing as an obstacle to go through before children could receive food and health services. While children were weighed, the purpose of the process was not explained to women so that they could understand the educational importance of growth monitoring.

Supplementary Feeding

Fieldwork revealed several problems in the use of supplementary feeding as a 'cure' for undernutrition. First, supplementary feeding was not targeted towards children whose growth was faltering. While the designers of TINP stressed that supplementary feeding was to be used as 'medicine' only for children experiencing growth faltering, all children who attended *angan-wadi* received the supplement. There are several possible explanations for this lack of targeting. At the level of the front-line community worker, one problem was that the reading and plotting of weights was frequently inaccurate. Because of the difficulty in weighing a child, plotting the weight, and interpreting the growth chart, it was easier for the worker to give rations to all children present that day. In addition, in the context of deprivation, albeit with slight variations in extent between households, it

127

was difficult to withhold food from children whose growth was considered satisfactory, yet who still expressed feelings of hunger.

Further, as with other stand-alone nutrition projects, what was intended as supplementary food for children turned into replacement food. Women attended *anganwadi* in the morning before work. Instead of the child being given the usual breakfast, the child received the supplement. In addition, while women appreciated that TINP included supplementary food, the majority of women in all caste groups preferred for their children to receive 'healthy foods' such as vegetables, dairy products, and eggs over the supplement. While the supplement was eaten because the children were hungry and it was free, when discussing the supplement with older children, they complained that it did not taste good and expressed a desire to have more variety.

Intensive Nutrition Counselling

A high rate of women in all caste groups could not report what they had learned in *anganwadi*, indicating that neither educational level nor income level had improved the receptivity to the nutrition worker's teachings in these communities. The designers intended TINP to be an education programme in which women would learn better caring practices through individual 'nutrition negotiations' with the health workers. But at the front line, the community workers did not have enough time to discuss caring practices with women. There also tended to be more emphasis placed on producing written educational materials than on actually speaking to women about health and nutrition. However, the written materials were not useful to the women who are illiterate.

In terms of the beneficiaries, many women preferred to take advantage of the supplementary food and health services provided by the *anganwadi* as opposed to discussing health lessons, and the fieldwork revealed several obstacles constraining their ability to comply with some of the behaviours the programme was trying to encourage. For example, a tribal woman was told that she should breastfeed her child. However, she noted that she was unable to comply with this advice during the day because she was a daily labourer. The practicability of other types of advice was also seen to be limited. A District Medical Officer reflecting on the limited applicability of nutrition advice stated, 'But they know it, they know that the child does not eat very well because it is the same meal every day. What are you going to propose? You are not going to propose anything because she won't have the capacity to apply it. This is a problem. Thus, I think that they are right not to come to be repeated the same thing again and again' (Roberfroid *et al.* 2005: 210). The effectiveness of the health education effort was thus hampered by the limited ability of the intended beneficiaries to comply with that advice, stemming from their limited purchasing power and weak labour market position.

Despite the problems with individual nutrition counselling, there was a high level of knowledge in all four caste communities on proper caring practices, as defined by the World Health Organization. Over 80 per cent of women in all caste groups had received three ante-natal check-ups as well as iron tablets during pregnancy. Over 90 per cent of women in all caste groups reported that it was important to take rest during pregnancy, although fewer actually did so. The structural constraints of lack of time and money were the primary reasons given for not taking rest. In addition, most women in all four groups ate more during pregnancy, were aware of colostrum, and knew about the recommended breastfeeding duration.

The main sources from which caring practices were learned, other than kinship networks and *anganwadi*, were television and women's groups. The primary beneficial aspect of TINP at the local level was the creation of women's groups by community workers. These groups gave women the space to share educational lessons along with social and economic empowerment activities.

In these communities, inadequate knowledge and ignorance were not the main causes of high rates of child undernutrition. Rather, those high rates could be put down to inadequate purchasing power and alcohol consumption by males. The major household expenditure in all four castes was food, with a significantly higher number of tribal households compared to forward caste households reporting food as their primary expense. In addition, there was a significant difference in the number of meals eaten per day according to caste, with a higher percentage of tribal households eating two or less. The expressed desires for food suggest that most people wanted more rice, meat, and vegetables, indicating that given an adequate income, households would aspire to a more balanced diet. Since inadequate knowledge and child care practices were less responsible for child malnutrition rates in these communities than inadequate purchasing power and gender inequality, the TINP tools of growth monitoring and nutrition counselling were not effective for the reduction of child undernutrition in Tamil Nadu, while the creation of women's groups had beneficial effects. Despite their lack of effectiveness, TINP cannot be seen as a total failure.

While it achieved less than originally envisioned, it did introduce women's groups and provide supplementary food.

Importance of Local Circumstance

The disconnect between the three levels of policy indicates the importance of incorporating local circumstance when designing projects. Reflecting on stereotypes in development, Olivier de Sardan (2005: 76) notes that 'Superstitions, customs, mentalities are repeatedly and routinely called upon to account for the "backwardness" of peasant populations, their inertia or their resistance to development operations.' Culture tends to be viewed as a barrier to progress. According to van Hollen (2003: 187), there is the conflation of superstition, backwardness, immorality, and criminality. As one health worker said to a mother: 'You are doing wrong (*tappu*). You are not giving what you should give to the child and yet you are saying that you are not doing anything wrong' (van Hollen 2003: 187).

In my sample, the main constraint on improving child nutritional outcomes seemed to be of a more structural and gendered nature, with inadequate purchasing power perceived as a major problem. On average, the community researched spent 47.8 per cent of its income on food, and food was cited as the primary expense by 73 per cent of households. 95.4 per cent of women contribute to household income; however, only 43.7 per cent of women reported having control of household expenditure.

A major household leakage was alcohol, which 31.8 per cent of households reported as a problem. Men were found to make the decisions regarding food and resource distribution in 56.3 per cent of households. An average of 39.8 per cent of all household income was reported to have been spent on alcohol by the men. I assume that the actual rates of alcohol consumption were much higher, since women do not usually report alcohol use fully due to its taboo nature. Alcohol affects child nutrition through two pathways. Economically, it is a major leakage of income. Socially, it exacerbates gender inequality within the household and reduces the ability of women to care for their children.

In this community, women thus have knowledge about childcare, yet are constrained by lack of control over income and time. Women often mentioned lack of time, money, or control over household expenditure to explain why their child was not healthy. For example, when a woman stopped breastfeeding before the World Health Organization's recommended twelve months period, it was usually because she had limited time, insufficient milk, or because she was sick. Many of the low caste and tribal women had to work in the fields all day and upon returning felt that since they had been separated for more than eight hours from their child, their breasts were engorged and the milk had become sour. Instead of asking the health workers for more formula, out of fear of being chided, mothers would hide the fact that they were not breastfeeding. As a result, they would end up giving the baby sugar water, or cow or water buffalo milk (van Hollen 2003). These substitutes tend to increase the risk of infection and are even more detrimental to child health than formula. But the health workers were more preoccupied with the value of breastfeeding itself in poor communities than with acknowledging the social conditions which forced poor women into forms of labour that did not provide them the time or space for breastfeeding (ibid.).

It has been shown that in many developing countries men are the decision-makers in the household (Harriss 1991; Mencher 1988; Fapohunda 1988). Despite their dominance within the household, men are not included in nutrition education efforts. In addition, mothers-in-law wield enormous power. Women had to bring their child into the *anganwadi*. Only in rare instances did a man bring his child in because the programme was promoted as a 'woman and child' intervention. Thus women must go to work and earn money in the public sphere as well as take full responsibility for the health of their children. In these four caste communities, it was predominantly lower caste women who worked. While it has been argued that work strengthens a woman's position, there is evidence that working women have less time for child care. Lower caste women, who were on average less well-off, thus had to use their already constrained time to go to the *anganwadi*.

The continual emphasis placed on changing the caring practices of mothers can be viewed as part of a framework of blame. Essentially a mother is admonished by health workers who simply assume that an undernourished child is the result of a mother's inadequacy. Biha, an agricultural labourer, apologized for not being able to take better care of her children, saying 'I am sorry for working, but I have no choice. I have to leave my children alone.' Since undernutrition was seen as preventable, women had to bear the burden of the responsibility for it. Women not only faced a double bind of having to do both public and domestic labour, but also faced another burden in that they were blamed for not having certain attributes, such as knowledge or patience, to care properly for their children. This was one of the unintended negative consequences of TINP.

The Paradox

My findings on the structural determinants of undernutrition in India reveal that a key characteristic of the TINP was that it did not take into consideration local conditions. This characteristic can be seen as a result of the World Bank's reliance on rational blueprints and universal models, and it is a prime example of the arguments that James Scott (1998) makes in *Seeing like a State*. Scott argues that the reasons why government policies so often fail is that there is an excessive focus on modernization and rational tools resulting in homogenization. The corresponding neglect of local conditions results in failure over and over again. Scott claims that, 'designs inevitably leave out elements essential to actual functioning', and policy-makers have 'little confidence... in the skills, intelligence and experience of local people'. He concludes that, 'formal schemes are untenable without some elements of practical knowledge they tend to dismiss' (1998: 7).

The findings reported here are similar to those of White (2005) and Nahar *et al.* (2009) for the Bank's Bangladesh project and to Gopalan's (1992) and George *et al.*'s (1993) for TINP. Despite the problematic features of the model, a similar blueprint has been continually used to fund stand-alone community projects in several different countries. While economic and biomedical ideology shaped the design of the policy, the resilience of the TINP model points towards organizational and bureaucratic incentives to stick with existing blueprints. As Woods (2006: 63–4) has noted, this 'faith-based blindness is a result of the Bank's reliance on a template, which guides staff all over the world. The benefit of a template is that it permits the Bank to stand above local knowledge, to claim universally applicable expertise, and to show that it treats all borrowers the same.'

To understand the Bank's use of a template for nutrition it is helpful to examine the history of nutrition and poverty concerns in the Bank. The World Bank was established at the Bretton Woods Conference in July 1944 to finance European reconstruction after the Second World War. The first Bank loans were given to Denmark, France, Luxembourg, and the Netherlands in mid-1947 (Ayres 1983: 1). Unlike other UN agencies, the Bank initially raised funds through donor contributions from wealthier countries and private financial markets. This procedure allowed it to raise money to provide interest-bearing and interest-free loans, credits, grants, and technical assistance to countries that could not afford to borrow money in international markets. The Bank's Articles of Agreement focus on productivity, investment, capital accumulation, growth, and balance of payment.

In the 1960s, with the creation of a new branch of the World Bank, the International Development Association (IDA), the Bank turned its focus to development which was internally and internationally conceived of as economic growth to be achieved through industrialization. The IDA financed these projects through interest-free credits to poor countries as opposed to the International Bank for Reconstruction and Development (IBRD) which functioned purely as a bank for middle-income countries. Between 1961 and 1965, the IBRD loaned 76.8 per cent for electric power and transportation and only 1 per cent for projects in the social sector; even the 'development-focused' IDA spent a little under 3 per cent for social services (Ayres 1983: 3).

Robert McNamara sparked global interest in social sector investment and nutritional investment in developing countries when he became President of the World Bank. McNamara arrived at the Bank in 1968 after serving for seven years as US Secretary of Defense under Presidents Kennedy and Johnson (Schechter 1988). He brought to the Bank an agenda outlining the moral imperative of foreign aid both for humanitarian and national security purposes. He then attempted to institutionalize these ideas at the Bank, as Martha Finnemore notes, 'Ideas need to be institutionalized for maximum effect' (Finnemore 1997). McNamara formally addressed world poverty in his Nairobi Speech to the Board of Governors on 24 September 1973 where he spoke of improving living conditions, expanding education lending, and focusing on basic nutritional requirements. There he outlined a two-pronged approach to development. His first objective was to scale up Bank lending and to increase Bank staff at least five-fold. In fiscal year 1968, the Bank's new commitments were $953.5 million; by 1981 total cumulative lending reached $92.2 billion (Ayres 1983: 6). McNamara's second objective was to further the Bank's control on the way aid was used by borrower countries; specifically he wanted to have greater Bank influence on project design. Greater influence would be achieved through the institution being framed as a technical assistance agency that would show countries the 'western way of doing things' through providing advice, furnishing consultants, and giving training, at the expense of the borrower country (Schechter 1988: 115).

However, as he endeavoured to reconfigure the Bank's direction, McNamara faced an organizational constraint in that poverty-oriented projects required more staff, more work, and more attention to detail. The Bank was torn between being a bank and being a development agency, between spending effectively and moving money fast. The Bank was set up to be a financial institution which valued investments that showed a measurable and direct monetary return. Yet, McNamara wanted to redefine the Bank as a credible development agency. Despite the move to poverty-alleviation projects, he still increased pressure on staff to move loan money for projects fast to meet the year's financial goals. 'The new style ... entailed lending for small projects based on less information, using less well-developed techniques, and involving more costs and benefits that were difficult or impossible to quantify using standard economic tool analysis' (Finnemore 1997).

The Bank's staff, predominantly trained in economics, regarded themselves as technicians providing rigorous scientific analysis of development. They had difficulty applying their technical econometric models to soft issues of health and social welfare. Other difficulties with the change were McNamara's desire for quantification of targets and outputs as well as short-term results. The fast-paced progression of projects did not give staff adequate time to address local concerns and complex social realities such as kinship, caste, and local governance structures.

The tension between moving money fast and poverty-alleviation still remains today in the Bank's nutrition operations. One staff member recounted difficulties with the way the Bank 'thinks' in nutrition and more generally in its project loans. In his words, 'The Bank likes to think big, because otherwise it is not worth the time of staff if they're not going to move lots of money.' In addition, as the Bank runs out of borrowers, he noted that the Bank is forced actively to 'sell' projects to governments. In the case of nutrition, if there is no real commitment on the part of the government, then it will not work. The workload on staff has been steadily increasing over the past half century. In 1981, a Bank staff member remarked:

Every few years there is a new factor that we must take into account, but we are not given more time or staff to accommodate it. This makes me think that the Bank's senior management is responding to outside pressures by delegating the hard choices to us. I don't have any clear understanding of whether we are supposed to pay lip service to, say, the environment or the role of women in development, or to take them seriously. Even worse, I don't know to what extent the Bank wants me to take any one of these things seriously when they conflict with one another. I can make up my own mind on this, but am I supposed to? (Ascher 1983: 430)

Reflecting on the Bangladesh nutrition project in 2005, the former head of nutrition at the Bank noted,

I think, firstly, that it's clear from the ICR [the Implementation and Completion report of BINP] discussions within the Bank that there's no doubt that with hindsight we all agree that moving forward with NNP too quickly was a mistake. The Bank has said so publicly, has written it down. There is no doubt about that. That there were very strong political reasons for doing that is also a reality, and I think understanding some of that, and acknowledging some of that, and how do we as technical people respond to those kinds of realities I think is something we all need to deal with.

If a project takes too long or costs too much, it is seen as a failure on the part of the staff. Spending too long on local complexities is considered as creating a problem and hampering the real work of the loan point-person. One staff member stressed to me that the purpose of the Bank's mission is not to create a 'Bank' project. He said, 'So, whatever, at the end, is done or not done, these things are due to the government.' This claim was contested by an individual who works with the Bank in nutrition. She stated,

What we seem to be seeing . . . is the reliance on people coming in from outside into the country for very short periods of time, engaging in very rapid consultation processes and writing design documents often outside the country leads to a situation where it's very difficult for national stakeholders to actually challenge the approaches which are being put forward. Blueprint approaches.

During interviews with Bank staff, I received mixed messages about the flexibility in the policy process for the borrower country to make changes.

The pressure to move money fast puts staff in a difficult position. They are required to produce an enormous amount, travel often, all in an environment in which every interview, journalist, or researcher, could potentially result in a public affairs debacle. Designing a project is a long and arduous process and staff simply do not have time to put together a whole new project. They already have project recipes that can be exported to every country. In a larger study on the evolution of IMF and Bank policies and how the institutions can reform, Ngaire Woods notes:

Junior officials are regularly sent to far-away places to analyze rather alien and difficult solutions. As mentioned above, a clear blueprint of models and policies provide the Fund and Bank staff with a well-structured starting point from which to define the problem, map out the stakes, prescribe the solution, evaluate the chances of success, and assess the implications of their prescription. Obviously, the simpler and clearer the model the more usefully it fulfils these functions. (Woods 2006: 55)

In a way, staff are forced to use a blueprint despite acknowledging that the blueprint is flawed. Reflecting on negative evaluations specifically for nutrition, a Bank staff member noted:

And I would also say that stopping implementation of projects, if there is the concern that great harm will be done if one goes forward — let's say we're building a dam and there are very serious design questions — that certainly is an appropriate remedy. If the concern is that we're not being as effective as we ought to be, that's a different threshold where I would say the remedy might not necessarily be to impose a moratorium.

In addition, as Ngaire Woods's study shows, staff face a strong personal incentive to stick to the blueprint; 'If all staff speak with one voice and prescribe the same things, then it is the institution as a whole that must bear the brunt of any criticism' (2006: 63), not the individual. There is little incentive for staff to try something new since the Bank will not take responsibility for a novel approach. Thus many staff are reluctant to work in an unfamiliar field especially if there are no career benefits arising from this (Heaver 2006: 19). Staff are concerned with protecting their jobs, thus they are likely to stay within the existing structures if they offer some sort of security. The World Bank is a rational institution in that policy is guided by organizational factors (bureaucratic incentives) in the superficial or real service of given fundamental values and principles (economic and biomedical).

Conclusion

This chapter has argued that there is a mismatch between how malnutrition is defined, measured, and evaluated by the Bank, and how it is lived and experienced in affected communities. While the biomedical approach to undernutrition might be suitable in the setting of a clinic, it is problematic when exported to stand-alone community nutrition projects such as TINP. TINP defines undernutrition as a medical disease resulting from women's lack of knowledge on proper child care practices. The disease can be visually detected in the child through the use of growth monitoring and promotion. Community workers determine if the child is 'sick' (i.e. undernourished) and in need of treatment through the use of growth monitoring. The 'cures' promoted for this disease are educational tools: growth monitoring to show a mother her child's growth is faltering, supplementary feeding for 90 days to teach mothers that small amounts of additional food can 'cure' their child, and nutrition counselling on hygiene, food quality and quantity. However, as fieldwork in Tamil Nadu revealed, these educational tools are not effective at addressing undernutrition in India.

Two conclusions can be reached from the findings of this research which reflect the unintended consequences of public policy initiatives and reforms. First, unintended consequences of the type discussed here will arise when policy-makers fail to address the structural determinants of malnutrition, in this case involving the circumstances within which households and individuals make choices. Second, such unintended consequences will arise when policy-makers fail (in *Seeing like a State* fashion) to take account of local conditions, in this case involving women's position in society, and thus avoid policy options such as hunger reduction strategies that can increase not only household purchasing power, but also improve the position of women, through schemes such as cash transfers and the creation of women's groups.

8

Integration at Any Price

The Case of the NHS National Programme for Information Technology

Justin Keen

Editors' Overview

In this chapter, Justin Keen looks at the unintended consequences of a huge technology-based modernization project: the NHS National Programme for Information Technology in England. The project was envisaged by policy-makers in the Department of Health as a major rationalization of the NHS, gathering together all patient information in a single record for every citizen, accessible to health practitioners from across a range of services. It relied on the development of a huge, centralized, integrated IT system that would be used by all health practitioners. But the NHS is a collection of organizations with a troubled history of failed information technology projects and a complex legacy of multiple systems for specific tasks, operating in parallel. There are also successes in some areas, where important links between systems have been developed and fostered over many years. Modernization plans introduced in the 1990s ignored these previous on-the-ground efforts, with policy-makers taking a fatalist view of the ad-hoc untidy nature of existing arrangements and the lack of integration between systems. Policies were aimed at 'tying down the future' with a new 'gold standard' of a centralized, integrated system which would radically simplify the organization of health information.

Seven years after its conception, and a huge outlay of resources, the project remains only partially implemented and appears to have introduced additional complexity and uncertainty to the NHS information environment. A national 'spine' of basic information about citizens exists, but none of the stakeholders seem to know what kinds of patient information should be attached to it. The future is more uncertain than ever, as policy-makers continue to devote resources to the project, seemingly playing for time as they wait for an appropriate problem to fit the technological solution they have bought into. Modernization in this project rested on integration, to be achieved through a central IT system and 'ruthless standardization' of behaviour. Yet nearly ten years on, neither integration, nor standardization, nor the benefits they were supposed to bring, have been attained. Centralized plans ignored the reality of 'local' conditions as in many of James Scott's examples, but here the local actors were inside the state: professionals in hospitals and primary care who did not use the systems in ways that designers and their political backers envisaged.

Introduction

None of us is surprised when we hear that a major project is running late. We tend to assume that it will be completed eventually, or abandoned if problems prove to be insuperable. But what are we to make of a project which is costing billions of pounds, but has no clear end date, and yet there is no sign of it being abandoned? That, in essence, is the fate of the NHS National Programme for Information Technology in England.

In order to understand how the NHS National Programme has arrived at this point, we need to go back in time and retrace the steps taken by the key parties involved. It turns out that there are two distinct tracks, which only really merged when the NHS National Programme was announced in 2002. One track leads us through developments in computing in NHS organizations. The NHS can claim a creditable track record in implementing information technology (IT) systems for general practitioners (GPs), though a more patchy one in hospitals, and many nurses and other clinical professionals still make limited use of IT even today.

The other track is the one trodden by policy-makers down the years. While there are clear and unsurprising differences between the earliest IT policies in 1990 and those of today, there are also important continuities. For example, it is possible to trace a growing commitment to the belief that it is possible and desirable to integrate all of a patient's personal data in single electronic health records. Similarly, it has always been assumed that doctors and other clinicians will collect data for their own use, but that key data will also be passed to and used by central government. The NHS is funded mainly through general taxation, so it is reasonable for governments to monitor the use of public resources. As we shall see, though, fundamental disagreements about the nature of that monitoring have cast a shadow over NHS IT policy-making for the last fifteen years.

The two tracks lead us to the central paradox in the NHS National Programme, and indeed in the aspirations of health policy-makers in many other countries. Modern centralized, integrated IT systems are viewed, by their proponents, as technologies which *reduce* complexity. This was certainly the view of the cheerleaders for the National Programme at the start, who spoke about 'ruthless standardization' of behaviour through the use of integrated IT systems (Department of Health 2002), and rapid — unproblematic — procurement and deployment (Brennan 2005). It was as if they believed that they could see into the future, to a world where large-scale integration had been achieved. Yet one of the most distinctive features of the internet and other large-scale electronic networks is that they *increase* complexity. That is, the more one tries to integrate services the greater the challenges of dealing with heterogeneity and scale. In the NHS, integration requires coordination across professional and organizational boundaries, and across large geographical distances. Yet it has always been difficult to achieve effective coordination. Services are inherently uncertain: healthcare is not a uniform process, akin to a car production line. Professional boundaries are jealously guarded. The realization that this was an important consideration in the NHS came late in the day (Nicholson 2008). The integration promised by IT networks has run into severe coordination problems, in part because organizational and professional boundaries are deeply entrenched and stoutly defended.

The next section sets out the political contours and administrative context of the NHS and other healthcare systems, as it is not possible to understand IT developments without some understanding of the landscape. This is followed by brief accounts of the development of selected IT systems, and then a retracing of the tracks laid down by policy-makers. The final section sets out the central paradox, and argues that it rests on deeply held beliefs about the potential of IT networks to enable policy-makers to impose tight control over the behaviour of doctors and other clinicians and standardize behaviour in the collection and use of personal information.

The Political Landscape

Three general characteristics of the NHS are relevant to this account. First, all healthcare systems in developed countries are based on long-term political settlements between the most powerful interests. Moran (1999) argues that the state, clinicians (particularly doctors), and technology suppliers are locked into a long-term triangular relationship with one another. The arrangement has been stable over long periods because each party derives benefits from the relationship. For example, pharmaceutical firms have access to markets to sell their products, doctors can use those products to provide high-quality care, and governments benefit by being perceived to have supported a valued service. By comparison with GlaxoSmithKline and other pharmaceutical firms, IT suppliers in England have historically been minor players, but the amounts of money committed to the NHS National Programme for IT suggests that they now have a place at the top table.

It is important to stress that the triangular relationship has not always resulted in services that serve the wider public interest, however that term is defined. For example, there is clear evidence that doctors — who control the majority of resource allocation decisions in practice — are reluctant to work in more deprived areas (Acheson 1998). Given that health problems increase with decreasing household incomes, the result is that service provision is inversely related to need. There is also good evidence of unjustified variations in both the content and quality of care across the country (Dixon *et al.* 2007).

Second, the NHS is a bureaucracy, but one with some peculiar characteristics. In the early 1990s the NHS was subjected to a New Public Management makeover. A number of structural innovations were made, including the introduction of an 'internal market' wherein the purchasing and provision of services were separated from one another. The story of the rise and fall of the internal market has been told elsewhere (Klein 1998; Moran 1999) but the essential point here is that it kick-started a drive to increase the amount and quality of detailed information collected about services being provided. The NHS has been subjected to successive rounds of reforms — upheavals might be a better term — ever since, and at present it is in the grip of overt moves to contract out health service provision to private firms. As with the internal market these policies have been both controversial and at best partially successful. Indeed, far from devolving authority the 1990s reform programme led to centralization (Hacker 2004). The reforms greatly strengthened the hierarchical relationships from hospitals and other provider organizations upwards through district and regional general management tiers. One important result is that the government has been able to introduce strong top–down performance management.

Third, the NHS has always been riven with inter-professional problems, with increasing professionalization over the last twenty years contributing to coordination problems on the ground. Throughout this account, it is

141

important to bear in mind that the state may have a legitimate interest in monitoring and evaluating the work of doctors and other professionals.

Information Technologies on the Ground

Throughout the last twenty years, most IT investment decisions have been made by individual NHS organizations. For straightforward reasons, relating to the scale and complexity of healthcare, IT solutions developed along functional lines. Discrete systems have been developed for GPs, for out-patient clinics, operating theatres, and so on. At least until recently, NHS managers and clinical staff have not had to wait for national initiatives, so that these various systems have diffused across the NHS or faded away without central intervention. This section sets out a number of thumbnail sketches. The accounts show that there have been some important successes, as well as the inevitable false starts and failures. Crucially for this chapter, the successes highlight the ways in which initiatives on the ground have grown up in a piecemeal way, with few links between them. Looked at as a whole these local arrangements form an important legacy and a major coordination challenge for the new centralized plans laid out in the National Programme for IT.

GP and Pathology Systems: Two Successes

Around 90 per cent of all contacts with the NHS are in primary care, and the great majority of these are with general practitioners (GPs) and practice-based nurses. Twenty years ago, there was little in the way of IT in primary care. But change was under way. The Department of Health paid for the development of a system for remunerating GPs, who are independent contractors and who have always been paid through a complicated mix of flat fees and tariffs for specific activities (such as providing health screening services or minor surgical procedures). In the late 1980s a number of small specialist IT firms worked closely with GPs, and developed early commercial systems, which were useful for automating the complicated 'back office' administration of GPs' incomes, and resulted eventually in GPs being able to submit claims electronically.

From the start, the firms and the GPs envisaged that their systems should also be integral to clinical work, and so hold all of the data that GPs would need to diagnose and treat their patients. During the 1990s, more and more GPs purchased systems, so that by the end of the decade the great majority of GPs had them on their desks. Today, it would be a rare event to see a GP without a computer system playing a role in the consultation. However, as we shall see, these systems do not link with one another, and there are still only limited direct links between GP practices and hospitals.

A similar story can be told about pathology systems. Hospital doctors and GPs are both heavily dependent on pathology services to help them with diagnosis and treatment. A typical hospital pathology department undertakes millions of tests each year for its own doctors and for local GPs. In the 1980s, a number of pathologists who had active interests in IT began to develop systems and communications standards that would allow their colleagues to make electronic requests for pathology tests, and for them to receive the test results once they were available. Pathology department systems — the machines that analysed samples — were becoming progressively more automated, but were producing paper printouts which had to be sent out in hospital internal mail or by post to GPs.

It seemed a natural, if big, step to link the analysers to IT systems in order to capture results and send them to the people who had ordered them electronically. Pathologists and interested GPs worked with small specialist IT firms, initially to develop electronic links within hospitals and to small numbers of practices. As with the development of GP computing, pathology test reporting became more popular over time, so that pathology departments have gone a long way to removing paper from their reporting processes. This said, and echoing the situation with GP systems, the links are still one way: in most places GPs cannot make electronic requests for tests (Carter 2008).

In both GP and pathology computing, it is striking that developments have been professionally led, and have diffused across the NHS steadily over a period of twenty or so years. Over time, more and more GP practices have received pathology test results electronically, with the results being entered automatically into GPs' patient records. In the last five years the development of electronic communication of pathology data has been supported by the NHS National Programme, an example of a quiet development away from the limelight.

A Mixed Picture

There are further successes to note. Twenty years of NPM-inspired reforms have resulted in a service with solid finance systems, which have developed in parallel with increasing demands on the quality of financial information. Similarly, the basic administrative systems in hospitals — called patient administration systems — were first implemented in the 1970s. These systems support mundane, but vital, functions such as booking of out-patient appointments and admissions. However, many patient administration systems are still based on 1970s technology, have not kept up with wider technological developments, in many hospitals have not been replaced, and have to be continuously patched up.

This brings us to the strange case of parallel information systems in healthcare, and to structural problems of the kind that generate paradoxes of modernization. While there have been successes in primary care and in 'back office' hospital systems, the fact is that hospitals and community health services — district nursing, health visiting, and the like — are still awash with paper. Principal among these are the medical, nursing, and other records that professionals use when they see patients, and the forms and letters that hospital doctors send to GPs. There are two consequences of reliance on paper-based systems. The first is that they do not aid the kind of coordination required for safe care. (This observation underpins all thoughtful arguments for electronic patient records: they may not turn out to be achievable, but the basic premise is perfectly reasonable.) The second is that the records are disconnected from the administrative and finance systems, which effectively work in parallel in most places. Upwards reporting to the Department of Health is based mostly on the administrative and finance systems, so that central returns do not directly reflect the data in clinical records.

The problems involved in the operation and use of multiple parallel systems within and across specialist areas of the health sector are well illustrated by the case of radiology systems. Broadly speaking, radiology services are similar to pathology services. Radiology departments provide diagnostic services to both GPs and to hospital colleagues, though in their case the services are based on making and interpreting medical images including x-rays, CT scans, and MRI scans. Yet the trajectory of technological development has been very different. Radiology information systems have been available and routinely used since the late 1980s. They were developed as local versions of patient administration systems, and used for booking and tracking patients through radiology services.

Then followed the move from film — including x-ray films, the films that are stuck up on light boxes in any self-respecting medical soap — to computerized imaging, and on to systems which hold all types of images in one place, called Picture Archiving and Communication Systems (PACS). PACS were first available in the early 1990s, but were expensive, costing several million pounds per hospital, and a lot of money for what are essentially storage devices. Images were typically only available within a radiology department, and possibly in the one or two specialities that were the heaviest users of imaging services such as orthopaedics and general surgery. In contrast with pathology services, the focus was on capturing and storing radiology images rather than on communicating results — radiologists' interpretations of images — to medical colleagues. The result is that, in many hospitals, radiologists' opinions were — and still are — dictated, transcribed and then posted to the doctors who have requested opinions. In other words, radiology departments have maintained the separation of clinical and administrative data.

In order to round out the picture, it is important to note that there were many calls for system integration in this earlier period. Papers setting out ideas for electronic patient records were first published in the 1960s. In the UK the Department of Health published a report (the Tunbridge Report) proposing electronic medical records as long ago as 1965. Since that time there have been dozens of initiatives supporting the design and implementation of electronic records technologies. As we have seen, the result is some successful stand-alone records systems. As the next section shows, though, *shared* electronic records have proved to be a graveyard for the ambitions of policy-makers.

A similar situation prevails in telemedicine — this being an umbrella term for using electronic networks to allow remote consultations or advice giving. The first formal studies of telemedicine systems were reported in the 1970s (Moore *et al.* 1975; Dunn *et al.* 1977). There have been technological improvements over the years, and a progression from 'near-laboratory' applications, through early commercial systems using proprietary technology, to solutions which use cheap and reliable mass-market equipment over the internet. In spite of the reduction in costs, the diffusion of telemedicine applications in clinical practice has been slow and take-up is still very patchy. The history is one of large numbers of initiatives, most of which have failed to diffuse beyond small numbers of enthusiastic users (Coiera 2006; Wootton 2001).

IT Policies since 1990: From Technicians to Technocrats

This section covers the IT polices that prevailed in the NHS from the 1990s. It shows that there were two distinct phases of policy-making. The first phase was characterized by central exhortation to design and implement new systems to support both administration and the delivery of services. In the second, the most recent plans have sought to impose reforms on the basis of central technology-focused objectives, rather than building on the best of the endeavours on the ground that were described in the last section.

As noted earlier, the milestone White Paper, *Working for Patients* (Secretaries of State 1989), set out proposals for an 'internal' market' in the NHS. Policy-makers in the Department of Health realized that the new arrangements would require detailed information about the health of local populations, so that purchasers could allocate resources to where they were most needed. Providers would need to collect data on the volume, cost, and quality of services and use it as the basis for negotiations with purchasers. They would have to show what they had done in order to persuade purchasers to pay for it. The view was taken that these new requirements could only be met by using IT systems. The drive came from politicians and civil servants who wanted the reforms to work, and so were motivated to produce their own plans. The first result was the Framework of Information Systems in 1990. This was followed by the more detailed Information Management and Technology (IM&T) Strategy in 1992.

The dominant theme was centralization. Both the 1990 and 1992 policies emphasized the importance of ensuring that the Department of Health would have the data it needed, which would be derived from local systems across the NHS (contradicting the new era of NHS managers freed from central control, presaged in the *Working for Patients* proposals). What is more, the fact that important early IT development was already under way in the NHS was ignored: policy was not connected to realities on the ground. There were no detailed statements on the usual bedrock of IT policies, such as standards for inter-operability of systems; in this sense the plans appeared to propose standardization without standards. There were no convincing statements about the ways in which IT would support the key *Working for Patients* policies in practice. It is one thing to say that IT will support a policy, another to explain to NHS managers and clinicians which systems they should buy, and why. This was policy-making of the vague exhortation variety.

Unsurprisingly, the consequence was that not much happened, at least in the arenas of interest to policy-makers in London. In the event, everyone was let off the hook because the NHS internal market experiment was slowed down and then quietly dropped around 1995. (This era has been reviewed elsewhere, see Webster 2002.) But the IT supporters at the Department of Health had secured a foothold in the policy firmament. One tangible result was that, in 1994, they were able to sign a contract with suppliers including BT and Cable and Wireless for an NHS network, NHSnet, which we would now recognize as an intranet.

NHSnet was little used initially but carried substantial volumes of email traffic — up to one million emails on a working day by 2002. It was not used to exchange clinical information, though, partly due to a recommended boycott of NHSnet by the medical profession (Anderson 1995), and partly due to the realization by civil servants that data within NHSnet were — as doctors' representatives claimed — not secure. Both then and now, NHSnet is only accessible on NHS premises, so that staff cannot access it 'on the move' or in their own homes. The Danish network, in contrast, carried both clinical and administrative data, so that by 2002 the majority of prescriptions, as well as hospital referrals, were handled electronically.

During the period to 1998, as we have seen already, implementation continued on the ground in a gradual, unfussy way. We cannot mention this period, however, without also mentioning the list of NHS IT disasters. Four in particular hit the headlines, each of which further emphasizes the top–down, technology-driven thinking that was prevalent at the time. The first was the Wessex region IT programme, started at the end of the 1980s, where the (then) Wessex Regional Health Authority signed a contract with IBM to implement region-wide finance, HR, and hospital information systems. Major elements of the project never got out of the starting blocks, and millions of pounds were wasted. This was followed by the Department of Health-supported Hospital Information Support Systems (HISS) programme. The HISS programme was intended to provide hospitals with high-quality communications infrastructure, so that pathology, radiology, prescribing, and other data were all available at a single terminal. (The thinking here was broadly similar to that surrounding electronic health records, though with a stronger focus on communications than creating single databases of individual patient data.) A National Audit Office report concluded that the programme had spent £103m and achieved savings of £3m. (Arguably, allowing the £3m claim was if anything generous.)

Next came the London Ambulance Service (LAS). The Service awarded a contract for a new IT system for routing ambulances following emergency calls. The contract was poorly specified and awarded to a company that had simply bid too low. When the system was introduced it quickly led to chaos, with stories quickly appearing in the media of patients dying while waiting for ambulances that never arrived. The system was quickly scrapped (though it is worth noting that a new system was introduced with barely a ripple three years later). The scandal over the Read Codes was different in nature, but contributed to the general malaise. Dr James

Read, a Loughborough GP, had developed a clinical coding system for use by GPs. Coding is important because counting, and identifying groups of people with particular problems, really does matter in healthcare. If you want to target people with diabetes in a new education campaign, you need to know who they are. It transpired that Dr Read had been paid substantial sums for a new version of his coding system which was not delivered, and had presided over irregular financial and HR practices. All of this was exposed in another NAO report.

These failures, combined with the observations about the fragmented nature of developments on the ground, help us to identify two points that are relevant in the next period, from 2002 onwards. First, the NHS has historically lacked project management skills, and has a poor track record in negotiating with large private firms. Combined with naivety in policy-making, this has led to large, inflexible projects which are beyond the skills of the organizations involved to manage (Collingridge 1992; Collingridge and Margetts 1994). Second, the policies in this period tended to ignore the practical realities on the ground: the inherent complexity of healthcare delivery, and the IT successes and failures. This situation occurred in spite of the fact that some of the initiatives, including GP and pathology computing, were supported by some civil servants. There appears to have been a disconnection, within the Department of Health, between the civil servants who interacted with and supported NHS developments and those who wrote the policy documents.

Into the Limelight: Connecting for Health and the National Programme for IT

The change of government from a Conservative to Labour administration in 1997 did not lead to early change. The next policy, *Information for Health* (Department of Health 1998), was published in 1998. One noteworthy development was explicit support for integrated electronic patient records, presented as part of a move to more patient-centred care. Documentation was, though, vague about the content of the records, or who would use them. Overall, the document represented a continuation of earlier policies, in both its focus on central requirements and in the absence of money for purchasing new systems. A later policy (Department of Health 2001), intended to show how IT would support the NHS Plan, Labour's principal early policy statement, merely reaffirmed earlier policies, and there was still no money.

And then something happened. There was a marked change in IT policy-making during 2001 and 2002. The period included a high-profile meeting between Prime Minister Blair and Bill Gates. The Wanless (2002) report on the NHS for the Treasury concluded that the NHS had seriously underinvested in IT over many years (though it should be stressed that the report failed to offer any compelling evidence for this view). Management consultancy reports on NHS IT were prepared for the Prime Minister and others (Craig and Brooks 2006). It all culminated in a meeting at 10 Downing Street in May 2002, the result of which was a decision to provide funding for an ambitious IT infrastructure for the whole of the NHS, to cost around £2.3billion and to take two years and nine months to introduce (Brooks 2007). These examples show that the Prime Minister and Chancellor dominated decision-making: accounts from senior Department of Health officials confirm this, with those officials travelling to Downing Street for key meetings (Brennan 2005).

What happened next puts all previous NHS IT disasters — indeed IT disasters anywhere — in the shade. In brief, a new Director General of IT was appointed, on a salary higher than both the Prime Minister and the Chief Executive of the NHS. He headed a new Agency, Connecting for Health. The Director General decided to strike long-term, and highly inflexible, contracts with large IT firms. The contracts were agreed between Connecting for Health and the contractors — the NHS had no direct input into the process. Initially there were five ten-year contracts, each for a region of England, for electronic health records for every patient. A sixth contract was agreed for a national system called Choose and Book. This was intended to allow GPs, or patients, attending hospital for a first appointment to book that appointment themselves. This was viewed as a key technology underpinning the Labour government's commitment to ensure that patients could exercise 'choice' between hospital services. A seventh contract was, in effect, an extension of the earlier NHSnet contract, designed to allow patient data to be available anywhere in the NHS. All data would be routed through the network — now called The Spine — even if it was only being sent from a GP practice to a hospital a mile away. Later, contracts were awarded for a national system for the electronic transfer of prescriptions from GPs to pharmacies and for the implementation of PACS in radiology departments. All hospitals were expected to implement PACS by the end of 2007.

Accounts from key participants at the time show that the National Programme was based on three key ideas. The first acknowledged the historical lack of funding and weaknesses in procurement (Brennan 2005;

Department of Health 2002). The second was that IT contractors would have the knowledge needed to deliver the Programme. The National Programme reflected the ideological belief, originating under Mrs Thatcher's premiership, in the ability of large private firms to help to solve perceived problems in public services. The third idea was that the centre wanted more control of doctors and other clinicians. This played into the centralizing tendency under both Conservative and Labour governments, and has arguably been the principal driver of IT policy-making over the last twenty years. As noted earlier, this is a reasonable policy position — the question is whether top–down IT policies could ever help to achieve the desired control in practice.

Things have not gone well. The Choose and Book technology, strongly championed by ministers and civil servants, was perceived to be difficult to use in both GP surgeries and hospitals. There was considerable initial resistance from many GPs, but the system has been implemented in some areas, partly because clinicians and managers know that the technology is intimately related to a key government target that no patient with an initial diagnosis should wait longer than eighteen weeks from first GP referral to hospital treatment. Work on the electronic prescribing service (EPS) started later than Choose and Book. The pattern looks similar to GP and pathology computing in earlier times; NAO reports and deployment statistics (http://www.connectingforhealth.nhs.uk/newsroom/statistics/deployment) show that there was a slow start, attributable to extensive negotiations with GPs, pharmacies (from Boots to single shops), and pharmaceutical firms, and then increasing uptake. PACS have been successfully installed in all NHS hospitals, though as noted earlier these are stand-alone systems, and contribute little to system integration. The main problem concerns the flagship of the programme: the five contracts for electronic health records, worth over £5bn. Five years in, systems had been implemented in a handful of hospitals in the south of England, and in single departments in two hospitals in the north.

The main bright spot, if you are a policy-maker, is the N3 network, the Spine. N3 works, in the simple sense that GP computing systems can link to it, and pathology services now run over it. However, because of problems elsewhere, connections from hospitals are few and far between. As a result we are still a very long way from the avowed goal of accessing a patient's details anywhere, anytime, via the Spine. Indeed, it is still not clear how patient data will be integrated. Government policies flip-flop between proposals for creating summary records with just a few data items (a patent's current prescriptions, for example) and making full clinical details available to clinicians (Ministerial Taskforce 2006; Anderson *et al.* 2009). Taking a detached view, the success with N3 is important because central agencies such as the Information Centre for Health and Social Care, and primary care trusts, now have access to detailed patient-level data from primary care, where most care is provided, and which can be used for planning purposes.

The mystery is why anyone thought the National Programme would work. There was ample evidence of the risks from the start, and much critical commentary in the early days of the Programme. Some journalists deserve credit for identifying problems early on and for doggedly exposing problems in the first two to three years, when Connecting for Health was both secretive and aggressive in the face of the slightest criticism. Similarly, a number of academics and other commentators (Cross 2006; Guenier 2002) expressed concerns early on, and set out alternative strategies. Indeed, it is worth pointing out that the evidence base was very thin. In healthcare, new drugs and devices are routinely subjected to cost-effectiveness assessments, in the NHS and many other countries, and yet there is almost no evidence for IT investment. Systematic literature reviews of evidence about electronic patient records show that there is, at best, limited positive evidence for effects on the working practices of clinical or administrative staff Anderson (Delpierre *et xal.* 2004; Poissant *et al.* 2005; Ross and Lin 2003). There is, similarly, little empirical evidence to support investments in communications technologies in healthcare (Whitten *et al.* 2002).

Conversely, there has been a failure to learn positive lessons from some other countries. Arguably the most impressive example is in the Danish health service, where patients can view their own electronic health records on the internet. Work began in the early 1990s on the development of communications standards. Sustained development and implementation effort has led to a situation where almost all communications are handled electronically across the country. It needs to be stressed that Denmark has pursued a policy of supporting communications through clearly defined and agreed standards, as opposed to pursuing the technology-driven policies preferred in England.

When it became clear that all was not well the NAO announced that it would investigate. Its first report in 2006 (NAO 2006) looked suspiciously like a whitewash, stating that the National Programme was experiencing problems but could still be successful. The report did, though, show that progress had been slower than had been claimed, that the lifetime costs of the Programme had risen to £12.4bn, and it stated that Connecting for Health had been unable to identify significant benefits, even in principle.

Rumours circulated of stormy meetings with Connecting for Health, and of deadlock over agreeing the text lasting several months. Politicians, including members of the Public Accounts Committee, were unhappy with the first report and quickly announced a second one. The second report, in 2008, was more forthright and appears to have led to the resignation of the Director General in advance of its publication. Progress was still very slow, and timescales for electronic health records were stretching out into the next decade. By 2009, the National Programme was little more than a source of easy sound bites for opposition politicians, and a continuing source of stories for journalists. There was always something going wrong, and there were persistent rumours about renegotiating some of the contracts altogether.

This state of affairs raises obvious questions about the responses of Connecting for Health, the NHS, and supplier firms. Connecting for Health is still in place. While there have been regular calls to scrap the National Programme, the fine print in ministerial speeches and policy documents points to the continuing belief that the NHS needs more IT investment. The NHS National Programme is properly viewed as the culmination of policies which have brought IT policy-makers and suppliers to the top political table. It may be very uncomfortable to be there, given the endless criticism, but at least they are there.

NHS organizations waited for these systems initially, but many are now pursuing their own plans outside the NHS National Programme. Having been promised new 'base' systems, such as patient administration systems — remember that many of these were ageing at the start of the Programme — many hospitals are now procuring their own systems, in the same way they would have done before the National Programme. In GP computing a new firm, TPP, has produced a system that is popular with GPs, particularly in the north of England. This system can pass data upwards to the NHS Spine, but connections to hospital departments are still few and far between. In short, local managers, informatics managers, doctors, and others have concluded that it is no longer sensible to wait for the long-promised national solutions.

As for the National Programme suppliers, some firms walked away, arguably retaining some dignity (Accenture), while others had contracts terminated (IDX). One of the key firms became embroiled in internal governance problems (iSOFT), and these appear to have significantly affected its ability to deliver promised systems. With the exception of BT, who are responsible for the Spine, we can conclude that firms could not solve the technological and implementation challenges in the NHS, as the politicians and civil servants had hoped. In retrospect it seems that the firms had different motivations for participating in the National Programme, and to some extent this has influenced their subsequent behaviour. For example, Accenture seems to have taken a straightforward business decision to join and then to walk away: the National Programme looked like a good opportunity, but just wasn't in practice. Other firms such as Cerner are more committed, commercially, to the healthcare IT market and have found it more difficult to walk away.

Conclusion: Standardization without Standards

This story started with a number of professionally driven initiatives, where policy-makers were excluded from decision-making and implementation, at least in the early stages. The period before 2002 offers an important lesson, which is that the successes followed professional and organizational contours, notably in the cases of GPs and pathologists. If technologies did not fit these contours — telemedicine is one example — then they failed time after time. Yet in spite of the evidence of practical successes and failures, a stream of criticism and critical official reports, and the absence of cost-effectiveness evidence, policy-makers have consistently pursued top–down, centralized, integrated solutions. Archetypal modernists, they believed that they could see the future, or at least believed that people working in large IT firms and management consultancies could do so. They foresaw a world where large-scale systems would guarantee two types of coordination. Health services would be coordinated through 'ruthless standardization' of professional behaviour. Coordination of routine data collection would facilitate collection of data required by the Department of Health, which could use it panoptically to monitor and evaluate NHS activity. In short, integration would be achieved through standardization, and lead to a reduction in the complexity of managing the NHS.

These beliefs led the Department to strike large, long-term, and tightly defined contracts with suppliers, and to employ large numbers of management consultants within Connecting for Health. The National Programme policies looked simple, but this was only because they omitted to address the complexities of the NHS. It was assumed that the contractors would deal with the complexities in the design and deployment of their new systems and would apply standards to the collection and storage of information. As we now know, this belief was misplaced. The contractors could not see into the future after all. Even now it is unclear whether the contractors ever believed that they could replace existing systems. They may have been believers, or felt forced to suspend disbelief, because the commercial risks of being excluded from the Programme were too high.

The real task facing the contractors was to overlay their new systems on the existing patchwork. Indeed they faced three challenges: securing the commitment of all key groups of health professionals and managers, integrating new and existing systems, and integrating the new systems with one another, requiring coordination between the contractors. The result has been the opposite of the original intention, with the National Programme adding a new set of coordination problems. There has been an increase in complexity, reflected in continuing difficulties with implementation. The National Programme contained the seeds of this increased complexity from the start, with its commitment to technological integration aimed at standardizing behaviour, rather than the Danish model of long-term, sustained development of agreed standards for electronic communications. A more modest policy of standard setting for local initiatives, rather than the ambitious attempt to impose standardization through integration at the centre, might have had more success in incentivizing professionals on the ground to change their behaviour in the collection and use of information.

There is some evidence that this point is now (belatedly) understood. For example, in his evidence to the Public Accounts Committee in 2008, the Chief Executive of the NHS stated that the National Programme was more complex than anyone (in his milieu) had realized (Nicholson 2008). In addition, Connecting for Health has been considering opening up the market for electronic health records and other services to all comers, thus breaking the monopolies created in the initial contracts. Policy-makers may now appreciate that they cannot see the future after all. Tightly drawn contracts cannot be used, and contracting parties will in future need to enter into long-term relationships with one another, and deal with the inevitable unexpected turns of events through negotiation.

The National Programme seems to be stuck in a sort of Never-Never Land. The belief within political elites in the potential of large-scale integrated systems seems unshakable. Shared electronic patient records even rated a mention in President Obama's (2009) inauguration address. While some policy-makers have come to realize that IT increases complexity in healthcare, recent history shows us that it will be difficult to resist the desire to control the future, and the pouring of more money into IT investments in the hope of doing so.

9

Post-Second World War British Railways

The Unintended Consequences of Insufficient Government Intervention

Timothy Leunig

Editors' Overview

In this chapter, Tim Leunig analyses investment in Britain's railway network over the years since the Second World War, during a period when the railways were run by a state-owned statutory corporation (referred to here as 'British Rail' for convenience, though it had three slightly different names between 1947 and 1995) for nearly fifty years until a form of heavily regulated and subsidized privatization replaced the earlier regime in the mid-1990s. Successive governments left railway policy to the managers who ran the system and saw railway modernization essentially in engineering terms that favoured technically complex and prestigious 'grands projets' over more incremental and technically feasible but mundane improvements. Leunig argues that one of the unintended consequences of this policy was that it paradoxically led to outcomes in railway investment that were neither economically rational nor politically beneficial to incumbent governments.

That outcome can hardly have been intended by the architects of post-Second World War railway nationalization, since it neither followed an economic logic of investment in projects that concentrated on those parts of the rail system which yielded the bulk of passenger fares nor the political logic (often observed in other nationalized industries in the 1960s and 1970s) of rewarding key electorally favoured areas at the expense of economic efficiency. That engineering view of modernity which came to prevail as the default position in British rail investment led to a concentration of investments in the longer-distance intercity lines rather than on the commuter lines around London that in many cases carried far larger volumes of traffic, and on which passenger speeds could have been greatly increased by technically feasible options such as a investment in lighter electric trains with multiple doors, more station platforms, more imaginative timetabling and use of 'slip' trains.

Introduction

There are many ways in which passenger transport can be improved: it can be made safer, faster, or more comfortable. Safety has improved steadily on Britain's railways over time, and is essentially taken for granted by passengers except when something goes wrong. In the post-war era Britain's railways have had their share of fatalities, but they have not been characterized by fatality rates out of keeping with international levels (Evans 2005: 3–9).

In contrast, comfort and speed are more obvious. There is considerable evidence that almost all travellers are concerned about speed. We see this in individual behaviour: people overwhelmingly take the fast train rather than the slow train, just as they choose to drive longer but faster routes. We can also see evidence of this preference for speed statistically: house prices close to good transport links are higher (Gibbons and Machin 2005: 148–69). Speed has frequently been an important part of rail advertisements.

Although, other things equal, customers prefer a more comfortable service, there is little evidence that comfort is valued highly. Few choose to travel first class, particularly when they are paying their own fare, irrespective of the distance travelled. Although getting a seat is important on long journeys, people seem prepared to stand for surprisingly long distances, and moves to squeeze in more seats, or to replace seats with standing room, appear to have no discernible effect on the number of people who take the train. This finding is not specific to train travel: coaches consistently offer relatively little legroom, even on routes characterized by high-income travellers, the vast majority of people travelling even very long distances by plane do so in economy class, and the most successful new transport company in recent years — Ryanair — places emphasis firmly on price, not comfort.

For these reasons this chapter is concerned with the performance of Britain's railways, as measured by the speed of travel. It will look at the post-1945 period, and assess not the overall gains in speed, but the distribution of those gains across different routes. In short, did British Rail invest in the right lines?

We first demonstrate that there was considerable heterogeneity in the extent to which speeds improved on different lines. We then go on to show that this cannot be explained by *ex ante* and unalterable technical factors. Nor is it in line with an equality-based social welfare function, or obvious commercial criteria. Having shown that there is no compelling reason for what we observe, we go on to show that different patterns of improvement were possible. We argue that decisions on where to invest were made by British Rail management, before indicating that Government, acting in accordance with political incentives, could have produced a railway system that better met the needs of those who travelled on it.

Methodology

Railway journey times between any two places can be found in past editions of railway timetables. Although not all trains run to time, there is no reason to think that the timetable is more or less accurate in one year versus another. For that reason changes in the timetable are likely to be an accurate reflection of improvements that passengers would have experienced.

Even today there are more than 2,500 stations in Britain, generating more than 6 million possible journeys. It is not possible to computerize that many journeys, and nor would it be sensible to do so. Many of those possible journeys are never undertaken: given that only ten people boarded a train at Buckenham in Norfolk in 2007, and only fifteen disembarked at Coombe Junction Halt, in Cornwall, it is most unlikely that anyone travelled from Buckenham to Coombe Junction Halt (Office of Rail Regulation 2006–7). The speed of trains between these two places is irrelevant to an understanding of how the railways performed.[1]

In addition to publically available data on the number of people using each station, the Association of Train Operating Companies kindly made available a list of the 1,500 most important journeys, as judged by ticketing data.[2] Urban journeys are generally less well-recorded, because passengers use 'Travelcards' and similar regional tickets that do not state their destination. For that reason the ATOC data overstate the importance of long-distance

---

[1] According to the thetrainline.com website, the fastest service on this route takes eighteen hours and involves seven changes and an overnight sleeper from London. The price is a very reasonable £28. Although faster trains might lead to this journey becoming coming more common, the chance that it would ever be important is very remote.

[2] The data cover all routes with more than 110,650 passenger journeys per year.

journeys, for which 'point-to-point' tickets that allow accurate record-keeping are more usual.

These data demonstrate the well-known importance of London: journeys that begin or end in the capital account for three-quarters of the top 1,500 journeys, a figure that is likely to be broadly representative of the railway as a whole. Table 9.1 shows that the most popular journeys are relatively short: the most important journey is not London to Manchester, but London to Croydon.

The top twenty routes are all commuter routes as opposed to intercity or regional routes. The busiest intercity route is London–Manchester, which is ranked 27 (1.9m). The only other intercity route in the top fifty is London–Birmingham, at 49 (1.4m), while the only non-London routes in the top fifty are Glasgow–Edinburgh at 21 (2.3m) and Glasgow to Paisley Gilmour Street at 44 (1.5m). More generally ninety-one of the top hundred routes are London commuter journeys.

Nevertheless, restricting ourselves to looking only at London commuter routes would not capture the full range of services offered by British Rail in the post-war era, and would not be a fair measure of performance. For that reason we computerized train times for three different types of journey: commuter routes into London, long-distance intercity routes into London,

Table 9.1. The busiest twenty rail journeys in Britain

Rank	Route	Total journeys
1	London to Croydon	6,312,433
2	London to Wimbledon	4,660,406
3	London to Brighton	4,080,586
4	London to Chelmsford	4,075,772
5	London to Reading	4,054,617
6	London to St Albans	4,028,130
7	London to Gatwick Airport	3,977,792
8	London to Clapham Junction	3,566,754
9	London to Surbiton	3,519,943
10	London to Woking	3,353,360
11	London to Richmond	3,134,516
12	London to Milton Keynes Central	2,885,066
13	London to Orpington	2,749,904
14	London to Stansted Airport	2,719,266
15	London to Cambridge	2,630,082
16	London to Sevenoaks	2,609,140
17	London to Guildford	2,584,549
18	London to Southend	2,517,048
19	London to Bromley South	2,461,965
20	London to Romford	2,376,434

Source: ATOC. A journey is a single journey in either direction. Journeys to Croydon and Reading cover all stations in the Croydon and Reading BR groups respectively; journeys to Southend are specifically to Southend Victoria.

and regional routes. The details of these forty-one journeys can be found in the appendix. For each of the seven years in our data set, we computerized every train on each route, before deleting trains overtaken en route: if the 1230 departure is overtaken by the 1240 departure, we would expect passengers to ignore the 1230, and so we ignore it as well. We average the speeds of the different trains, taking into account that trains at some times of the day are more important: for example, a fast train at 6 p.m. is of greater benefit than one at 6 a.m.[3] We convert the time taken to a speed by dividing the route mileage by the time taken. We use route mileage rather than straight-line distance, as although customers care only about the straight-line distance, it is not reasonable to expect train companies to have provided completely new infrastructure in the post-war era. Thus we judge rail companies by their performance in improving speeds on the tracks they inherited at the start of the period.

We also consider train frequency. A more frequent service is, in some sense, a faster service. A person who wishes to catch a train at 10 a.m. may well be indifferent between a slow train leaving at 10 o'clock, and a faster train leaving at 10.30. We follow UK Department of Transport conventions on this subject. In essence, a wait of up to ten minutes is considered to be equivalent to a journey that takes the same number of minutes longer. In contrast a wait of an hour is less bad than a train that takes an extra hour, since passengers can and do delay their journey to the station. If the train is not leaving for another hour, people can stay at home and get something done, or stay in the office and get something done. For that reason, a train leaving hourly but making the journey instantaneously would be considered a faster service than a train leaving every second, but taking an hour. The results do not generally change by including waiting time and we only quote results including waiting time when they alter the results.

Results

The expectation is that train speeds will have improved between 1951 and 2008. After all, this fifty-seven-year period saw significant technological change. The most obvious is the replacement of steam by diesel and electric trains, but there were many other technical improvements that we would expect to increase speeds. These include the ability to use lighter,

---

[3] The results are not at all sensitive to this assumption. More details of the methodology can be found in Leunig (2006).

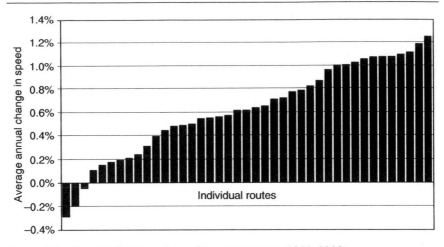

Figure 9.1. The distribution of speed improvements, 1951–2008

Sources: National Rail timetables, 1951 and 2008.

monocoque aluminium bodies in place of steel panels built on a separate chassis, improvements in signalling, as well as general improvements within any given type of technology. The potential benefit of incremental improvements should not be understated: both the 1950s Ford Anglia and today's Ford Focus are petrol-engined, steel monocoque cars, but even the lowest powered Focus will accelerate more than twice as quickly and has a much higher top speed. In addition to technological progress, we would expect willingness to pay to increase: people are richer and travel further than ever before. This combination of technological change and a willingness and ability to pay leads us to expect transport speeds to have increased over time.

Although most journeys have seen improvements in speeds over time, we find that contrary to expectations this is not true for three out of the forty-one routes studied here. Trains from London to Wimbledon, Surbiton, and Richmond all saw speeds fall.[4] Taken as a whole there was considerable heterogeneity in the results: the worst performance was a fall of over 0.2 per cent a year, while the greatest improvement was over 1.2 per cent a year. This means that the best performance was sufficient to halve journey times over the period, whereas the worst performance added 18 per cent to journey times. The typical journey time of trains in this sample fell by just over a quarter. The full range of results is given in Figure 9.1.

---

[4] This remains true if waiting times are included.

Explanations

There are a number of potentially valid explanations for the fairly dramatic variation in performance by route. The first is technical: some lines might be intrinsically poor, with tight curves and steep gradients. If that is the case, we would expect to find that being slow in 1951 would be a good predictor of few improvements after 1951. Second, it could be that the nationalized rail operator and its political masters were concerned to be fair to people across Britain, and therefore strove to ensure that everyone had access to an equally good rail network. In that case we would expect to find that speeds in 2008 were more homogeneous than in 1951, at least when the type of journey is taken into account. The third hypothesis is that British Rail responded to demand, and improved the speeds of the most intensively used lines. As we shall see, none of these hypotheses is upheld.

Instead we shall show that British Rail was an engineering-led organization with its own conception of what a railway should be. That engineering conception of modernization had little connection either to the business case for the railways or to social equity. In fact, we shall argue that one of the problems was that the government was unwilling to set out a clear rationale for the railways, and to hold the railway to that rationale. Indeed, we will show that if the government had set out to manipulate this public service for the purpose of winning over 'swing' voters, the outcome would have been more economically rational. An unintended consequence of leaving the modernization of British Rail to the managers who ran it, and who supposedly understood how to modernize it, is that Britain ended up with a less useful rail system than had politicians tried to modernize the system for narrow electoral advantage.

Intrinsic Quality of the Line

The intrinsic quality of the line is an important determinant of train speeds. Trains work best when the track is flat and straight. The low level of friction between a train wheel and a metal rail is the key to both smooth high-speed travel and energy efficiency, but reduces the ability of trains to climb steep hills effectively. For that reason gradients slow trains down significantly. Sharp curves are also inimical to rapid rail travel. Train carriages are relatively long, and even with articulated bogies they are not well-designed to go round sharp corners. Furthermore, the intrinsic quality of the track is relatively difficult to improve. It is, of course, possible to build new track,

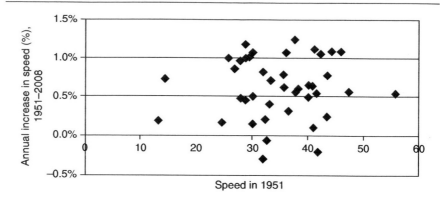

Figure 9.2. Were improvements determined by infrastructure fundamentals?
Sources: National rail timetables, 1951 and 2008.

but it is very expensive, especially if new civil engineering features, such as bridges or tunnels, are required. As a result, we are left to a large extent with the routes bequeathed to us by the Victorians. It is not realistic to expect, for example, that British Rail would have removed the very sharp curve on the Gillingham to London Victoria line, west of the River Medway, as this would have required building a new bridge. In addition, some routes have only two tracks: one 'up', and one 'down'. Such routes will almost always be slower than those which have two tracks running in each direction, since faster trains cannot overtake slower, stopping trains as easily. Again, the Gillingham to London Victoria route has only one line in each direction for most of its length, and the cost of acquiring the land for an extra two tracks would be huge, especially in urban areas. For these reasons, it is unlikely that trains from Gillingham will ever be as fast as trains from Reading, given that trains from Reading have two lines in each direction, and the route is relatively flat and straight. We can get some measure of the quality of the route by looking at the speeds at the start of the period. It is likely that routes that have intrinsic problems will have had relatively low speeds in 1951, constraining what could be achieved since that date.

As Figure 9.2 makes clear, there is no relationship between the speed at which trains travelled in 1951 and subsequent improvements in speeds.[5] It remains the case that absolute speeds at the end of the period will be constrained by the routes bequeathed to us by the Victorians, but there is

---

[5] This is confirmed by regression analysis: speed in 1951 is not a statistically significant predictor of changes in speed 1951 to 2008, with a t-statistic of 0.3, and a negative adjusted R^2.

no evidence that these constraints prevented significant improvements to journey speeds for any particular type of journey.

Equal Speeds for All

We can imagine that a state-owned rail company might wish to ensure that everyone has equal access to fast trains irrespective of where they live. If this were the case, we might expect train speeds to be more homogeneous at the end of the period than at the beginning. As Table 9.2 shows, we find the reverse: the coefficient of variation increased from 0.24 in 1951 to 0.32 in 2008.[6] Nor is this result caused by a handful of long-distance intercity routes becoming much more rapid, increasing the overall diversity of speeds across the country. We find the same result when we look separately at commuter and long-distance journeys, although the coefficient of variation for regional railways remains unaltered.

One aspect did become more equal: the number of services on each route. As Table 9.2 shows, there was considerable convergence in the number of trains per day on the routes studied. In essence, routes that previously had

Table 9.2. Was equality the goal?

	Coefficients of variation	
	1951	2008
Train speed		
All routes	0.24	0.32
Commuter	0.17	0.31
Long distance	0.05	0.09
Regional	0.31	0.31
Service frequency		
All routes	0.92	0.19
Commuter	0.76	0.4
Long distance	0.19	0.07
Regional	0.57	0.41
Total journey speed		
All routes	0.32	0.39
Commuter	0.21	0.34
Long distance	0.06	0.11
Regional	0.37	0.36

Source: Author's calculations from British Rail timetables.

[6] The coefficient of variation is defined as the standard deviation divided by the mean. It is more useful than the standard deviation in this context, because standard deviations cannot be compared if the means of the samples are different. In contrast coefficient of variation is designed to be comparable irrespective of differences in the underlying data.

very few trains gained additional trains. Nevertheless, increasing frequency on previously neglected lines was insufficient to outweigh the greater diversity of speeds of the trains themselves: total journey time heterogeneity increased over time. In short, there is no evidence that British Rail acted to ensure that people in Britain, wherever they lived, had access to trains of equal speeds.

Responding to Demand

A third possible hypothesis is that British Rail acted as a commercial firm, improving the service on lines that were heavily used. Although we do not have data on passenger flows for the earlier part of the post-war period, the increasing importance of both London in general, and of commuters into London in particular has been well known for many years. For that reason, we use present-day numbers of passengers per route as a proxy for the post-war period. Figure 9.3 shows the improvement in train speeds on individual routes compared with passenger numbers for that route.

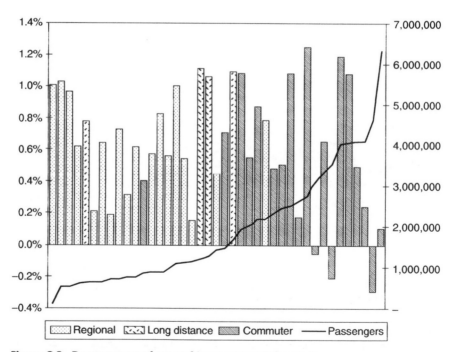

Figure 9.3. Passenger numbers and improvements by route
Sources: National rail timetables 1951 and 2008, route data from ATOC.

Figure 9.3 shows that overall there is no relationship between the number of people on a route, and increases in the speed on that route. In addition, there is no sense in which commuter routes, taken as a whole, were improved at a faster rate than regional routes or intercity routes, even though commuter routes generally have much higher levels of traffic. Indeed, taking a simple average of routes of each type, we find that commuter routes improved slightly less quickly than regional routes, and significantly less quickly than long-distance intercity routes. A weighted average makes the picture even starker, with commuter routes' underperformance more pronounced.

Third, when we look at performance within each of our three sectors, we find evidence of British Rail responding to demand only in the case of long-distance routes. Here, the least heavily used route, London to Bristol, has improved less rapidly than the other three routes. The picture is much less satisfactory in the other two sectors. The second most important commuter route as judged by passenger numbers, London to Wimbledon, saw the service slow down significantly between 1951 and 2008, and more generally three out of the top ten commuter routes saw speeds fall, with another one — the busiest journey in the UK — seeing only trivial improvements.[7] Again, when we look at regional routes we discover that the three least busy regional routes saw speed improvements dramatically better than either regional routes as a whole, or the network as a whole, despite their relative unimportance.

Could Suburban Services have been Made Faster?

Clearly, any claim that BR's engineering approach to modernization failed to produce an economically (or politically) rational outcome is contingent on it having been possible to run faster trains on commuter routes. This chapter is not the right place to look in detail at engineering solutions, but it is worth setting out some of the many things that could have been done. We divide the comments into three parts: infrastructure, rolling stock, and operation.

---

[7] London to Wimbledon, Surbiton, and Richmond became slower, while London to East Croydon improved only fractionally. The finding that these three routes are slower now than in 1951 is robust to including service frequency: the total time to make this journey including waiting time has increased in this period.

The biggest infrastructure improvement for suburban rail is replacing steam and diesel power with electricity. Electric trains are generally lighter, which allows faster acceleration and braking. This, rather than a high top speed, is critical for rapid commuter services, particularly on stopping lines. The privately owned Southern Railway electrified most inner suburban services in the pre-Second World War era, yet it took its nationalized successor a further fifty years to electrify all suburban trains from Kings Cross, while electrified lines from Paddington still extend only to Heathrow (Gourvish 2002: 92–3). Suburban electrification north of the Thames could have been started much earlier, and been more comprehensive.

Although it is generally hard to improve infrastructure in built-up areas, some improvements could have been made. For example, the speed of services to and from Waterloo is limited by the number of platforms available at Waterloo.[8] But we know that additional platforms could have been provided, because this was done for the Eurostar train service through the Channel Tunnel to France and Belgium in the early 1990s. That preparedness to invest in additional capacity at Waterloo for a big prestige project contrasts sharply with the unpreparedness to do likewise for suburban services. Indeed, today there is even an unwillingness to convert the already-built Eurostar platforms for suburban use several years after the Eurostar trains have been diverted to St Pancras International, leaving the Waterloo platforms unused and boarded up. What better symbol can there be of the way in which long-distance trains receive investment, but commuter trains continue to be neglected?

A major constraint on rail operations is trains needing to cross over other tracks. In Britain trains, like cars, usually run on the left. Thus a train turning right has to cross over the path of trains coming the other way, creating a timetabling constraint ('fewer train paths'). This means that short sections of elevated track, allowing trains turning right to go over, rather than across, the opposite track have considerable benefits in busy areas. Yet track configurations on busy sections of track such as at Woking and Reading require trains to cross over at the same level, reducing the number of trains that can travel in the opposite direction, creating timetabling constraints, and making it more likely that a delay will have knock-on effects.

Rolling stock is expensive to replace when existing stock is operating satisfactorily, but periodic replacement allows for upgrades at relatively low

---

[8] Today e.g. each Waterloo platform handles almost three times as many people as each Euston platform.

cost. Suburban trains need to accelerate and brake quickly, as well as allow rapid boarding. The solutions are lightweight aluminium bodies, powerful motors driving all axles, and at least three sets of doors per carriage. British Rail considered building such a train in the late 1970s for inner suburban services, but settled for steel trains, with only one carriage out of four powered, and with only two sets of doors per carriage.[9] The result of that decision is a slower service on almost all suburban routes, in London and elsewhere.

Potential gains can also come from more imaginative timetabling. On lines with only one track in each direction the current options are two-fold: either there are plentiful but slow stopping services, or the fast train cannot leave until the previous stopping service has got a considerable distance ahead, allowing a faster but infrequent service. Passing loops can give limited flexibility, but severe constraints remain. A more innovative approach would be to note that asymmetric passenger flows mean that trains to London ('up' trains) are more important in the morning than 'down' trains. Average journey times for passengers would fall if the slow 'up' train moved onto the 'down' track whenever the fast 'up' train needed to pass. This would both increase the speed of fast trains and allow more fast trains to be run. On safety grounds 'up' trains on the 'down' line probably preclude fast 'down' trains operating in the morning peak, and would require slow 'down' trains to stop as necessary, but the asymmetric passenger flows mean that the net speed gain for passengers would be considerable. The reverse would occur in the evening rush hour. This would require additional points, but the cost of such investment is trivial compared with the number of people travelling on many core commuter routes.

Second, 'slip trains' could offer large benefits for Britain's commuter railways. Rather than having one long train that runs all the way from terminal to terminal, the train would split along the route, either in a station, or in motion. This would allow dramatic increases in service frequency, since additional train paths for the busy section near the London terminal would not be required. Instead, for example, of running separate trains half hourly from Waterloo to each of Chessington South, Dorking, and Guildford via Epsom, there could be a train every ten minutes splitting at Motspur Park and Leatherhead and so serving all three destinations. Clearly there is a cost from having additional drivers, but this cost would be divided between large numbers of commuters at peak times. Splitting trains at off-peak times

---

[9] The so-called class 445/446 PEP train, compared with the subsequent second-generation EMU class 455 and AC equivalents.

would generate savings, since three separate trains every half hour could be replaced by one splitting train. This would reduce energy, rolling stock maintenance, and track access costs. There are many destinations that could gain a more frequent service if splitting trains were more common.

Splitting trains in motion would allow faster as well as more frequent services. Wimbledon, for example, has gradually lost its non-stop service. This could be preserved by 'slipping' the rear portion of a fast train just before Wimbledon. The slipped section would immediately move onto the slower suburban line, preserving the fast line's capacity. It would then call at Wimbledon and (say) stations to Kingston and Shepperton, reducing journey times to these places as well. This is even easier beyond the London boundary, where tracks are much emptier and slots on the slow line easier to obtain. It is not difficult to split trains, either in stations, or in motion. The Victorians slipped individual carriages from steam trains to serve individual stations. It is harder to join trains especially in motion. But even if British Rail had managed only to split and not to join, commuters would at least have enjoyed significantly faster and more frequent journeys home from work.

British Rail in the Post-Second World War Period

We have seen that improvements in train speeds were heterogeneous, and that that heterogeneity cannot be explained either by underlying technical factors, by a search for equality, or because the railway system was responding to demand. Further, we have seen that different patterns were possible. We therefore need to explain why the observed patterns occurred. There are in essence two possibilities: government and management. It could be that government, for whatever reason, directly or indirectly caused the patterns of service improvements that we observe. Or it could be that government stepped back, and so management was responsible for the decisions made. In order to understand the decisions made, we first look at the nature of relations between government and the railway, before looking at British Rail's approach to running the network, and the government's attempts to respond.

The Nature of the Relationship between Government and Railways

The post-war era saw a huge expansion of government control and influence over what are now referred to as 'public services' and the 'commanding heights' of the economy more generally. The 1945–51 Attlee government not only created the National Health Service, the concept of cradle to grave social security, and so on, but it also nationalized many firms and industries whose connection to 'public service' was limited — the creation of the National Coal Board, for example. Nationalization was enshrined as 'Clause 4' of the Labour Party's constitution, and was seen as a source of technical efficiency, as well as a way of ensuring equality and preventing workers being exploited (Tomlinson 1997: 68–123).

The standard form of state-owned industrial enterprise in Britain was the so-called 'Morrisonian Corporation', named after Herbert Morrison. As well as his general interest in state-owned enterprises, Morrison was Transport Secretary in Ramsey MacDonald's short-lived Labour government, leader of the London County Council in the late 1930s, author of the 1933 book *Socialisation and Transport* and the 1938 pamphlet *British Transport at Britain's Service*. As Transport Minister and LCC chair he was instrumental in creating the London Passenger Transport Board, which transferred many private-sector transport undertakings to the London County Council. Although Board members were appointed by the LCC, the company was run on commercial lines on a day-to-day basis. Morrison said that the Board combined 'public ownership, public accountability, and business management for public ends' (Tomlinson 2002: 96). This model drew widespread support from across the political spectrum, with the then-backbench Conservative MP Harold Macmillan endorsing it as 'forced on us not by theoreticians but by facts' (Macmillan 1933: 28).[10]

This approach was replicated in contemporary thinking about the railways. The 1931 Royal Commission on Transport advocated state ownership of the railways, as part of a unified transport system dedicated to minimizing social costs. Critically an addendum, submitted by members appointed to the Commission by the Labour government, argued in favour of a large, managerial firm, arguing that: 'The growth of the big business has only been made possible by the emergence of big men — great organisers who represent high standards of training and skill — of men with a genius for organisation — whose aim is proficiency in the administration of industry and in public utility enterprises' (1931: 229). Such managers, the authors argued, could be found in the railways: 'There is perhaps no better type in the country of the organiser trained by experience, without possessing necessarily any particular professional or technical qualifications, than is

---

[10] Macmillan (1933: 28).

represented by the general managers of the railways' (1931: 229). Arguing that, 'Their capacity would probably be more conspicuous if they were not restricted in their executive actions — in taking speedy decisions and in the control of their staffs — by the day dilatory methods of unwieldy boards of directors' (1931: 229), the addendum noted that 'it is imperative that the national transport trust should be free from Treasury control', and more generally that 'the trust would be free from all political influences and government interference in administrative matters' (1931: 231).

British Rail was designed from the outset to be run along these lines, that is, by management and not by government. In many ways this reliance on experts — 'big men' — was similar to the post-war consensus not only for nationalized industries but for public services as a whole. It was not until 1988, with the Great Education Reform Bill, that Britain adopted a standardized national curriculum and standardized national testing, and only with the creation of the National Institute of Clinical Excellence in 1999 did doctors lose their unfettered right to prescribe medicine as they felt appropriate.

The government gave the railways only very general guidance. The 1947 Transport Act created the British Transport Commission of which the railways were a constituent part. The Act stated that 'The Commission shall have power to carry goods and passenger by rail, road and inland waterway, within Great Britain' (Transport Act 1947 10 and 11 Geo 6, Ch 49, Part 1, Section 2). Later on, the Act specified that 'It shall be the general duty of the Commission so to exercise their powers under this Act as to provide, or secure or promote the provision of, an efficient, adequate, economical and properly integrated system of public inland transport and port facilities within Great Britain for passengers and goods', noting that 'for that purpose it shall be the duty of the Commission to take such steps as they consider necessary for extending and improving the transport and port facilities within Great Britain in such manner as to provide most efficiently and conveniently for the needs of the public, agriculture, commerce and industry'.[11] The fiscal requirement to ensure that 'the revenue of the Commission is not less than sufficient for making provision for the meeting of charges properly chargeable to revenue, taking one year with another' was imposed, but no other guidance given (Transport Act 1947 10 and 11 Geo 6, Ch. 49: 9). *The Economist* (7 December 1946) noted that such a set up would allow management to follow 'the settled habits of mind of railway men',

[11] Transport Act, 1947 10 & 11 Geo 6, Ch 49, Part 1, Section 3, p. 8. Available at http://www.railwaysarchive.co.uk/docSummary.php?docID=67.

but as Gourvish (1986: 27) notes, what mattered to the government was not whether the system would work, 'what mattered was political and administrative expediency'. The Commission delegated operational control to the Railway Executive, staffed by 'railway men' — only one of the six initial members came from outside the industry, while the remaining five averaged forty years' railway service, with a majority having worked for only one company (Gourvish 1986: 35–6).

The distinction between strategic and operational issues is never clear, and the Railway Executive — as *The Economist* predicted — ran the railways on traditional lines, and strove to gain power at the expense of the Commission. It did this by withholding information from the Commission, so that the Commission would not have the knowledge with which to challenge the Executive's decisions (Gourvish 1986: 47–9). Although the Executive was later abolished, this idea of maintaining control by restricting information was to be repeated at a number of different levels over the subsequent fifty years. Twenty years later, for example, H. R. Gomersall, British Rail's New Works Chief Officer, noted that the method by which BR received approval from government for investment projects 'also has the advantage that it is not necessary for us to give to the Ministry any information other than that strictly necessary' (Gourvish 1986: 522–3). On the other side of the relationship, we find the Treasury lamenting in 1955 the railways 'failure to provide detailed costings of individual projects' (Gourvish 1986: 271).

British Rail's Approach to Running the Railway

British Rail's determination to restrict information, combined with government's reticence to force it to divulge more information, meant that British Rail had considerable *de facto* freedom. It used that to pursue a traditional railway, characterized by extensive scope, and the pursuit of a particular definition of modernity. We will look at each in turn.

Nineteenth-century railways were extensive because, excepting urban journeys, railways were the best means of getting around. In contrast, post-war railways lost out to road-based traffic in both freight and passenger markets. Road haulage proved more effective except for bulk ('trainload') freight such as coal. Similarly rail lost much of its passenger traffic to road, with the two notable exceptions of London commuters and intercity business travel. Even among intercity business travel, rail was much more successful in retaining travel to and from London, where the flows of passengers remained sufficiently high to warrant a fairly frequent service.

Given these changes, the optimal scope for the passenger and freight railway system clearly fell over time. As Stewart Joy, former BR chief economist, stated in 1973, 'The real question [at the time of nationalization] was "how much rail service does the nation need?"', but such a question was never posed (Joy 1973: 23).

The original 1947 Transport Act permitted the Commission to reduce services as the country's needs changed. Having set out the general duty to provide an adequate system of transport, the Act explicitly noted, for example, that 'nothing in this subsection that shall be construed as (a) imposing on the Commission any obligation as to the provision or continued provision (either at all or to any particular extent) of any, or of any particular form of, goods transport service between any particular points' (Transport Act 1947 10 and 11 Geo 6, Ch 49: 9). Nevertheless, this was not an option that British Rail intended to follow. Instead British Rail consistently overstated the importance of freight, and defended uneconomic lines for which the fixed operating costs were divided between very few passengers (Pryke and Dodgson 1975: 5, 10; Gourvish 1986: 265, 279–80, 415). As Joy (1973: 92–3) stated: BR management believed that 'the Nation wanted to have a comprehensive railway service, regardless of its cost'.

Modernization was rightly part of the post-war railway's aims, but its choices reflected a particular approach to modernization. The Commission's 1955 *Modernisation and Re-equipment of British Railways* set out a plan to invest £1,240 million pounds to modernize Britain's railways (£24bn in 2009 terms if uprated by RPI, £64bn if uprated in line with earnings) (Officer 2009). Before we look at its recommendations, we need to understand the advantages and disadvantages of different forms of motive power. Steam trains can be replaced with diesel or electric trains. Electric trains are much more expensive initially, since lines have to be electrified, either using overhead wires, or 'third-rail' systems. Against that, electric trains are lighter, and therefore can accelerate considerably faster. For these reasons electric trains make most sense for dense commuter lines, where acceleration is more important than top speed, and where passenger numbers are high enough to make the cost of electrification relatively low per passenger.

This underlying rationale explains why the first lines to be electrified were commuter lines. Here there was a split between the pre-war companies: by the outbreak of the Second World War, the Southern Railway — covering routes south of London — had one of the largest electrified networks anywhere in the world. The Great Western Railway, London Midland and

Scotland, and London and North Eastern Railway, in contrast, made very little effort to electrify their suburban tracks, so that only 1 per cent of the rest of Britain's railways were electrified (Johnston 1949: 328).[12] This general disinterest in electrification does not suggest 'men with a genius for organisation — whose aim is proficiency in the administration' were common across Britain's railways.

That electrification led to higher speeds on suburban routes is confirmed by this research, and was acknowledged in the modernization report, which stated that 'There is a wide and accepted field for electrification in suburban services.' Despite this apparent acknowledgement, the plan included very little electrification of commuter routes into London: only 200 miles of tracks into North and East London, and an additional 250 miles of track in East Kent and East Sussex were listed for electrification. Out of the £1,240 million package, only £43 million was assigned to electrify track for London commuter services, with a further unspecified amount needed for new electric trains (British Transport Commission 1955: 6, 14, 15).[13]

Instead, the drive for modernity emphasized electrification for more glamorous long-distance services, even when there was no technical, economic, or business case for doing so. The modernization plan called for the electrification of long-distance mainline trains from King's Cross and Euston. The plan was to electrify what is now called the East Coast main line as far as Doncaster and Leeds 'and (possibly) York', with the West Coast main line electrified from Euston to Birmingham and Crewe, Liverpool, and Manchester. In addition the main line from Liverpool Street to Ipswich, Clacton, Harwich, and Felixstowe beyond the suburban section was to be electrified (British Transport Commission 1955:15). The estimated cost of electrifying the track for these schemes was £125 million, with a further £60 million needed to purchase electric locomotives for long-distance trains on these routes (British Transport Commission 1955: 15). Thus the modernization plan involved spending approximately three times as much on electrifying long-distance lines as on electrifying suburban lines in the London region.

It is quite striking that the modernization document contains no consideration of the relative merits of electric and diesel power for long-distance services. Indeed, when assessing the plan, the House of Commons Select

---

[12] Johnston (1949: 328).

[13] In total £285m was listed for the purchase of new multiple unit electric and diesel trains, the modernization of existing locomotive-drawn passenger carriages, and improvements to passenger stations and parcel depots. No breakdown is given for this £285m.

Committee wrote that 'Your Committee are astonished at the way in which the Commission has been able to set in motion great modernisation schemes, without the department comparing the economics of them with those of the possible alternative schemes; that in giving a banker's sanction to the expenditure on the London Midland electrification, for example, the ministry did not know what the alternative expenditure in using diesel locomotion would be' (Select Committee on Nationalised Industries 1960: p. iii). Richard Beeching — later to head British Rail — argued for diesel as part of the Government's Stedeford Advisory Group Inquiry into rail investment, but British Rail refused (Gourvish 1986: 303).

The failure to consider electric and diesel trains as alternatives reflects a lack of underlying rigour in the report. The 1955 modernization plan aimed to create 'an efficient and modernised railway system' (British Transport Commission 1955: 5), and argued that current problems were 'mainly' caused by insufficient investment. The Commission itself later admitted that 'There was no attempt made in the earlier estimates to make a precise calculation of the return' (Foster 1963: 95). The Stedeford Inquiry, although cautious in challenging the conclusions put forward, noted that British Rail developed plans on the basis of technical merit, not commercial considerations (Gourvish 1986: 301–3). This view was echoed by Christopher Foster, who noted that the total budget 'was arbitrary' (1963: 25).

Thirty years later the story was repeated on the East Coast main line. As mentioned, electrification had been the aim since the modernization plan, and was finally approved in July 1984 (Gourvish 1986: 263; 2002: 163). The initial construction costs meant that the financial case was never strong, as British Rail admitted in the late 1970s (Gourvish 2002: 92). Instead it claimed without evidence that electrification would create a 'halo effect', in which the total benefits to the network were greater than the sum of the individual benefits (Gourvish 2002: 92; Pryke and Dodgson 1975: 113–14). Not only was this false, but the benefits of electrification were miniscule even for the relatively limited number of people travelling on that line. An analysis of railway timetables shows, for example, that electric trains save only three minutes on the journey from London to York.[14] Given that the East Coast main line required high levels of initial investment in infrastructure, as well as the design and construction of locomotives specific to that

---

[14] Electric trains are used for ECML services unless the destination is Aberdeen or Inverness, in which case diesel trains are used for the entire journey. As a result both diesel and electric train times to York can be found in any given year's timetable. The difference is typically three minutes.

Table 9.3. Investment per passenger mile by sector

	Intercity £m	Commuter £m	Regional £m
BR non-freight investment	1,029	454	185
BR actual passenger miles, 1972	7,370	8,170	2,560
BR predicted passenger miles, 1981	9,500	9,900	3,200
Investment per actual passenger mile 1972	14.0p	5.6p	7.2p
Investment per predicted passenger mile 1981	10.8p	4.6p	5.8p

Sources: Pryke and Dodgson 1975: 28, 34, 38, 102. Investment includes everything except investment explicitly required for freight. Allocating Intercity systems, operation, and HQ expenditure in proportion to passenger and freight rolling stock investment for that sector lowers the passenger investment by 14%.

route, and given that the resulting time saving was under 1 minute per 60 miles travelled, it cannot be likely that electrification would pass cost-benefit analysis. It is overwhelmingly likely that the same investment would have saved far more passenger minutes had it been spent improving commuter services.

The neglect of commuter routes can also be seen in the aggregate numbers. Pryke and Dodgson (1975) produced figures for BR's investment by sector for the 1970s. As Table 9.3 shows, British Rail planned to invest 2.5 times as much per intercity passenger mile as per commuter passenger mile. Even taking into account BR's predictions of growth in intercity traffic, the investment level per head is still 2.3 times that of commuters.[15] Regional rail investment per head fell somewhere between these two figures.

It is worth reiterating that commuter routes' failure to receive high levels of investment was not caused by an absence of investment opportunities. As we argued earlier, there are many speed-improving commuter projects that could have been undertaken. More generally, this was the period in which BR simultaneously spent over £100m on an unsuccessful tilting 'Advanced Passenger Train' designed for the West Coast main line, while deciding not to replace 5,000 mark 1 'slam-door' commuter trains, whose life was instead extended to forty years (Gourvish 2002: 87, 223). British Railways' priorities were apparent to anyone.

The Government's Response

We noted earlier that government never set the railways a clear mandate against which their plans and performance could be judged. Instead, government's involvement occurred primarily when the railways losses were

[15] Pryke and Dodgson (1975: 34–5, 40) also judged BR's intercity forecast to be optimistic.

larger than expected. This involvement was rarely strategic. Thus, for example, Gourvish characterizes government's response to financial difficulties in the late 1950s as 'notably feeble' (Gourvish 1986: 293).

The exception, of course, was the government's choice of Dr Richard Beeching as the first head of the British Railways Board, which replaced the British Transport Commission in January 1963. Drawn from the private sector, and on a private-sector salary, Beeching was clearly expected to run the railways much more like a private company. He had been the most effective critic of the way the railways were run in the late 1950s, in his role as a member of Stedeford Advisory Group. His appointment, *de facto*, signalled a change in the government's approach to the railways in keeping with a more aggressive approach to nationalized industries as a whole, set out in the White Paper *The Financial and Economic Obligations of the Nationalised Industries* (Select Committee 1961). At one level Beeching was successful: many little-used loss-making routes were pruned in what was widely known as the 'Beeching Axe'. But there were two senses in which Beeching changed nothing. First, there was no sense that British Rail now made information on costs and revenues available to those outside the organization, so that others could accurately assess its investment decisions. Indeed, Beeching himself was reluctant to share information with ministers (Gourvish 1986: 442).

Second, and perhaps more importantly, the Beeching Axe was seen by both government and the industry as a one-off event, rather than as a potentially ongoing process under which services with only trivial levels of usage are abandoned, releasing investment for other areas.[16] As Joy (1973: 82) remarked, Beeching's 'concentration on the obvious loss-makers blinded the management to the increasingly unhealthy state of the whole railway'. Indeed, the government legitimized the preservation of all remaining routes by creating an ongoing subsidy for 'public service' routes (that is, services that the public chose not to use).[17] In 1970, despite evidence from its own economists to the contrary, the BR Board persuaded

---

[16] Beeching found that 50% of stations accounted for 2% of revenues. Today 50% of stations account for 3% of journeys, and probably a lower share of revenues, suggesting that today's situation matches that of the era immediately before Beeching remarkably well. Had Beeching's methodology and central intuition been accepted, it is almost certain that the 177 stations used today by fewer than ten people a day would have been closed long ago, fairly likely that the further 465 used by fewer than 100 people a day would have been closed, and probable that some of the additional 726 used by fewer than 500 people a day would no longer exist (Office of Rail Regulation 2006–7).

[17] There are now more stations operating than after the Beeching Axe, with e.g. 23 new stations opening in the early 1990s (Gourvish 2002: 303).

government that the current network would minimize subsidy. As Pryke and Dodgson (1975: 19) note: 'It seems incredible that the civil servants who examined the Board's studies should have accepted that a railway system from which a large number of unprofitable services had been excised would be not more profitable than one which contained them. Yet in their report they do not even express surprise that the Board should have come up with this startling result.' The commitment to preserving uneconomic branch lines reduced investment available for busier parts of the network.

An Unexpected Consequence

Many working in public services fear government intervention. They see the danger that government targets will force them to do things that are popular, but not actually in the best interests of those who use the service. For example, it is commonly claimed that centrally imposed service improvement targets can distort decision-making (see Hood 2006). Here however we have the reverse: by leaving the railways to railway management, Britain ended up with a railway that suited railway managers, and one in which investment was based on the pursuit of engineering excellence, whether or not that was feasible (the Advanced Passenger Train fiasco) or warranted (electrifying the East Coast main line).

Although the first-best policy would be managers who put the public interest first, in this case politicians using railway investment to 'buy votes' and 'reward supporters' would have given Britain a more sensible distribution of railway investment. It is clearly crude to say that politicians use investment to try to buy votes, or to reward their own supporters. Against that, we know that decisions about investment in marginal constituencies can and are made with at least an eye on the political effect, and that parties can and do reward groups that vote for them — few would contest that the Tories are more likely to cut the top rate of tax, and Labour to raise the minimum wage, for example.[18]

We know that some voters have particularly strong allegiances, while others — so-called swing voters — change the party for whom they vote. It is this group that politicians need to target. At a first approximation it was London commuters who were neglected by post-war rail management. The

[18] Macmillan's 1957 splitting of the fourth steel strip mill serves as an example of politicians making decisions on grounds other than efficiency (Owen 1999: 128).

question then is whether London commuters are likely to be swing voters. Clearly, we do not have voting or polling data specific to this group, but we can approximate it by looking at the rates of swing between elections for commuting and non-commuting areas. The Nuffield College British General Election Studies Series gives data for the Conservative–Labour swing in each election. Swing data work best when there are only two parties, and for that reason we look at the period 1945–1979. The UK swing between one change of government and the next averages 6.4 per cent, whereas the swing for the South-East is 7.1 per cent and the swing in outer London is 8.4 per cent.[19] Thus we find that outer London and South-East voters are less loyal and — potentially at least — more able to be 'bought' with public-service improvements that benefit them. A greater concentration of investment in commuter areas, rather than electrifying trains travelling through less-populated Lincolnshire, or north of Manchester, should have been electorally advantageous to either major party, as well as being a better use of government money when judged by more traditional public policy assessment criteria.

Similarly, given that the Conservatives have been the predominant party of power in post-war Britain, we would have seen better distribution of investment had the Tories viewed the act of governing as a way to reward their own supporters. Most of the trains from Waterloo journey to solidly Conservative constituencies, and yet it is journeys to these constituencies that have been most neglected in the post-war era, even though affluent areas such as these may well have been prepared to pay for a faster service. Rewarding supporters would have generated a more rational allocation of investment than leaving the railway to railway management.

Conclusion

Technological modernity in state-owned and influenced industries in post-war Britain all too often proved to be an obsession with the newest of the new, irrespective of whether it was appropriate or economic. We think, for example, of Concorde and advanced gas cooled reactors (Edgerton 1996). British Rail's emphasis on electric rather than diesel long-distance trains, and the tilting Advanced Passenger Train in particular, fit into this pattern.

[19] Nuffield Series, various dates.

But trains are not, in essence, high technology products, but rather products in which the greatest returns generally come from incremental improvements. As such they are like motor cars, or even civil aviation. In that view, British Rail should have concentrated on heavily used London commuter routes to a much greater extent. Trains to Waterloo, Victoria, and Liverpool Street are the backbone of the British Railway system. During the pre-Second World War period when railways depended on passenger fares, and not government subsidy, railway management responded to that fact: Liverpool Street had the densest service in Britain prior to the First World War, and extensive electrification arrived first on routes to Waterloo and Victoria between the wars (Austin 2008: 6–7).[20] But this focus was lost after the Second World War both under British Rail and under the essentially state-directed Strategic Rail Authority and Network Rail. As a result less well-used long-distance and regional routes received disproportionate levels of investment, while heavily used commuter lines were neglected. The paradox is that if governments had tried to appeal to swing voters, or if Conservative governments had set out to reward their supporters, then we would have ended up with a pattern of rail investment that would have been much more rational.

Acknowledgements

Over the years I have learned a lot about British railways from Mike Anson, Chris Austin, Dudley Baines, Nick Crafts, John Dodgson, Roy Edwards, Terry Gourvish, George Muir, Jim Steer, Alan Taylor, and Kevin Tennent, all of whom have been extremely generous with their time. I also thank seminar audiences in Oxford, London, and Cambridge for their comments. My team of research assistants deserve much praise for entering timetable data: Shimon Agur, Clarissa Brierley, Ahmad Bukhari, Alejandro Casteneda, Naomi Fish, Jordan Nebuya, Ellie Newman, Gabriel von Roda, Kevin Tennent, and particularly Christopher Fish, who not only entered data, but also ensured that each sheet was comparable, and extracted the data from them. Finally, I am grateful to the Association of Train Operating Companies for supplying me with data on the most frequent journeys on the network today. None of these people, or organizations, are responsible for the conclusions that I have drawn. Finally, of course, I am grateful to the ESRC PSP for funding this research.

[20] Austin (2008: 6–7).

Appendix 1: Routes Covered

Type of journey	*Route*
Commuter	London to Brighton
Commuter	London to Orpington
Commuter	London to Reading
Commuter	London to Richmond
Commuter	London to Shenfield
Commuter	London to Southend
Commuter	London to St Albans
Commuter	London to Surbiton
Commuter	London to Watford Junction
Commuter	London to Wimbledon
Commuter	London to Woking
Commuter	London to Bromley South
Commuter	London to Cambridge
Commuter	London to Chelmsford
Commuter	London to Colchester
Commuter	London to Ealing Broadway
Commuter	London to East Croydon
Commuter	London to Gillingham
Commuter	London to Milton Keynes Central
Long distance	London to Birmingham
Long distance	London to Bristol
Long distance	London to Leeds
Long distance	London to Manchester
Regional	Birmingham to Coventry
Regional	Glasgow to Stirling
Regional	Leeds to Bradford
Regional	Leeds to Huddersfield
Regional	Leeds to York
Regional	Manchester to Birmingham
Regional	Manchester to Bolton
Regional	Manchester to Leeds
Regional	Manchester to Sheffield
Regional	Reading to Wokingham
Regional	Birmingham to Selly Oak
Regional	Birmingham to Wolverhampton
Regional	Bristol Temple Meads to Bath Spa

Regional	Cambridge to Ely
Regional	Cardiff Central to Newport South Wales
Regional	Durham to Newcastle
Regional	Glasgow to Edinburgh
Regional	Glasgow to Paisley Gilmour St

IV

Modernization of the State

10

The Paradox of Performance-Related Pay Systems

Why Do we Keep Adopting Them in the Face of Evidence that they Fail to Motivate?

David Marsden

Editors' Overview

In this chapter David Marsden analyses the case of pay for performance in the British Civil Service since the 1980s, which progressively moved from a nineteenth-century classified pay system (in which pay rises came either from promotion to a higher grade or from incremental progression on a given grade) to one in which a fifth or more of pay was obtained by discretionary bonuses. Linking reward to work done or value added rather than paying public servants a fixed wage for grade irrespective of their individual performance can be considered to be a quintessentially 'modernizing' project insofar as it was at the core of Bentham's eighteenth-century principles of rational public management and was the central tenet of the 'Scientific Management' movement developed by Frederick Winslow Taylor from the 1890s, with the same basic ideas appearing in many different guises since then.

Marsden argues that pay for performance (PfP) in the British Civil Service produced consequences that were both positive and negative, that some of those consequences were anticipated but not intended by the 1982 Megaw committee that argued for the introduction of PfP as a major component of UK Civil Service pay, and that some of those consequences were neither anticipated nor intended. A negative effect that was anticipated (notably by the authors of a key report on Civil Service pay in the 1950s) but not intended by the 1980s architects was the failure of pay for performance schemes to motivate public servants, according to the results of attitude surveys, because of what was perceived as arbitrariness and unfairness in the implementation of PfP schemes. However, in addition to this well-known finding, Marsden argues that PfP had the effect of improving performance by mechanisms other than improved motivation, by making public servants work considerably harder for their pay and by the way PfP interacted with other processes, leading to stronger alignment between goal setting at the individual and organizational levels. Marsden argues that this effect of PfP seems to have been less anticipated (though it may possibly have been intended) by the 1982 Megaw committee, and that it can be seen to be generally positive. Further, PfP seems to have had the effect — neither intended by its original architects nor anticipated either by those architects or by their opponents — of increasing individual employee 'voice' in the determination of work objectives in the Civil Service — a consequence that can be considered positive or negative, depending on the viewpoint adopted.

Introduction: What was the 'Decision Problem'?

Pay accounts for a very large fraction of public expenditure, and therefore its potential use to motivate performance has long attracted interest. Its long-established predecessor, 'pay for grade', was widely thought to take people's motivation for granted. Although administratively simple, to most employees, it offered only a small number of seniority-based pay increments within grades coupled with limited opportunities for promotion. The Priestley Commission had observed in 1955 that arrangements for departing from the normal rate of pay and pay progression were 'directly related to special duties or specific qualifications' although increments could be withheld for 'serious inefficiency or disciplinary offences' (Priestley 1955: 21). Priestley had considered pay for performance, but rejected it on practical grounds: in most Civil Service jobs the merit of individual contributions could not easily be identified, and the inevitable involvement of the staff associations would lead to discussion of its application to individual cases (1955: 24). The Commission did envisage one exception: that of draughtsmen whose increased proficiency could be ascertained by additional qualifications (1955: 319). Nevertheless, the idea of pay for performance was taken up again by a series of government pay bodies before it became one of the key recommendations of Megaw in 1982. Thus, although recent debates have tended to associate the principle of linking pay to performance with the radicalism of Margaret Thatcher and John Major, concern about the underlying issues has a long history. Moreover, interest has not been confined to the UK. A major OECD study (Landel and Marsden, 2005) shows that many OECD countries have experimented with different methods of linking pay to performance in recent years, as well as with many different ways of implementing it. Therefore, if we are to understand the paradox behind the question in the subtitle, we need to look for longer-run concerns than the passing political ideologies of particular governments.

The Megaw inquiry provides a good starting point because it gave the final push to implementing performance-related pay systems on a wide scale in the British public services. It summarized the key arguments in their favour put forward in the evidence it received. In themselves, those arguments offered nothing particularly radical or new. It would be desirable to have a 'more effective means of rewarding good performance and penalising poor performance' than promotion and downgrading. It was inequitable to reward good and poor performance equally. The limited number of promotions in the Civil Service meant that promotion alone could not be expected to motivate the majority of staff. In the Civil Service in the 1980s, promotion into middle management jobs was very slow for most employees, and would have been exacerbated by 'de-layering' of middle management jobs in the following decade.[1] Finally, many private-sector organizations operated successful performance-pay systems (Megaw 1982: 326). The first three arguments identify the decision problem as dealing with a reward system that was failing to motivate public employees, and whose inequities could quite conceivably demotivate them. The final argument really takes up the practicalities that had led the Priestley Commission to reject linking pay to performance: if private firms, which are themselves often large bureaucracies, can operate such reward systems effectively, then surely the practical problems are soluble.

The emphasis in Megaw, as in much subsequent discussion of performance pay, has focused on individual employees, their incentives, and equity considerations. There is another important strand in the theoretical literature on performance, from organizational economics, namely the structure of principal–agent relations within large sections of the public sector. It is argued for example by Tirole (1994) that the multiple demands

---

[1] Using data from the National Audit Office, in the 1980s, the period leading up to the introduction of performance pay, in the UK civil service administrative group, a newly promoted Senior Executive Officer could expect to wait, on average, over 20 years to be promoted to Principal, the first grade with significant managerial responsibilities. Promotion rates into the SEO grade were even slower (NAO 1989).

on government organizations often lead to a lack of clarity in organizational goals. Multiple principals, or in the language of politics, multiple stakeholders, mean that large government departments responsible for administering a wide range of services often face contradictory goals, and that demands from one set of stakeholders often override those of others partway through the process of implementation. In the UK, clarifying the role of the principal was really the job of the Ibbs 'Next Steps' report of 1988, which proposed that central government should be restructured into a set of bodies each with a clearer and more limited set of goals (Efficiency Unit 1988).

On the whole, the Megaw and Ibbs reports did not devote much thought to the link between performance pay schemes for the great majority of public servants and the restructuring of organizational goals. Yet, it is evident that if organizational goals are unclear, it is going to be hard to be clear about the job-level objectives of individual employees. Indeed, it is notable that when the Megaw report discussed performance measurement at the individual level, it did so in terms of making use of the existing employee performance appraisal system and adapting it. This graded employee performance according to a number of department-wide criteria. It is as if employee performance could be embraced within the American public-service concept of 'neutral competents' (see Kaufman 1956: 1060; Heclo 1975: 81): within the government machine each employee has a predetermined job to be done, like a cog in an engine. This may be undertaken with varying degrees of competence and motivation, just as cog in an engine might encounter varying degrees of friction which affect overall efficiency. However, as with a car, direction is determined by the actions of the driver, and the parts of the engine continue to function in the same way. As we shall see later, one of the innovations with performance management has been to focus more on job-level objectives and how they can be adapted.

This chapter argues that the *intended consequence* or perhaps more correctly, *anticipated* consequence of performance-related pay — to improve the motivation of public servants — has proved elusive. When a policy is the result of decisions by many actors, it is not clear whose intentions were paramount. In contrast, the *unintended* or *unanticipated consequence* was that, although performance appears to have improved in several cases, it did so by other means than motivation. Notably, it came about because of the emergence of processes facilitating convergence between goal setting at the individual and organizational levels. These have supported a renegotiation of performance standards and priorities at the individual level. This did not come about overnight, but progressively as successive governments and generations of managers grappled with the need to make performance-related pay work in a public-service environment.

The Story

The story of performance pay in the UK Civil Service comprises two sub-plots: one at the individual level, and the other at the organizational level. At the individual level, the big step forward in the introduction of performance-related pay came just after the General Election of June 1987, which gave the government scope to proceed with its policy of focusing pay on 'merit, skill and geography'. The Civil Service unions' campaign of industrial action came to an end after the election, and within a short space of time, several major unions had reached pay agreements with the Treasury that accepted some elements of pay for performance. An agreement with the FDA (top civil servants' union) accepted a merit points system for senior managers, an agreement with the Institute of Professional Civil Servants in 1987 accepted performance pay for non-industrial civil servants, and an agreement with the Inland Revenue Staff Federation in 1988 saw the introduction of performance pay for middle-ranking Inland Revenue staff, responsible for assessing and collecting taxes (IDS 1987, 1988). The latter two agreements introduced the first large-scale performance pay schemes for British civil servants in the twentieth century. Among the stated aims of the Inland Revenue agreement were: 'to provide incentives for improving and maintaining efficiency in the Inland Revenue' and 'to reward sustained high performance' (Inland Revenue 1988: para. 5). In both agreements, the system consisted of provisions for accelerated annual pay increments and additional increments for those at their scale maximum, based on performance appraisals by employees' line managers.

Improvements in the Link with Appraisal

A notable feature of these early performance pay schemes was expressed in the words of an official of the then IRSF: they had been 'bolted onto' the existing employee performance appraisal system, in the manner originally envisaged by Megaw. The operation of one of these was studied in detail by the Centre for Economic Performance (CEP), that of the Inland Revenue. The 1991 study was funded by the Inland Revenue Staff Federation but with full cooperation from Inland Revenue management which distributed the questionnaire and allowed staff to complete the questionnaires during working time (Marsden and Richardson, 1994). CEP researchers went back to the Inland Revenue five years later, in 1996, with a similar survey of the revised and restructured performance pay scheme, introduced in 1993 (see Marsden and French 1998).

The initial experience of public service performance pay was summarized by a government report, surveying both academic research findings and inside management information, which observed a 'stark contrast between approval of the principle and disenchantment with the practice of performance pay' (Makinson 2000: 3).[2] The CEP found that in the Inland Revenue, the Employment Service, and two NHS hospital trusts it surveyed, around 60 per cent of employees expressed agreement with the principle of performance pay, while the figure among head teachers was about half of that. Much smaller percentages of employees (about one-fifth) thought that it had motivated them. Compared with that, high percentages of employees in each service covered thought that their scheme was divisive and unfair in the way it operated. Between roughly 50 and 85 per cent of employees in the organizations surveyed by the CEP thought that performance pay had caused jealousies in their workplace (Marsden and French 1998: 8). Even taking account of the more positive findings of Dowling and Richardson (1997) among NHS managers, the commonest failing appeared to lie in a widespread dissatisfaction with the operation of performance pay. It would be tempting to stop the story here, and conclude that the Priestley Commission had been vindicated: the practical difficulties of making performance pay work in a public-sector environment were too great and the numbers of employees who were motivated by it too small to justify all the management time and effort required to make it work.

However, this was not Makinson's conclusion in 2000, nor was it that of a Cabinet Office report produced about the same time (Bichard 1999). Both recommended further development and experimentation with different forms of performance pay, albeit along different paths. How could this be so? Two clues could be found in the CEP's study of the Inland Revenue's 1988 scheme. The first harks back to the inequities of the old system that were noted by Megaw. A majority of the respondents agreed with the principle of linking pay to performance, around two-thirds in the Civil Service departments, and rejected the idea that it was fundamentally unfair

---

[2] Among the surveys to which Makinson would have had access were those of local government employees by Heery (1998) and Thompson (1993), of Amersham International (Kessler and Purcell, 1993), and NHS managers (Dowling and Richardson 1997), and the Employment Service, NHS non-medical staff, and primary and secondary school head teachers (Marsden and French 1998).

(between a half and two-thirds). It might be the lesser of two evils when compared with the perceived inequity of pay systems that reward equally poor and good performance, and the limited scope for promotion for most employees. The second lay with the line managers, who carried out the performance appraisals, and whom the CEP researchers had asked about the impact of performance pay on their staff. A substantial minority of these managers (22 and 42 per cent respectively in the 1991 and 1996 Inland Revenue surveys) reported that the pay system had led their colleagues to work harder. Similar findings emerged from other parts of the public service covered by the CEP. Later CEP research on school teachers in England and Wales, for whom a form of performance pay was introduced in the autumn of 2000, similarly found that despite fairly widespread scepticism about its fairness and effectiveness among both classroom and head teachers (e.g. Wragg *et al.* 2001; Mahony *et al.* 2002 and 2003), other researchers found that there had been a positive effect on pupil outcomes (Atkinson *et al.* 2004; Marsden and Belfield 2007). The first of these studies, emphasizing incentives, found that pupils of teachers who were eligible for the new performance increases fared relatively better than their peers, and the second, emphasizing improved goal setting, found that schools in which performance management had been more effectively implemented appeared to perform better than their peers in terms of pupil performance. In other words, despite apparent divisiveness and a failure to motivate, there were signs that performance pay was somehow contributing to improved performance. To understand this paradox, we need to return to two important strands of the overall story. The first is that 'performance pay' has not been static, and has evolved as managers and other stakeholders have learnt from past problems and mistakes. The second is that performance measurement and goal setting at the organizational level itself has also evolved in ways that are important to the success of employee-level performance.

One reading of the development of public-service performance pay systems over the period since the late 1980s is that there has been a process of experimentation and learning leading to successive improvements. The first performance pay schemes had been 'bolted onto' the pre-existing performance appraisal systems that had not been designed for pay purposes. Indeed, their results had often been secret, and 'open reporting' only became widespread with the introduction of performance pay and the consequent need for greater transparency. The Inland Revenue appraisal scheme in force in 1988 assessed employees on about a dozen criteria common to the whole department, such as diligence, cooperativeness, and initiative, and for many jobs, only a few of these were relevant. Appraisals were treated like 'tests' in which employees were graded, to use the metaphor proposed by Folger and Cropanzano (1998). In contrast, a 'trial metaphor' could be more appropriate because of the need for procedural fairness. Some of the problems encountered by the first schemes arose because the linking of performance pay to these appraisal systems was felt to be inappropriate and unfair. Many of the criteria of good performance were irrelevant to many jobs, and even where they were relevant, too little recognition was given to the different abilities of employees. The standard criteria were likely always to reward the same employees, while others felt that no matter how hard they tried, their efforts would go unrecognized.

The 1993 revised system, 'Performance Management', sought to address a number of these weaknesses, particularly the perceived lack of fairness. The most important innovation of the new scheme was to adopt a 'contractual approach' based on agreements about work objectives for the coming period to be concluded between individual employees and their respective line managers. Their performance at the end of the year would be assessed against agreed objectives. This addressed two fundamental questions. The first was that employees had different abilities, and that it was just as important to motivate those in the middle as the high flyers. The second was that the 'test metaphor' was inappropriate for adapting employee performance to new needs, and the multiple criteria gave little guidance as to work priorities. By holding a discussion with each employee to agree objectives, managers could now use the appraisal process to address new work priorities. The new scheme also marked a definitive break with the practice of length of service increments for employees as they progressed up the pay scale for their grade. Pay progression within grades would be subject to performance. Nevertheless, the CEP surveys found considerable scepticism among employees as many thought that the contractual approach existed in name only, and that many line managers gave everyone the same quantitative goals (Marsden and French 1998: table 2.8).

The link between performance pay and goal setting figured even more strongly in the performance management schemes for head teachers in primary and secondary schools in England and Wales which took force progressively from 1995, and for classroom teachers from 2000. In this case, the goals might be specific to individual schools and so vary more with local conditions than in large bureaucratic agencies. The accepted wisdom on performance pay for school teachers had been that it was inappropriate for their kind of work, and it was summarized by Richardson (1999) in a paper commissioned by the largest teachers' union, the National Union of

Teachers, and by Dolton *et al.* (2003). Nevertheless, the government pressed ahead, capitalizing on the earlier experiences by emphasizing the place of performance pay within a wider system of performance management, which put as much emphasis on goal setting as on evaluation for pay. Performance management in schools comprised two components: systematic goal setting and appraisal for all teachers; and the extension of the old classroom teachers' pay scale with a new 'upper pay scale' on which pay increments would be performance-based, combined with a 'Threshold Assessment' required for progression onto the new scale. The new appraisal system placed a heavy emphasis on personal objectives and development needs, and how these fitted into the goals and priorities of the school as embodied in each school's School Development Plan. The CEP surveys found that over 90 per cent of teachers responding reported that they discussed and could influence their objectives, that they agreed them with the team leaders, and that they referred to items in their School Development Plan. Such an approach stands in marked contrast to the approach to performance appraisal of the first-generation performance pay schemes.

A general weakness of pay-for-performance systems, when they depend on judgemental assessments, and on agreeing objectives with line managers, is that they can easily revert to pay for grade and seniority in practice. Line managers depend on the cooperation of their subordinates to get their own jobs done, and this can create a bargaining relationship in which it is tempting to use appraisals and easy objectives as a means of buying cooperation. If line managers lack support systems from senior management, then they are often isolated, and it must be tempting to collude with their subordinates: to go through the motions and fill in the forms for goal setting and appraisal but not to worry about the reality. Megaw noted the rarity with which pay increments were withheld for poor performance, but did not address the organizational pressures which stand in the way of withholding increments.

Improvements in Organizational Measures

The second strand of the story relates to the organizational level, to clarification of organizational objectives, for which decentralization held the key, and to stronger pressures on line managers to take performance seriously, for which better indicators and benchmarking were important. As noted earlier, the 1988 Ibbs 'Next Steps' report began the movement to simplify the structure of the 'principal' within the public services, each agency or department having its own set of goals and performance criteria. Pay delegation enabled these bodies to begin to tackle the task of aligning their reward and employee management systems with their newly clarified objectives. The government's defeat of the Civil Service unions in 1987 represented the end of central bargaining over pay, and the beginning of a large-scale movement of decentralization of human resource management, thus enabling closer adaptation of reward systems to the performance demands of each unit. A study by one of the public service unions documents how from 1987 pay became increasingly 'delegated' to departments and government agencies, following the logic of the Next Steps process (PTC 1996). The same study showed how pay arrangements had become increasingly diverse between agencies. In effect, the new organizational structures, which were geared towards providing a narrower and more specific set of services, had begun to acquire greater autonomy over their human resource and industrial relations systems. Although at the time it was common to associate these moves in the contemporary public debate with privatization, in fact, some countries, such as Sweden, had long used an agency-based structure for the delivery of public services without any hint of privatization because of its greater role clarity.[3]

Another important factor in increased organizational efficiency in public services, which has also attracted a very bad press for its dysfunctions, is the use of performance targets for organizations (e.g. 'Target Practice', *Guardian*, 30 Apr. 2005). Yet good statistical performance measures are also at the heart of coordination within large multi-unit systems, such as the national office networks of public agencies, and the school system. Without benchmarks between units, higher management faces an almost insoluble problem of information asymmetry *vis-à-vis* lower levels of management. How can a minister or a senior manager judge whether a tax office or a hospital is being run efficiently unless its performance can be compared with that of similar units elsewhere? Just as with individual employees, performance measures can be used both to rank achievements, and as a diagnostic tool, enabling top management to ask the right questions of local management. It also enables it to identify good local practice that might be generalized, and weak local performance that might call for assistance.

The Inland Revenue provides an interesting example. When the author was looking for measures of organizational performance that might be compared with the appraisal scores awarded to individual employees across

---

[3] I am indebted to Niels Schager of the Swedish Agency for Government Employers for this observation.

units and over time, it became clear that fundamental changes had occurred. Just as the first employee performance measures had built on the pre-existing system for grading employee performance according to fixed criteria, so the first organizational measures had focused on accounting measures of performance. The Inland Revenue's annual reports in the late 1980s, when dealing with efficiency, focused on finance and on volumes of work handled within particular deadlines, such as the percentage of tax returns processed within x weeks. By the mid-1990s, as performance management became better embedded, the Inland Revenue was also reporting performance measures based on statistical sampling, such as the percentage of work done right first time. If employees are given incentives to 'clear post' under performance pay, then there is an obvious risk that quality will suffer. Yet without comparative measures of error rates it is hard for senior management to gauge whether the higher rates in one office are due to the complexities of the work or to poor management. Local managers might also be under pressure from their staff to turn a blind eye to errors in order to help them meet volume targets and qualify for performance pay.

Narrowing down the functions of the principal, and developing more reliable and more relevant measures of organizational performance, assists central management in sustaining the performance of local management. It also provides local management with the guidance and discipline needed to operate goal setting, appraisals, and performance pay at the local level. Arguably, it helps local managers to resist the organizational pressures towards indulgence mentioned earlier.

Schools represent an interesting further development of this convergence between individual and organizational performance management. This convergence occurs formally in the references in individual teachers' priorities to the objectives outlined in School Development Plans, but also through the pressures of the 'quasi-market' that exists within the school sector to attract pupils as a consequence of parental choice (Glennerster 2002). The 1988 Education Act devolved a number of powers from local authorities onto schools and their governors, thus giving them greater autonomy. At the same time, the government developed a national framework for schools in England and Wales, including establishment of a national curriculum, a system for assessing school and pupil performance, with publication of performance tables, and external evaluation by inspectors from the Ofsted (Office for Standards in Education). The changes were aimed at informing parental choice, and so providing quasi-market discipline on school managements. Thus local management had the autonomy to manage key resources in schools, but was subject to the pressure to attract pupils. Schools with good academic results, or which offered special facilities, could hope to attract more and better pupils as well as per capita funding. Although schools were not allowed to select, attracting a large number of applications from families that value their education increases their chances of receiving more able and more motivated pupils. Equally, schools which fail to attract such pupils will find themselves recruiting from a more limited pool of applicants. Thus, such a quasi-market puts pressure on the management teams in schools to ensure they attract motivated students and their families.

Against this background, the introduction of performance management for classroom teachers provided the missing part of the jigsaw for those schools that wanted to use it positively. Pupil progress had been pressed by the government as one of the key performance criteria for teachers. It is one of the few measurable outputs that are relatively independent of management indulgence, and it has a special significance for families making their choices about which schools their children should attend. At the outset, there was widespread concern that using pupil progress would mean a return to a discredited system of payment by test results that ran from 1863 to 1890 in England (NUT 1999: 4) or that the link would be applied in a formulaic way in many schools.[4] The arguments against, summarized by Richardson (1999) and Dolton et al. (2003), were that pupil progress depends on the contribution of many teachers, and that pupils' socio-economic background and their own motivation were factors that influence progress but over which teachers have little control. Linking pay to pupil performance would induce teachers to 'teach to the test'. In practice, the good practice case studies used as guidance by the Education Department highlighted a rather different approach, at least in theory, using data on pupil progress to diagnose problems, for example, with the attainments of particular categories of pupils, and to work out strategies for addressing them which could form part of a teacher's individual or team objectives for the coming year (DfEE 2000). The CEP's interviews with practitioners and its own panel survey work suggested that growing numbers of schools, albeit a minority in 2004 (the date of the last survey wave), were gradually taking advantage of the new system to integrate classroom performance

---

[4] For an account of the 19th-century system, see Nelson (1987). The operation of the scheme was the subject of several government reports. The detailed evidence of the Newcastle Commission of 1859 provides the background of why it was set up under the Revised Code of 1861. The Cross Report of 1887 provides the detail of why it was disbanded. I am grateful to Peter Dolton for this information.

management with school goals and priorities, and that those that did so were achieving relatively better pupil test results.

The Consequences

Summarizing the academic research and private management and union information then available, the 2000 Makinson review outlined a number of benefits that could accrue to organizations when performance pay schemes are operated well, and by implication, that the schemes then in force were failing to achieve. To paraphrase: well operated schemes clarify objectives and engage employees more directly with the goals of the organization; they motivate employees by linking an element of compensation to the achievement of targets rather than length of service; they reward achievement and identify areas of underperformance; and they foster a culture based on teamwork and fairness (Makinson 2000: 2).

How much a government should be concerned by such consequences is unclear. One argument put to the author in an academic seminar was that if the government was using closer monitoring through appraisal to pressurize employees to work harder, then many of the negative employee judgements reported could be expected. It is the price for making people work harder for the same general level of pay. Over time, those who were really discontented would leave, those who remained would grow accustomed to the more demanding work routines, and new recruits would not know any different. In our conversations with some managers, it was acknowledged that staff were working harder and efficiency had improved, but there was also concern about sustainability over the longer term.

The reason for concern became evident in the light of events that occurred in 1997, shortly after the CEP's survey at the then Employment Service, and which were reported in the *Guardian* and *Financial Times* newspapers. The scheme in operation there had shown many of the signs of disenchantment, perceived unfairness, and the feeling that performance objectives were just a numbers game. Job placements were one of the key performance indicators for both individual employees and for their offices. In contrast, many employees replied that what they liked about their work was helping unemployed people find new jobs, and thought they were contributing to a valuable public service (Marsden and French 1998). The way their performance pay scheme worked was that, if they took too long with their placement interviews, which might help job seekers find a more suitable job, they would risk missing their targets, and their pay would suffer. Thus when interview times were squeezed, many felt that they were being asked to go for volume rather than quality of placements. There is a grey area in recording placements that lead to a job: does one record sending someone along to any potential employer as a placement, or does one count only successful placements? And should one count placements that last only for a couple of hours, because the job seeker realized the job was not suitable? Under normal times, employees are held back from manipulating placement data by their view of the intrinsic value of their work. If this is eroded, then one might expect more opportunistic use of their discretion. A few weeks after the CEP's survey, a number of reports in the *Guardian* and *Financial Times* appeared to the effect that employees and offices in the agency were systematically over-reporting job placements, according to the journalist, by up to one-third. In some cases, according to the *Guardian*, offices were double-counting placements with major employers, not just within but also between offices. The issue was discussed in Parliament and an internal inquiry set up, but it was allowed to lapse after the General Election.[5]

The lesson would seem to be that if management pressure employees too much, then some of the safeguards against abuse that arise from the intrinsic value of the work, such as belief in providing a public service, can be undermined. In the Employment Service, it could be argued that these beliefs held potentially opportunistic behaviour in check — if you believe your job is to help people then there is no point in faking the numbers. If the intrinsic value is downgraded, and if employees are also penalized for giving attention to that rather than sustaining the desired case throughput, then the system can tip out of control, as appeared to happen on that occasion.

The Paradox: Unintended Consequences — Renegotiation of Performance

If intended consequences are anticipated, then one might take Megaw's statement of the argument as an indication of the likely results anticipated

---

[5] After the union drew their attention to the *Guardian* reports, the CEP researchers tried on several occasions to investigate this further after the election, but it seemed that neither management nor unions wanted to rake this up again for obvious reasons. See *Financial Times* (29 Mar. 1997), 'Labour Paves Way for Anti-Sleaze Fight', and *Guardian* (29 Mar. 1997) 'Jobcentres "Fiddled Figures to Boost Employment Statistics"', and (1 Apr. 1997) 'McDonald's Job Data "Abused"'.

at the time should performance pay be adopted. The committee's consultations had been widespread, and the case was a reasoned one. If there was a gamble over risk, it concerned whether managers would have the ability and resources to be able to find solutions to the problems that could be expected to emerge on the way. Priestley bet one way, and Megaw the other. As can be seen from the story so far, the risks were high: potential demotivation of individuals, and the possible loss of control of whole performance management systems. On the other side, there were the risks from doing nothing: with motivation undermined by limited advancement, by the inequities of good and bad performance being equally rewarded, and by lack of opportunity for management to underline new work priorities. So far, we have seen that management has been able to learn from experience and revise schemes, so there is some justification for Megaw's optimism. This much, one could argue, was anticipated at the beginning.

There were, however, consequences sketched out neither by Megaw nor by Makinson, but which I should like to argue could prove of fundamental importance. This concerns the issue of renegotiation of performance standards and priorities, and the creation of channels in which such renegotiation could become an ongoing process as organizational goals evolve. In some cases, this could provide the means for an integrative negotiation between management and individual public employees. This could be important also for the private sector, but arguably is more so in the public sector where employment protection is stronger, and it is harder to dismiss employees who lack motivation or who refuse to accept new work priorities.

A first clue is provided by the Inland Revenue's experience in which productivity and performance seemed to have increased with the development of performance pay even though staff found the system divisive and un-motivating. Part of the evidence for this was that, depending on the organization, between a quarter and a half of the line manager respondents to the CEP surveys thought that performance pay had caused employees to work harder (Marsden and French 1998: 8). Their view is significant because they carried out the performance appraisals on which performance pay was decided. Other organizational indicators were also reviewed in Marsden (2004), where the author sought to reconcile these two apparently contradictory observations. A key part of the underlying story was about renegotiating performance standards rather than motivation. The decisive change came with the introduction of annual agreements on work objectives and appraisal and the attribution of performance pay according to how well these agreements were achieved. As suggested earlier, the previous system generally assumed that the job determined the different dimensions of performance, and employees might work more or less well. Its successor introduced the idea that, within the job, employees might have different and variable priorities, and that these could be adjusted by the goal-setting process. Clearly, the findings of the second CEP survey of the Inland Revenue show that many employees thought their line managers still functioned according to the old model, applying the same targets to everyone, and that these were quantitative. But not all employees reported things being this way, and substantial numbers experienced the new system of agreeing work priorities and goals in a positive way, and they tended to achieve better performance levels as measured by their appraisal scores.

In many respects, the CEP study of classroom teachers provides a better illustration of this process, in part because of the design of the research, and in part because schools offer multiple units in which management actions as well as employee responses can be studied in conjunction. In schools too, the initial emphasis had been upon rewards and motivation. When introducing the new performance pay package, the Education Secretary spoke of the need to motivate: 'we can only realise the full potential of our schools if we recruit and motivate teachers and other staff with the ambition, incentives, training and support' (DfEE 1999: 5). In the first year of operation, 2000, the reaction to the new performance management system and the threshold assessment in the great majority of schools was to fill in the government's forms and take the money. This may have been partly due to conservatism, but partly also because many schools needed the pay increase simply to retain staff. Without adequate numbers of teachers, the finer points of performance management seemed irrelevant in many schools. However, interviews with the organization responsible for implementing the threshold indicated that some schools were using the new system not just to 'firefight' but as an opportunity to reform the way they were managed.[6] In particular, some head teachers saw it as a way to start to refocus the classroom activities of their teachers on the collective goals of the school. This line of enquiry was followed up by the CEP survey, which found that growing numbers of schools were beginning to use it as a means of aligning teachers' classroom activities better with the school's own objectives. By the fourth year of operation, the authors estimated that around 20–25 per cent of the schools in their sample had moved to this 'reformer' strategy. Moreover, the schools that did this tended to outperform their peers in terms of the test results of their students (Marsden and Belfield 2007).

---

[6] Cambridge Educational Associates.

Industrial relations theorists have developed an elaborate theory of problem-solving, or 'win-win', bargaining at the collective level. Thus Walton and McKersie (1965) contrast this form of 'integrative' bargaining with the more familiar form of 'distributive' bargaining that occurs in pay negotiations. The same intuition can be applied at the level of individual employees within performance management as a way of analysing how performance management and performance pay can be used to reorder work priorities. The reason this has to be at the individual level is that job performance is delivered by individual employees, and although this may be influenced by the culture of the workplace, in many jobs information asymmetries mean that managers depend heavily upon the agreement of individual employees to work in a particular way. As an example, one might consider the problem in schools at the time of the 1999 Green Paper. Many teachers have a strong commitment to their professional ethic, and believe in the importance of educating the whole person. Speaking of 'teaching to test' is the common way of denigrating what is felt to be excessive emphasis on exam results. Yet, with the quasi-market, schools are under pressure to give more attention to pupil attainments in national tests and in exams, as they reflect a parental concern about their children's life chances. As mentioned earlier, head teachers could try to impose a greater emphasis on teaching aspects of their subjects that lead to exam success as opposed, say, to developing a deeper understanding of the issues. However, the monitoring costs would be high unless teachers focused on exam success voluntarily. Head teachers might ease the dilemma for their colleagues in the classroom by using other resources to free up more of teachers' time for both kinds of teaching, for example by reducing administration. However, there might be no guarantee that this would bring the school much closer to its targets for exam performance. Teachers might use most of the extra time for the more general aspects of their subjects. On the other hand, if the extra resources are made available as part of a problem-solving negotiation, with agreement on resources provided and a commitment to certain outcomes, then one can see a greater likelihood of a mutually beneficial outcome, for the teacher's professional satisfaction and the school's performance needs. What the goal-setting and appraisal discussions bring to the process is a framework within which such discussion can take place, and the outcomes monitored. Performance pay enters less as a source of motivation than as one of the resources management can bring to the negotiation.[7]

---

[7] This example and another example based on the CEP work on performance management in the NHS are developed in greater detail and more formally in Marsden (2007).

The unintended consequence of the long road travelled by performance-related pay and performance management in the public services has been the emergence of a new channel for employee voice, this time at the individual rather than the collective level. Voice mechanisms have been explored extensively in collective bargaining and in commercial relations,[8] but they have received little attention in individual employee–management relations. These have commonly been conceived as relations of subordination, and this type of thinking is prevalent in the idea that managers need to motivate their staff to perform and to define their work objectives. The emphasis on subordination obscures an equally important aspect of employment relations, namely, that the employment relationship is also a contractual form enabling agreement on the supply of labour services in exchange for a wage or a salary. Free labour markets and a high degree of skill and professional competence such as one finds among many public-sector occupations results in a considerable degree of individual-level bargaining power which is reflected in the discretion such employees can exercise in their work. When such employees accept a job offer, there is an agreement on mutually acceptable patterns of working. If the relationship is a long-term one, it is unlikely that the employer will find that these remain beneficial forever, and so it will need an opportunity to adjust them to new organizational demands. This gives rise to a need for renegotiation of the package of benefits to both parties. In the example from schools, the renegotiation has focused on adapting teachers' professional goals in the classroom to those of their schools. In the Inland Revenue, an important organizational goal was to try to adopt a more 'customer-' or 'citizen-oriented' approach towards taxpayers, which meant greater sensitivity to individual cases. Both involved changes in employees' work priorities. The CEP surveys caution against assuming this process has become generalized, and that former ways of managing, or not managing, performance have disappeared, but they do show the logic behind it which could lead to wider diffusion. Imposition and compulsory retraining can achieve a certain amount, but on their own, without agreement, it is an uphill struggle. Without employee agreement, there must remain doubts about sustainability, and loss of control like that at the Employment Service remains a constant threat.[9]

---

[8] For a recent example in employment relations see Willman *et al.* (2006).
[9] I should like to thank the participants in the Paradoxes of Modernization seminar series for their comments and questions, and especially the editors of this volume.

11

What if Public Management Reform Actually Works?

The Paradoxical Success of Performance Management in English Local Government

George Boyne, Oliver James, Peter John, Nicolai Petrovsky

Editors' Overview

In this chapter, the authors examine the Comprehensive Performance Assessment (CPA) regime in English local government, a scheme introduced in the early 2000s to improve performance across local authorities. The CPA represents the epitome of modernizing public management reform along New Public Management lines. A paradox lies in the fact that even though the CPA was a classical performance management system, overall it was a success, whereas most other performance measurement systems have failed or have been replaced quickly by systems of performance review. Although CPA was eventually replaced, it seems that its termination had been intended and anticipated by its original architects.

The scheme worked by improving the information environment for stakeholders, incentivizing poor performers to improve, and make a substantive difference to local authority performance overall. This result is surprising, particularly given some contradictory elements of the incentivization under CPA, such as a context where deprivation beyond local authority control influences public service outcomes and an asymmetric electoral response to performance — electoral punishment for low performance, but no corresponding reward for high performance. Yet the system actually worked, in spite of a volume of commentary and research on public management reform that says otherwise.

Introduction

English local government in the 2000s arguably saw the most highly developed system of published comparative performance evaluation for public bodies ever undertaken. The Comprehensive Performance Assessment (CPA) regime was the apotheosis of a modernist approach to performance accountability. It entailed the assessment of multiple services and capacities, which were aggregated to form scores for each local government unit. Most other innovations creating systems of performance reporting have been partial in scope, shallow in depth, or temporary, making it hard to examine how organizations respond to performance-led incentives. Many performance management regimes have been quickly reversed or substantially altered, for example because of information overload or perverse incentives; or they have been caught up in major reorganizations. Management reform in the UK National Health Service is a good example: from the early 1990s centralization was replaced by markets and then in turn by centralization; it then reverted back to markets once again in the 2000s. But the case of local government in England was different. The UK central government hit on a system of performance measurement for English local government that produced consistent performance information over time, from 2002 to 2009, a reasonably long period, or at least long by public management reform standards.

The CPA gave clear signals to local authorities about how to behave, with comprehensible comparisons between them. Consequently, it is possible to see what this rationalist conception of organizational behaviour did to the decisions of public managers and local politicians as they adapted to the scheme and to find out what followed when citizens got to understand it too. For here was a system whereby central government set the rules of the game, the organizations were free to choose how to manage (within limits) and citizens and other stakeholders made judgements on the performance of public services thereby influencing performance. The chapter shows that in many respects the system worked, giving incentives to poor performers to improve their performance by better enabling stakeholders to judge them.

To the casual reader or the practitioner in central and local government the success of a management reform might seem unremarkable. But when put against the large international academic literature that suggests that in general performance management systems do not work, CPA is paradoxical. A paradox is a joint occurrence of two statements that are both true but cannot be jointly true. Whilst the literature asserts that performance management systems do not work[1] the Comprehensive Performance Assessment did work. Our argument goes beyond the established argument that performance management systems run down over time, and lose their capacity to discriminate between successful and failing organizations (Meyer and Gupta 1994). Rather, we argue that the CPA made a substantive difference to the performance of local authorities, especially to those at the bottom end of the league table.

The chapter starts off by reviewing the literature on performance measurement in the public sector, examining the reasons why most assessments are that such systems do not work well. It then outlines the CPA scheme for English local government, revealing some key features of how it worked in practice, mainly by setting a national agenda for local authorities that constrained both local politicians and managers. It worked at one level in giving information to citizens, encouraging them to vote for administrations to 'up their game' in the face of poor ratings.[2] At another level it created professional incentives for senior managers working in those organizations to perform well, or risk losing their reputations and jobs. The next section discusses the incentive effects of the system, especially the issue of allocating managerial and political responsibility for performance in a context where deprivation influences public-service outcomes and in a context where CPA was associated with an asymmetric electoral response to performance — with punishment for low performance but no corresponding reward for high performance. This section draws both on quantitative evidence about the general pattern of relationships and qualitative case-study evidence from particular local authorities. The chapter concludes with some reflections on the motivations of senior managers in the English system of local government and a discussion of lessons that can be drawn from the success of the system.

---

[1] Boyne's (forthcoming) systematic review of the literature on performance management systems shows the widespread belief among the majority of public management scholars that these systems do not work. Boyne (forthcoming) concludes that the mostly conceptual criticisms of performance management systems should give way to empirical evaluations to see whether the widely held negative beliefs about these systems are warranted.

[2] Initially, the link to citizens was to be even more direct: the first plan for the CPA envisaged all households to receive a postcard with the CPA score of their local authority. For better or worse, the postcard idea was abandoned when the scheme was finalized.

Performance Management in Theory and Practice

Since the 1980s governments at all levels — local, subnational, and national — have attempted to implement performance management regimes. This is not to say that performance measurement did not exist before this time. It dates back at least to the scientific management revolution of the 1920s (Taylor 1967), then operations research (Churchman *et al.* 1957), management by objectives, zero-based budgeting and a whole series of schemes in the 1960s and 1970s (Draper and Pitsvada 1981; Rose 1977; Schick 1973). But it is only in the recent period that regimes were introduced based on the measurement of performance and targets. Mostly occurring in the United States and the United Kingdom, these systems gradually spread across the world as part of what was called new public management (Pollitt and Bouckaert 2004). Both the media and academic commentary have been rather critical of some of these schemes, and, as noted earlier, the apparent failure of several of them has led to frequent policy reversals. Hood (1998) argues that reforms of public management are often rhetorical, based on the excesses of management consultants and their supporters operating from one corner of the cultural map.

There are several sets of criticisms of performance management. The first is that performance is hard to measure or at least hard to quantify though grading and ranking schemes. This means that activities that bring performance rewards may distract the organization from realizing a variety of aims and concentrate only on those that are measured. The second is that there is an art to the measurement of such schemes, which means that organizations can game the results by behaving in such a manner so as to achieve the desired performance score rather than actually improving services. An often-mentioned example is the makeshift creation of fake hospital rooms on corridors by means of curtains in British hospitals in order to fulfil a national target (Hood 2006: 517). The third is that the act of meeting performance targets may result in an organization failing to protect important values, such as the public-service ethos, which may sustain organizations in the long run. The fourth is that performance management becomes a political tool for government seeking to be seen to be improving services, which means there is added pressure from the centre to force organizations to improve and meet the targets which may accentuate distorted goals. This typically leads to too high expectations, and often ends up in the target being abandoned. Finally, performance management suffers from regulatory capture: the people doing the regulating are likely to be composed of expert members of a regulated group which may be adept in lobbying. This means that performance management may be a game played from the topdown with the regulator pretending to be policing the regulated parties. It should also be added that performance management regimes are often (but not always) resisted by the groups who are being regulated, typically organizations in the public sector, who are much more concerned with administration than other publics, like consumers, and have effective professional representations to put forward their points of view. It is not surprising, therefore, that performance management regimes suffer from a bad reputation, are commonly expected to fail, and terminate early. In this context, it would be expected that a regime to calibrate local authority performance to a simplifying scale would suffer from all the familiar problems of distortion, over-ambition, and opposition, and that it would therefore fail to produce any tangible improvements in public services.

The Comprehensive Performance Assessment System

England has a unitary system of government subject to parliamentary control and where the central government executive exercises a strong degree of legal and financial control over local government (Stoker 2004; Wilson and Game 2006). It provides 74 per cent of local finance through central grants (CLG 2008). Local government consists of multi-functional organizations administering an array of services from education to the environment to public safety. Elected local politicians in 34 counties, 47 non-metropolitan unitary councils, and 69 metropolitan authorities, as well as the Greater London Authority and 238 districts, exercise limited discretion in implementing statutes subject to strict budgetary and legal control from parliament. Nonetheless, local authorities are political bodies that exercise a higher degree of discretion over the public policies they administer, more than most non-elected entities due to their control of bureaucratic organizations and the delivery of services.

Since the 1980s central government in the UK has created numerous performance indicators for English local government, much more so than for central government departments or other public organizations (Hood *et al.* 1999). Such concerns go back to the Conservative governments of the 1980s that sought to introduce value for money and service efficiency. They mandated an array of performance indicators, such as those measuring the speed of planning applications and other routine local authority activities.

In time these grew in sophistication and number, culminating in the plethora of measures that underpinned the 1997–2001 Labour government's Best Value regime introduced in 1999 (Boyne 2002).

In a rare moment of clarity, central policy-makers realized that the system was unmanageable due to a lack of easily understood and comparable performance information. In response, the government decided in 2001 to create the Comprehensive Performance Assessment (CPA), which applied to all the above authorities. From the outset, the government and the Audit Commission expected it to serve for a limited time (e.g. see Audit Commission 2002: 19).[3] Already in its 2002 publication *A Picture of Performance*, the Commission foresaw that the CPA would sooner or later turn into or be replaced by another system covering all relevant public organizations in a local area, not just councils: 'Over time, the Commission intends to give more weight to community leadership — to how institutions collectively, not just councils, contribute to desirable outcomes for localities.' Also it suggested that 'CPA should be viewed as a work in progress rather than as a final statement of the best way to measure council performance' (Audit Commission 2002: 19).

The CPA was a system of inspection and measurement that categorized performance into five categories: poor, weak, fair, good, and excellent, superseded by the star system as part of the *Harder Test* in 2005/6 (Audit Commission 2005). To generate scores, six-member inspection teams analysed performance along several dimensions including organizational activity, resource use, and service provision. The final score was a judgement equally divided between corporate capacity and local service performance.

At the time of introducing the CPA scheme, the White Paper *Strong Local Leadership — Quality Public Services* conveyed the idea that that such a measure reflected central government's perception of local government's complacency and the need for somebody or something to motivate it. The categories of 'high performing', 'striving', 'coasting', and 'poor performing'

---

[3] Additionally, Paul Kirby, Director of Inspection of the Audit Commission, testified before the Parliamentary Select Committee on Transport, Local Government and the Regions in mid-2002: 'Lastly, in terms of CPA I think we are seeing it as a one-off exercise. I would not want anybody to think that the book is closed on how it will be handled in the future. This is particularly an exercise which is bringing together existing information, existing approaches with the purpose of reforming the regulation rather than continuing it' (Select Committee on Transport, Local Government and the Regions, Minutes of Evidence, 11 July 2002, question 464). And Lord Rooker stated that 'CPA results are not the end of the process; they are the starting point for improvement planning that will demonstrate the Government's public sector reform agenda in action' and that 'There will be an immediate focus on the poor and weak councils, informed by the corporate assessment element of CPA' (House of Lords, Hansard, 11 Dec. 2002, cc. WA35–WA36).

summed up this view, particularly the penultimate term. After lobbying from local government, these terms were converted into the more neutral ones of 'excellent' to 'poor'.

From the outset CPA was very much driven by the Audit Commission. The government delegated both the design and the implementation of CPA to the Commission, within the broad guidelines set out in the White Paper (Dr Whitehead's testimony during parliamentary questions, Hansard, 5 Mar. 2002, c. 168W; Lord Filkins's testimony, House of Lords, Hansard, 6 Mar. 2002, c. 300).

During the consultation the Audit Commission carried out with local government, there was a lot of support for the new scheme. In its publication, *Change Here* (2001), the Commission drew on the leading thinking at the time about how to improve organizations: having an effective leadership team, creating ownership for change, sustaining focus on the key priorities, focusing on service users, managing change, using external help, and building the capacity for continuous improvement — all of which fed into the CPA criteria and the framework of the scheme (Audit Commission 2002). Many local authority chief executives agreed that something needed to be done about persistently poor-performing local councils. This consensus meant there was never much opposition to this kind of performance measurement. Local authority representation on the Audit Commission itself and the peer-review element of inspections that formed the basis of the scores would ensure that local authorities as a whole would not be damaged by the scheme (Bertelli and John 2010).

The Rational Basis of the CPA System: Incentives for Politicians and Senior Officials

Local authorities took the CPA scores seriously. CPA ratings at the extreme ends of the scale — either poor or excellent — were highlighted in the media and low ratings were a source of local embarrassment (Game 2006: 468; James and John 2007). As examples of the latter, newspaper headlines included 'City Ranks among the Worst' (*Hull Daily Mail*, 12 Dec. 2002); 'Shock at Poor Rating' (*This is Local London*, 17 Dec. 2002 — headline refers to Lambeth Council); and 'Poor Services Keep Brum in Drop Zone' (*Birmingham Post*, 16 Dec. 2004). Concern from lagging ratings was reinforced by central government interventions designed to reform management in the poorly performing authority. There were a variety of interventions that central government could and did carry out to change local service delivery. Even though some local authority officers and members welcomed the assistance they got from these special measures, which might have helped them to solve deep-rooted organizational problems, we can be safe in concluding that local authorities wanted to avoid a low score and the negative publicity and hassle this entailed.

Key benefits to local authorities from a good CPA score were public recognition for quality service and regulation, and possibly also a belief in favourable treatment by central government and access to more funding streams (Haubrich and McLean 2006). In fact, those benefits were less tangible that they might appear. The freedoms and flexibilities promised to the good performers never appeared. Nor did financial benefits transpire either. It seems the incentives worked more diffusely. Officers and members believed the CPA would be important in competing for rewards from central government. The local government world is tight-knit: officers in particular know about what is happening in neighbouring authorities and in their professional groups. Here the grading scheme attracted attention in this competitive world in a similar way that the Research Assessment Exercise (RAE)/Research Excellence Framework (REF) attracted attention from academics and university administrators far in excess of what would be expected from the amount of research money that the Higher Education Funding Councils distribute to universities on the basis of the scores. Like the RAE/REF and academia, CPA is part of the gossip-world of interested professionals, where both good and bad performance gradings affect the reputations of organizations and the careers of those working in them. We provide some examples of these views and motivations below.

In spite of the weak financial benefits and policy freedoms, there appears to have been an incentive for local authorities to improve performance and to worry about poor results. It seems that the central state succeeded in devising a low-cost incentive for slack public organizations to deliver services efficiently and effectively without a need for additional centralization and heavy steering. The bureaucratic actors feared the consequences of a bad score; they felt pride in a good score; and they competed with each other to obtain excellent ones.

We do know these scores improved over the period of the CPA, with the average level increasing each year. Of course this could contain an element of grade inflation. It may also reflect the diffusion of knowledge about how to prepare for an inspection. There could even have been an element of politics to the system as authorities that contained within their boundaries one or more marginal Labour seats in Parliament tended to achieve higher

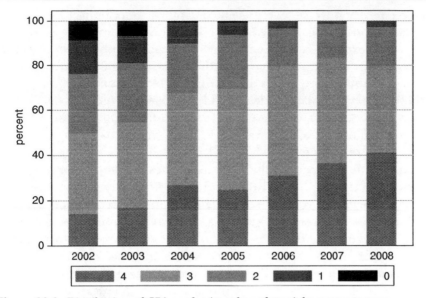

Figure 11.1. Distribution of CPA grades (number of stars) from year to year

scores, as shown in Bertelli and John's (2010) statistical analysis of the impact of the pork barrel on CPA scores.

As with all performance measurement systems, there is a debate about the extent to which the CPA was an unbiased measure of performance. There is the possibility that it might have sent incorrect signals. In particular, it was sometimes thought that the measures reflected the difficulties local authorities faced rather than a level playing field. This led to a debate as to whether the Audit Commission should adjust performance measurement scores to allow for the level of deprivation of English local authority areas, compensating them for the difficulty of administering services. The analogous argument was based on reporting deprivation-weighted examination score results because of the socio-economic characteristics of the communities where some pupils live. This policy option was discussed in Haubrich *et al.* (2008). Their paper shows that local authorities in deprived areas got worse CPA scores, which appears to be a result of the difficulty of administering services and the pressures faced by councils in these places. Haubrich *et al.* (2008) built on the earlier work at Cardiff Business School on the environmental constraints operating on the CPA (Andrews 2004; Andrews *et al.* 2005, 2006) as well as their own work (Haubrich and McLean 2006). All studies show the same pattern: local authorities in poorer areas got worse scores, even controlling for other factors, such as local authority type. So the system seemed biased from the start as a modernist experiment. If the performance of local authorities was partly generated from their environment, then the system did not reward the same amount of effort across the local public sector. As a result, the public and other external stakeholders would not have been able to evaluate the performance of their local authority in terms of the skill and leadership of the politicians and officers in charge. It might have been the case that local authorities were punished and rewarded for factors outside their control, with poor-performing local authorities receiving central government intervention through no fault of their own, or even when they had good management. And yet some highly deprived authorities that came under intervention subsequently managed to get up to three and four stars, even though their deprivation did not change and the Audit Commission did not adjust their scores upwards based on their poverty. Consequently, this particular asymmetric characteristic of the CPA system did not present as big a set of problems as it might appear. Indeed, compensating local authorities for their task difficulty would have weakened the electoral incentive for politicians to avoid low performance, which we discuss below.

One fact is certain: there was improvement at the poor end of the spectrum. Very poorly performing authorities, such as Hull, got better scores and a vote of approval from their electorates for the work of their incumbent administration after ending many years of poor performance. For the poorly performing local authorities, getting a bad score was a notice to voters and central government that the time was up or there would be changes at the top. These authorities also received interventions from central government, which were seen as legitimate, even by the politicians from authorities that were subject to them (IDeA 2009). Overall, there is evidence, including from longitudinal case studies, that the system worked well and did bring about true service improvements (Downe and Martin 2006; Martin 2008; Martin *et al.* 2009).

One of the attractive features of CPA, in contrast to the Best Value regime, which it built on, was that it offered a very clear — if broad-brush — assessment of how well local authorities performed and helped allocate responsibility for performance to incumbents. Everyone understood these grades, at least in outline. They had a reputational impact on the local authorities and associated stakeholders. For the winners, it spurred them on to keep succeeding, which became progressively harder to do as the others caught up. But it was not always so easy for those at the top for at best they could maintain their score or otherwise deteriorate. For the losers, the CPA acted as a spur to improve, exposing decades of poor performance to citizens, bureaucrats, and politicians, not just in the local authority itself, but on the national stage.

There is evidence that local electors used CPA results as a signal to kick out local administrations in councils only achieving the two lowest grades, with the relationship first observed in 2002 with the introduction of the CPA regime (James and John 2007; Revelli 2008). Looking at all 148 principal local authorities, of the ninety-two instances where a CPA rating of poor/zero stars or weak/one star was awarded between 2002 and 2006, in forty-eight instances an election was held the following spring (twenty-two whole-council elections and twenty-six elections by thirds). In thirteen of the whole-council elections and fourteen of the elections by thirds a single incumbent party faced the electorate following a negative Audit Commission verdict on their performance (CPA rating of poor/zero stars or weak/one star). The remaining councils were hung before the election. In four out of the fourteen whole-council elections (29 per cent) and in five out of the thirteen elections by thirds (38 per cent) the incumbent party lost power. This implies that there was a significant risk of losing power for an incumbent presiding over low performance. Revelli (2008) shows that this risk was significantly greater in the presence of low performance, and James and John (2007) and Boyne *et al.* (2009*a*) quantify the vote share loss for an incumbent party to be between three and six percentages points, a figure that could have been decisive in a number of authorities since majorities are often tight.

There is evidence from a randomized field experiment that the provision of performance information to citizens indeed influences their views of service performance (James 2009). Political change was also a signal to bring in a new management team (Boyne *et al.* 2010). With further data from the Economic and Social Research Council project, *Leadership Change and Public Services: Reinvigorating Performance or Reinforcing Decline* (2006–8), it has been possible to observe a chain from poor performance, to electoral change, to change in political leadership, to change in the senior management team, to improved performance (Boyne *et al.* 2009*b*), which complements other work showing that leadership and management matter for the CPA (Andrews *et al.* 2006; Gains *et al.* 2007).

One possible criticism of the CPA scheme is that it was not clear how the signals worked throughout the system. Most of all, the (electoral) reward system for politicians was asymmetric: the electorate punished poor-performing local authorities. We can show this from some case-study evidence collected from interviews with leaders, chief executives, and officers in five contrasting local authorities. We summarize the results in Table 11.1,

Table 11.1. CPA scores and trajectories and politician and senior manager responses

	Declining performance	Improving performance
High CPA score	Politicians not too concerned by small deteriorations, but chief executives strove to restore performance to the previous level. No change in political control, some limited change in senior managers below chief executive level	Politicians sought to preserve performance but did not make it the main priority, chief executive strove to maintain performance, some limited change in senior managers being poached
	Unitary, County Council, both in the south of England	*County Council in the south of England*
Low CPA score	Politicians and chief executive were both very concerned about performance. Change in political control and chief executive. New politicians and chief executive made wholesale changes to the senior management	Micro-managing incumbent politicians were voted out. New incumbents delegated far more to the chief executive, who sought to continue improvement. The former incumbent replaced the chief executive and there was also some change in senior managers
	Unitary in the south of England	*London borough*

which is a synthesis of these interviews in each authority. Politicians tended to respond only to low levels of performance or declining performance, with the largest response in cases where both of these factors were evident. In contrast, politicians in authorities that were good and improving tended to ease off, especially because it was difficult to make improvements at the top levels of performance.

As well as idiosyncratic differences between authorities, the response of politicians was conditioned in part by party-political affiliation. Interviewees commented to us that the CPA reflected, to an extent, the national Labour government's priorities and that this brought about more engagement from politicians in Labour authorities than in those controlled by the Liberal Democrats and the Conservatives. As the national Labour government's popularity waned, councils run by opposition parties were increasingly resistant to some aspects of the performance regime. However, this did not amount to a rejection of the system but a difference of emphasis. Some Liberal Democrat-controlled authorities were more resistant to CPA than those controlled by the two other main parties, not only because of policy differences, but also because the CPA's focus on corporate strategy and central direction of the authority was not always consistent with the mode of working of Liberal Democrats, which tends to have weaker central leadership and greater heterogeneity of outlook on policy priorities amongst the ruling group than other parties.

Table 11.1 demonstrates that in cases of poor and declining performance chief executives and senior managers were often removed from their post by politicians, although rather than outright sackings a range of strategies were pursued to ease people into early retirement or to encourage some form of voluntary departure. However, there are institutional safeguards for senior officials to protect them from dismissal, and these staff members have expertise which gives them some autonomy. Nevertheless, there is some evidence that political dismissals did occur (Boyne *et al.* 2010), and that performance incentives for senior management were strong. Classic theories of bureaucratic behaviour suggest conduct is influenced by a range of factors including professional motivations and career concerns. These may have given officials an incentive not only to avoid being in the worst categories of CPA, which could have been terminal for their careers and did not fit with professional motivations, but also to aim for higher levels of performance.

All the senior managers and politicians we spoke to agreed that the CPA focused the attention of local authorities on performance, although there was less consensus on the size of the effect. CPA appeared to have a greater effect on officers, particularly chief executives and those interested in becoming chief executives, than on members (Audit Commission 2008). A bad CPA result served as a wake-up call for both managers and politicians at one council and it stirred up the lowest performing service heads at another. The chief executive at a third council stressed that this was one of the virtues of CPA: it helped direct the attention of the organization to the weakest performing services. Even a chief executive who on the whole doubted that the CPA did much to move local government services closer to the needs of local citizens, nevertheless thought that the regime had some success, a fact that this chief executive felt to be an indictment of local government. While three chief executives suggested that the CPA had a greater effect on the actions of officers than members, there was agreement that it did also affect leaders and there was one case where the authority's Conservative leader was very focused on improving the authority's CPA score.

Officers' main motivation for focusing on the CPA and attempting to improve it derived from the way the labour market for chief executives responded to the scheme. It rapidly evolved to reflect the importance of either a track record on the CPA overall, or for more junior candidates, a record of improving a particular service in terms of the CPA. There is also evidence from all the interviews we conducted that chief executives cared about achieving higher level scores as well as getting out of the bottom category. They were keen to demonstrate improvements associated with their tenure, and in authorities performing above the lower categories this necessarily implied an interest in achieving high scores.

While the strong career incentives made the CPA centrally important to current and aspiring chief executives, whereas no such link at all levels of performance existed for politicians, there was also a difference in type between officers and members that made the former more receptive to the CPA. One chief executive vividly expressed this difference which several others, as well as a council leader had alluded to: 'Officers think in terms of reasons and systematic data, politicians think in anecdotes; [they] don't care about numbers. They care about the media, residents, and anecdotes.' This was not a uniform pattern but appeared to resemble the central tendency in English local government. Given the career incentives for officers and this tendency, one chief executive's suggestion that the CPA led to more delegation to the chief executive, particularly in initially low-performing authorities, is not too surprising. Also it hints at an interesting undercurrent and possibly deliberately designed mechanism in CPA: central government ministers tend not to trust local authority councillors. Therefore they created a system that would work towards more decisions being taken by officers, in an overall attempt to bring up and homogenize the performance of local government, which could be of a value in a country where the majority of the electorate is critical of a postcode lottery in public-service provision.

Despite the concerns about the impact of deprivation on performance of public services and associated difficulties of making assessments of political and managerial leadership competence that have been expressed in the academic literature, none of our interviewees considered the CPA to be biased against authorities in poor areas. One chief executive suggested that there was no evidence that the CPA ratings were politically influenced, although stated views on this topic may not reveal all of the processes at work on such a controversial topic.

The incentives in the CPA fed through the local authority organization to senior managers and below. It appears that the penalties for poor-performing service heads may have been even greater than for chief executives who could to an extent shield themselves from poor performance in the absence of a new set of politicians coming into power and demanding a shake up (Boyne *et al.* 2008). But these officials, too, expressed to us their concerns to raise standards of performance in their areas beyond the lower levels and also their frustration that politicians would not support improvements to services that were already seen as performing adequately.

Conclusion

The paradox explored in this chapter is this: performance management systems normally fail or at best make little impact, yet the Comprehensive Performance Assessment in English local government was successful. It did deliver performance improvements, especially to poor-performing authorities. This is because the electoral incentives of CPA for incumbent politicians were clear: do not end up in the lowest categories or lose votes. Beyond this level of performance the CPA did not seem to have much electoral resonance, and as the grades of councils improved over time the system had less influence overall even in this respect. However, career and professional incentives for senior managers, especially chief executives, did provide incentives to raise performance beyond this level, although these influences were kept in check by politicians who are ultimately in overall control of the authorities. The asymmetry of incentives for performance, the punishment of poor performance but lack of reward for excellence, would normally have been suggested to stifle innovation and service improvement. But in fact the evidence does not suggest this happened (Brannan *et al.* 2008; Audit Commission 2008). There seems to be a demand for innovation throughout local government, which in the case of CPA was largely driven by officers who had the most to gain from achieving a high performance score. Our findings show the power of the bureaucrats in the English system of local government, at least as far as the administration of performance regimes is concerned. Only a regime that appeals to their competitive instincts with each other is going to work, at least for the middling and well-performing authorities. Of course, there was an element of gaming in the system, and there might or might not have been an element of politics to the scores (see Bertelli and John 2010), but such detracting influences remained on the margins rather than core to the system.

In politics success is usually short-lived. The CPA was probably too successful as it created improvement across the board and thus removed the differences between authorities and the competitive drive inherent in the system. In 2002 one in five councils was in the lowest two categories, but 2008 it was just one in a hundred. The Audit Commission, which had always regarded the CPA as a temporary system, argued the system had achieved its objectives in its publication, *Final Score* (2009). It had already tried to raise the bar on performance in its review three years into the scheme reflected in *CPA The Harder Test* (2005). From April 2009, the

Commission introduced Comprehensive Area Assessment (CAA) (see Audit Commission 2009*b*), which evaluates performance across an area using a wider set of indicators. Even though many of the underlying performance indicators remain intact, the broad-brush five-point evaluation of councils has been dropped, which arguably was the driver to improve performance. Citizens will no longer be able to hold local politicians to account in this way because the CAA will be partly determined by local organizations that do not have a locally elected mandate. The clarity of responsibility has been lost. On the other hand, reporting of councils will continue, and the Commission will use red and green flags to give an overall view of performance, but the electoral incentive effects of the CAA are likely to be weaker — especially compared to the power of being labelled as a poor performer in the CPA.

It remains to be seen whether CAA will have incentive effects and performance improvements similar in strength to those of the CPA. Perhaps it too will be a public management reform that confounds academic expectations and works well.[4]

[4] Author order is alphabetical: all have made an equal contribution to the chapter. We thank the Economic and Social Research Council Public Services Programme for support (grant number RES-166-25-0026).

V

Conclusion

12

Modernization, Balance, and Variety

Helen Margetts, Perri 6, and Christopher Hood

This chapter asks three kinds of questions about the risks of unanticipated and unintended consequences arising from modernizing reforms. How do we understand and classify these risks? How should we best explain these outcomes, when they do arise? And can our explanations suggest anything important of a prescriptive character about how policy-makers might work to contain at least some of these risks? In this final chapter, we present a synthesis of what can be learnt from these case studies that might help to develop answers to these questions.

In Chapters 2 and 3, we developed a conceptual framework with which to understand the varieties of both modernization and of surprising results. Here, we show how the frameworks developed there can fruitfully be applied to the cases. We go on to examine the case studies to identify some of the causal factors contributing to surprising outcomes. Our aim is to develop theory. We cannot aspire here to test that theory adequately. Our sample of cases could not permit such an aspiration, nor could any such sample; there is no way to measure the vast population of modernizing interventions (let alone types of consequence) that could allow for probability sampling. We undertake only modest qualitative comparative case analysis to develop some provisional hypotheses. Then, we consider whether the sketch we offer of an explanatory account suggests any normative recommendations.

Applying the Framework

Whether they were reforms undertaken by government or innovations developed from within commercial or voluntary activity, each of the cases is modernizing in the loose sense of being presented as new, state-of-the-art, and offering improvements on previous arrangements or technologies. Their architects promised faster trains, a more efficient and responsive health service with improvements in health outcomes, a more motivated public service, better performing local government, enhanced information to assist prospective US university students in choosing their place of study, reduced rates of child malnutrition in developing countries, and a free, open, interconnected cyberspace for citizens to conduct their social and political life. Each rests on one or more of the pillars of modernization identified in Chapter 2 — namely, economic efficiency (including incentivization and instrumentalism), integration (including interconnectedness, central control, standardization, and formal rules), and specialization (which can include expert knowledge, scientific advancement, quantification, and technological development).

Our case studies have been chosen to provide adequate diversity across these three types of modernizing intervention. Some were reforms attempting to modernize the state itself: those policy-makers who developed pay-for-performance initiatives for state employees and the Local Authority Comparative Performance Assessment intended to improve government's efficiency and performance. Some were state-led initiatives aiming to modernize some aspect of society or at least with profound implications for society. Modernizing Britain's rail network was intended to improve transport; the NHS IT programme, it was hoped, would change both clinicians' and patients' behaviour as well as providing them with more integrated information management tools; the World Bank nutrition programme had ambitious aspirations to reduce malnutrition and change mothers' behaviour. Some are innovations developed within the state, but their rapid adoption by the wider society means that they look more like societal modernization. The internet protocol was originally developed from work undertaken within an agency of the US Department of Defense and Tim Berners-Lee's early work that led to the World Wide Web was done while working at the publicly funded research body, CERN.[1] Both developments had very wide social, economic, and political consequences, both benign and malign, yet also provided a vast array of new instruments for governments as well as new problems of on-line criminality that required further innovations for effective governance. One other innovation originated

---

[1] However, Berners-Lee was working as an independent contractor on a proposal of his own rather than from his client; therefore, the World Wide Web was further removed from government direction than was the development of the internet protocol on which it depends.

outside the state, but also had important implications for the public sector: new university ranking tables introduced by a US newspaper affected both state universities and government support for students across the sector.

Having been chosen to illustrate the variety of modernizing interventions, it is perhaps not surprising that our cases do not offer examples of every type of unintended, unanticipated, or unwelcome consequence identified in Chapter 3. We have two examples of surprises that are at least largely happy. The World Wide Web was an unexpected and unintended consequence of developing the Semantic Web: few would argue that the many sordid and criminal uses to which it has been put so outweigh its economic, social, and political benefits that the World Wide Web should be counted as a setback. Secondly, in some cases where it has been applied, at least after a time and some learning, pay for performance in the public sector has contributed to improvement. In two cases, the outcomes seem to be the result of risks knowingly run — namely, university rankings produced by a US newspaper and pay for performance, where such schemes failed to work. We have four bad surprises: these are the NHS IT programme, nutrition policy in the World Bank, cybercrime, and rail policy. Finally, and of particular value in comparative analysis for theory-building is the example of success, where the outcome seems to have been intended, anticipated, and welcome to the scheme's architects. This is the case of the Comparative Performance Assessment scheme for UK local authorities.

Not all these cases are paradoxical in the sense that their outcomes are perverse (Hirschman 1991), or actually the reverse of their goals. The most likely candidate for this 'brain-teasing' paradox category is the case of performance pay, where in spite of pay for performance schemes failing to fulfil their aims by motivating staff, they seem sometimes to improve performance. But all the cases fall into the looser definition of paradox that we provided in the Introduction. Each produced something contrary to opinion or expectation, at least to some important actors. Britons did not get faster trains on the lines that they use most, nor has the NHS IT programme led either to a more efficient health service or to improved health outcomes. Prospective students in the USA got more information, but they also seem to now be offered more cautious and less creative university courses. Performance-related pay has, in some instances, improved public servants' motivation but in others it has demoralized workforces. Spiralling cybercrime and the prospect of regulation to deal with it have dismayed the techno-utopians, although they had their playground for a while. Berners-Lee seems happy with the major social innovation that the World Wide Web has become, but he still strives to develop the

Table 12.1. Categorizing modernization reforms

Outcome	Success	Happy Surprise	Bad Surprise	Risks Knowingly Run
Pillars of Modernization				
A. Integration (interconnectedness, standardization, central control, formal rules)	Performance management for local authorities	WWW and Semantic Web	World Bank nutrition policy NHS IT Internet and cybercrime BR investment programme	
B. Economic Rationalism (incentivization)	Performance management for local authorities			Performance related pay University rankings
C. Specialization (scientific advancement, expert knowledge, technological development of quantification)	Performance management for local authorities	WWW and Semantic Web	World Bank nutrition policy NHS IT Internet and cybercrime BR investment programme	

Semantic Web, seemingly his original intention. Even our successful case of performance assessment in local government has been deeply surprising to academic researchers, contradicting twenty years of research evidence that such schemes always fail. The precise reasons for and timing of the eventual abandonment of the scheme that apparently worked so well leaves us with a further puzzle — if it was good, why stop making it? — even though it seems its termination was intended and anticipated by the architects of the scheme.

Table 12.1 summarizes how the cases fit into the conceptual framework.

Developing a Provisional Explanation

Can comparative analysis of these cases suggest common causal factors in the aetiology of surprise, or indeed, of success and failure?

Any explanation for an unintended or unanticipated consequence must address the questions, (i) why the reformers or innovators did not anticipate or did not intend that outcome, (ii) what features about the design of the action or programme contributed most importantly to the outcome, and (iii) what causal path was followed from the action, once undertaken. In any particular case, one or two of these issues may, as we argued in Chapter 3, have greater explanatory importance.

In this section, we develop the argument suggested in the Introduction, that successful modernization depends on *requisite variety*, or more loosely, as suggested at the end of Chapter 2, on 'balance' between both the three strategies of modernization, and the basic institutional forms of social organization.

As noted in the introduction, the concept of requisite variety was developed by the mathematician and cybernetic theorist, W. Ross Ashby (1956: 202–11). A commonly used informal statement of the law would be that 'The larger the variety of actions available to a control system [a regulator], the larger the variety of perturbations it is able to compensate [in the regulated system].' (http://pespmc1.vub.ac.be/reqvar.html). Requisite variety explanations represent a whole family of models, but they are quite distinct from other kinds of causal theory. One central point about these types of explanation is that they propose that the outcomes are brought about by redundancy, or an apparent excess of resources that might seem at any point to be inefficient because not all of them may appear to be used at any given time. In cybernetic terms, a strategy needs to be capable of a wide range of actions, in order to ensure even a small range of outcomes. Successful outcomes, these models suggest, are achieved by there being in place resources of *diverse* kinds, each of which may contribute only indirectly, or negatively, by enabling people to solve certain problems, should those contingencies arise.

Within the family of requisite variety explanations, we can distinguish some principal types of models. One kind of model proposes that the various elements (for example, strategies of modernization or institutions) among which variety is required for success should be in tension with each other. Requisite variety then calls for this tension to be maintained, and for no element to be so dominant, so that the set of resources drawn upon in — for example — modernization, is never completely mutually supporting or even consistent. That tension may itself, in some models, be creative. In others, it may be destructive, but the friction may just be a price worth paying for having the contribution that each of the diverse resources may bring. Another kind of requisite variety model would have the various

Table 12.2. Types of requisite variety

	Elements in tension	Elements not in tension
Enough and not too much of each	A. Countervailing relations (weakest requirements)	B. Diverse resources
Rough equality in the strength of the elements	C. Balanced tension	D. Balanced settlement (strictest requirements)

elements be in principle consistent with each other, or not in inevitable tension, but simply diverse in their content.

Requisite variety models differ on another dimension too. Some require, for a successful outcome, that there be 'just enough' but 'not too much' of each element to deal with particular risks or challenges. That allows scope for considerable inequality among them. Stricter models require that there be some rough equality in the degree to which each element (for example, each of the three strategies of modernization) is institutionalized. Although loosely we can speak of all requisite variety models as proposing balance, only these latter models rely on 'balance' in the narrowest sense of the term. For where variety requires 'just enough', we positively want an *imbalance* (see 6 *et al.* 2010 on balance; and 6 2003 for the definition of four general types of requisite variety).

This gives four general types of requisite variety (cf. 6 2003), shown in Table 12.2.

Of course, in the social sciences, it is often very difficult indeed to find comparable measures of the strength of institutionalization of such things as our three modernization clusters (economic efficiency, integration, and specialization) that would enable us to weigh them on the same scale. Nor can we readily be sure in advance of seeing just what risks actually transpire to a modernization project, whether the resources available in the programme were sufficiently developed in any of the three. But just because something is hard to measure, it does not follow that it is without meaning. In practice, we often work with different measures for each element, and people can often identify weaknesses in advance, because they can anticipate that some risks might well occur. Unanticipated consequences occur when institutions cultivate in people those styles of judgement that blinker their ability to anticipate certain types of risk. The capacity of social scientists to do better in overcoming those institutional blinkers, when judging in advance, than policy-makers, should surely not be over-estimated. But even retrospective explanation can represent real intellectual advance.

Here, we propose the following type of requisite variety explanation for successful outcomes from modernization reforms or innovations, before presenting some comparative analysis of the case studies examined in the preceding chapters, to make the case for this proposal.

Our hypothesis is that success in modernization depends on two fundamental *necessary* conditions, namely

(a) *Balance or countervailing relations among the three strategies of modernization* — economic efficiency, integration, and specialization; and

(b) *Counterbalance or countervailing relations from the elementary forms of social organization* (e.g. 6 2003; Verweij and Thompson 2006) — the hierarchy and individualism that both sustain the three modernization strategies and that they in turn tend to cultivate, but also enclaved and isolated orderings (egalitarian and fatalist in Mary Douglas's (1992) terms).

These two conditions are, we propose, necessary conditions for success in modernization reform. There may be ways in which these necessary conditions also become 'sufficient' conditions for a modernization project to be successful. First, looking at (a), the three clusters of modernization strategies can work in tension with each other (as in the example of some New Public Management reforms discussed in Chapter 2), be mutually consistent, or actually mutually supporting or reinforcing. The case where modernization follows a mixed strategy of economic efficiency, integration, and specialization, but where the causal mechanisms unleashed by the three strategies are mutually consistent and reinforcing, is one of particular interest. Here, as it were, we have all our ducks lined up in a row: these are the most favourable conditions for success. Second, if condition (b) is met then it may be that the particular mix of countervailing institutions or forms of social organization will maximize the possibility of effective feedback loops in a reform. The logic of the requisite variety argument suggests that one should persevere, if one has confidence in the variety of the resources deployed, but adjust, if the early feedback suggests that the modernization programme lacks sufficient articulation of one strategy or one form of institution. Unfortunately, people can readily be institutionalized into excessive confidence in their strategies so that they reject information that ought to suggest a change of course (Thompson and Wildavsky 1986; 6 2004; 6 *et al.* 2007). Yet we can also be institutionalized to exaggerate the significance of information, leading us to *over*-correct our course. The right mix of countervailing institutions or forms of social

227

organization should facilitate some chance of being able to offset each kind of blinkering with the others, so that we might be able to judge when it is best to persevere and when to adjust. So, where causal mechanisms released by the modernizing intervention are mutually consistent or reinforcing, and the mix of countervailing forms of social organization is varied enough to facilitate feedback loops, this should be sufficient for a successful outcome from modernization.

Comparing Cases

To support these hypotheses, we consider each of the cases in turn. The Comprehensive Performance Assessment (CPA) regime in English local government is the nearest we have found to a case of success. The regime's results were roughly what its architects intended and seem to have made a substantive positive difference to local authority performance overall, assuming that the performance numbers were meaningful. The outcome was a surprise mainly to those academic researchers who have produced volumes of material to suggest that such schemes rarely work. It was largely internal to the state, although there were incentives for societal involvement at the local level. It was a typical New Public Management reform, apparently similar to many failed schemes. Why does it seem to have succeeded? Boyne *et al.* show evidence that it rested on all three pillars of modernization. It was centrally controlled, with central government setting the rules of the game. There was standardization upon a national agenda for local authorities and a common approach to implementation expected of all local authorities. Quantification was central, providing both clear signals to local authorities and a mechanism to provide for easily accessible and understandable performance information (although the chapter highlights weaknesses in the allowances made for levels of deprivation in some areas). The scheme created organization-level incentives for authorities, by offering rewards for better performance, individual-level incentives for senior managers in local authorities through the managerial job market, and political incentives to citizens to use the published information to vote to punish administrations that failed to improve. Asymmetric elements in the electoral elements of incentivization (with authorities punished for poor performance and not rewarded for good performance) appear to have meant that incentivization worked better for managers than for members, but this may have been deliberate, given that central government ministers have long had limited trust in local councillors. The CPA seems to be an example of modernization with requisite variety, and with all the causal mechanisms working in the same direction. Interestingly, it also exhibits some variety in the elementary institutional forms of social organization. For the individual career incentives worked in significant part because the world of English local government is a densely enclaved community in which reputations are quickly known to all, and where generations of subordination to central government have sustained a degree of isolated coping and compliance with an unending series of new central schemes. This case alone can be no more than suggestive, but the hunch is given further support when we examine the cases which were subject to surprise.

Performance-related pay too affords an example of an internal state modernization reform. Because the architects of the scheme were aware of the risks of staff demotivation and of loss of control of whole performance management systems, we characterize it as an example of risks knowingly run. However, Marsden shows that disappointment with early experience led to subsequent improvements, but as a result of a different mechanism than that of individual monetary incentive, using standardized and quantified instruments. Rather, early experience led to greater efforts to specify individual and organizational levels. The earlier schemes gave way to schemes, developed after learning from early failures, which increased individual employee voice (Hirschman 1970) in determining work objectives and measures of collective as well as individual performance. This fostered greater teamwork and an enhanced perception of fairness. These strategies are less clearly modernizing than that of individual incentivization, but may have provided some element of enclaving at team and organization levels to perhaps act as a countervailing pressure to the otherwise exclusive reliance on individualistic institutions governing incentives. Thus, greater variety in organization seems to have been important, as well as the capacity of at least some organizations, such as the Inland Revenue and some schools, to remain open to information from early experience. As a result of this learning, multiple causal mechanisms were applied, in a mutually supporting relationship.

When villains rather than reformers or innovators learn quickly from early experience of modernizations that lack adequate variety, surprises follow. The case of cybercrime illustrates both the modernizing vision of the developers of the internet and the more postmodern vision of the techno-utopians. The original architects of the internet embarked upon a project to modernize academic, social, and also governmental activity, using sophisticated technology and highly specialized expert knowledge to connect networks in universities and military organizations that could not previously communicate. The project relied on integration, interconnectedness, specialization, and technological development. Economic efficiency played a lesser role, although there were undoubtedly cost savings to be hoped for from such a project. The techno-utopians, by contrast, had a more postmodern (or perhaps non-modern) vision of a highly disaggregated space, with no governance, no regulation, and few standards. They imagined that they could leave behind the nation-state, with its hierarchical organization and central control, so opening the way for social emancipation. Yet they relied on interconnectedness and the technical capabilities of the internet, which were the modern elements of the project. Although specialization seemed contrary to their goals of social equality and openness, these early users were themselves highly specialized.

Cybercrime was given its opportunity by the very technical and social freedom enabled by the technical architecture of the internet, originally designed to ensure security for military uses. Cybercrime today is an 'ultramodern' enterprise, with intense specialization, professionalization, and expertise. Arguably, for the pursuit of many of their own goals of orderly self-governing on-line communities, the internet utopians were not modern enough, in the mix of their strategies and especially in their lack of attention to economic rationality or incentives, for the arms race of technical modernization between government, criminal organizations, and ordinary users that ensued. Their own aspirations for reliance upon enclave, using technologies developed for hierarchical purposes that opened opportunities for individualistic exploitation, proved as lacking in variety in institutional organization as their mix of modernization strategies. Unable to adapt sufficiently quickly to information about the manner in which their vision was swept aside, the idylls of self-governing community have either atrophied or retreated behind rules and firewalls. Here, reliance upon technology was the single intervention, and the causal mechanism by which the utopians hoped that it might bring about the social developments they hoped for was insufficiently clear or developed.

The case of the World Wide Web and the Semantic Web are examples of happier surprises. As developed by Tim Berners-Lee at CERN, the World Wide Web was a modernist endeavour that emphasized integration and standardization, but lacked clear economic incentives. Moreover, its few formal rules were of a technical nature rather than about substantive use and, without central control, the internet-supported software program enabled people to find and organize information, by standardizing addresses and automating the manner in which users can move among pages. Wilks argues that Berners-Lee had sought and still seeks to develop a still more standardized, integrated, and logical system for organizing data than offered by the World Wide Web, the Semantic Web. It would be based on a web of machine-readable data coded in a standardized manner for their meanings. Berners-Lee's development of the World Wide Web was a happy surprise, in part the product of luck or serendipity, a less fully modernized spin-off from his pursuit of the Semantic Web. Like the internet, this technological innovation, devised for narrow and technical purposes, has had vast social spin-offs. In this case, unlike (say) the World Bank nutrition policy, the initiative was rescued by societal adoption of the World Wide Web when it was several steps away from becoming the Semantic Web. Here, the causal mechanisms changed over time, as Berners-Lee and his community of experts learnt from experience and from their own serendipity.

The World Bank's nutrition policy resulted in a bad surprise. We can treat it as a state-centred modernization programme, for in many respects the Bank acts as a kind of international public authority. Reliant upon a technology of biomedical and health economic models, based partly on expert analysis and knowledge, the programme was standardized and integrated. At an early date, information became available of its under-achievement, poor implementation, and weak incentives for mothers. Yet institutional constraints within the bank, emphasizing expert knowledge and statistical modelling, worked against the use of this knowledge. In some ways it is a case rather similar to those of James C. Scott (1998), in that the Bank failed to anticipate problems rooted in local culture and power structures. Failure clearly occurred locally, as in Scott's cases, with muddled incentives for local women to comply with the strategy. But perhaps more importantly, the Bank failed to change the programme when evidence of problems with existing blueprints started to emerge and this was caused by career incentives within the Bank to persist. Even had local incentives been provided, weak incentives within the bank for individual bureaucrats to pay attention to feedback information about how the programme was working would have worked against success. Priority was given to one pillar of modernization — namely, integration, standardization, and central control. Key elements in other pillars were ignored. Quantification was pursued without enough attention to even expert, let alone to lay knowledge, particularly in digesting feedback from the field. This was a one-club programme, reliant upon a single causal mechanism, a clear case of unbalanced modernization.

In some respects, the NHS IT programme in England is a similarly structured case of a bad surprise arising from state-centred modernization. Central control and integration were used to impose standardization across the service. Incentives for clinicians to work with the programme were weak. Economic rationality too was attenuated. There have long been notorious problems in justifying the costs of huge IT projects of this kind. Yet policy-makers accepted the programme's spiralling costs, in the face of sustained evidence that it could never repay in benefits. This suggests that economic rationale cannot have been a priority. Little thought was given to what patients and prospective patients wanted or how they would behave. Perhaps surprisingly, given the technological nature of the project, specialization seems rather absent from this reform. NHS managers driving the programme seem to have placed great faith in the ability of the suppliers to understand what was needed to provide the required solution, yet there is little evidence that the suppliers involved had a real idea of how the system could or should develop. Meanwhile, the views of professionals and experts within the NHS were more or less ignored. Feedback from early experience about the tendency of clinicians to circumvent the system was given short shrift. The principal difference between this case and those examined by Scott (1998) is that, here, the *mētis* or local knowledge ignored was that of state professionals rather than of local communities. Integration was used disproportionately, while the pillar of specialization was based on a generalist and non-expert view of what experts would say and was insufficiently articulated. Poor attention to the incentives of actors within the state to comply with central control meant that the economic rationalism pillar was hardly present. As with the World Bank nutrition policy case, feedback information on how the reform was developing was largely managed away, trivialized, and screened out.

That huge investment in Britain's railway network resulted in financial priority being given to the least used lines is another bad surprise for at least some policy-makers in the first decades of the post-war era. This was a state-centred modernization with little societal input about most frequently made journeys, most used lines, or passengers' preferences. Integration, central control, interconnectedness, and standardization were the key pillars of the modernization, over several decades. For example, track width was standardized during this period. Specialization was also critical in developing rail technology; professional engineering knowledge was central to the formation of rail policy. At first glance, this might seem to be a 'Scott case' of overweening faith in the expert knowledge of engineers. But a closer reading of Leunig's chapter suggests that it was in fact a misperception of expert knowledge that drove policy. Railway general managers, 'men with genius for organization ... without possessing necessarily any particular professional or technical qualifications', were the dominant influence on the strategy, with their own view of the best use of developments in rail technology. The specialization pillar was therefore rather shaky, resting on managers' desire for the fastest trains. These were neither economically efficient nor particularly desirable from an engineering perspective (Leunig suggests that the UK rail network's retention of steam trains for so long can be explained in the same way: steam trains were popular among non-specialists, but again are neither efficient nor desirable from an engineering perspective). In the period examined, professional engineers of the time had no training in cost-benefit analysis, and they faced few incentives to develop economic rationales for their investment plans. So the economic rationalism pillar was absent from the reform, as was any view of what would provide incentives for passengers to travel on particular routes or at times of lighter usage. The case represents, therefore, an instance of modernization that lacked requisite variety, with one pillar (specialization) based on very shaky ground and another (economic rationalism) almost entirely absent. Again, a single intervention of central planning releasing the single causal mechanism of directly managed investment was relied upon.

The US newspaper's ranking of universities can be viewed as a case of societal modernization, an innovation rather than a state-driven reform. A commercial enterprise, seeing the growing popularity of rankings as a decision-making tool for consumers, saw both prospects of additional sales of newspapers and a valuable aid to prospective students in choosing universities and courses. Both those aspirations were achieved, but this success is of less interest for our purposes than the risks presumably knowingly run that universities' behaviour would change as a result of publication, including gaming and a degree of isomorphism, as universities avoided adventurous but risky changes to their programmes. Modernization rested mainly upon quantification. Other elements of this pillar were underplayed. Indeed there is evidence in this case that the rankings led to reduced specialization, as rankings tended to stabilize over time and led to institutional isomorphism. The newspaper's own economic rationale is clear, but there was no intention to save the universities money. Indeed, they seem to have spent substantially to keep their place in the tables. This shows again the risks of reliance on a single pillar, intervention, and mechanism, and of the impact on public and non-profit bodies of societal modernization initiatives.

The analysis suggests that, perhaps, if these cases are illustrative of wider trends, at least sometimes lack of adequate variety may be less important in societal modernizing innovations than in state-centred modernizing reforms. For in neither the US university rankings nor in the development of the Semantic Web, was exclusive reliance on a single pillar so damaging as in other cases. Even the emergence of cybercrime has hardly so damaged the usability of the internet that people are willing to eschew its use: rather the contrary. On the other hand, state-centred reforms that lack adequate variety can only compensate for this by being led by people working within institutions that sustain their openness to information from the field that might indicate the need for change, development, and compensating initiatives, as the case of NHS information technology suggests.

Conclusion

We have disentangled a notion of modernization from the vast volumes of words crafted in the name of the concept. This definition is not so empty as to include every kind of reform (if it did it would be meaningless), but is reasonably precise and distinct. Modernization can, we argue, usefully and practicably be understood as consisting principally of strategies of reform and innovation that rest on one or more of three basic clusters of strategies — namely, economic efficiency, integration, and specialization. This definition has been extracted from the history of modernization theory of macro social and political change and may be used to characterize more limited modernization reforms, both to discern whether a reform may be labelled as modernizing and to determine what kind of modernization reform it is. Modernization under such a definition is dislocated from its original temporal location and is not confined to recent times; indeed, the great civilizations of antiquity all provide excellent examples of each type.

Modernization is clearly not an unambiguous boon from every reasonable perspective, even when it is successful in the narrow sense that its objectives are fulfilled without unanticipated, unintended, or unwelcome consequences. No one celebrates when tyrants modernize their repressive apparatus or their military capabilities; even the successful modernization of entirely civilian activities can prove to be a wasteful dead end, having to be replaced by other modernizations that may prove more durable platforms for sustained development. Although modernization has been hugely attractive to policy-makers at various times, it has not always been viewed as a trump card, and other rhetorical justifications have been used for a wide range of reforms.

Nearly all of our cases of modernization reform have resulted in some kind of unintended or unanticipated consequences which cannot be simply explained. Even with this limited set of cases, we can find no single 'law' of unintended consequences: there is no single general explanation for all the types of case. Modernizing reforms and innovations have no monopoly on unanticipated or unintended consequences, but these surprises are at once common, explicable, and found in a limited but classifiable variety of forms. Nor is it convincing simply to assert that the peculiar vulnerability of modernizations to surprise is the consequence of their uniquely great *hubris*. For other kinds of innovations and the strategy of eschewing change can be at least as guilty of that sin, and by no means all of our examples of modernization show particularly great *hubris*.

We do not argue that any algorithms will be found that will enable the designers of new initiatives to achieve surefire success in designing out 'bad surprise' by avoiding excess and insufficiency of any of the critical elements of modernization. Policy-makers and innovators alike work under institutions that limit their scope to reimagine, let alone to redesign, their relations with others and their own thought patterns in ways that might break free of the constraints that make for surprises. On the other hand, we have seen that modernization is not a one-track, one-way road to disappointment, failure, and unhappy surprises: some modernization projects actually work! Although we cannot suppress all unanticipated or unintended or unwelcome consequences, we might reasonably hope to learn how to strike better trade-offs in selecting particular risks to reduce, even at the price of running still others. At the very least, we can hope that sometimes, converting what might otherwise be unanticipated outcomes into risks knowingly run might be worthwhile.

Tentatively, we propose that the pursuit of adequate variety in strategy and social organization should be a priority for would-be modernizers. First, modernization reforms should not rely heavily on just one of the three 'pillars' of modernization. That is, we suggest that modernization reforms should include strategies from more than one of the clusters of economic efficiency, integration, and specialization. Second, reforms may need variety from outside modernization. That is, the three 'pillars' we have identified are dominated by the worldviews of hierarchalism and individualism. Modernization reforms may need a 'counterbalance' or countervailing influence from other worldviews, something provided in some of our cases by 'enclaves' or 'isolates'. Of course, variety can be at most a necessary and not a sufficient condition for success. Although we do not examine them in this book, there will surely be cases where adequate variety is found, but where other factors led to failure. The precise way in which the three pillars of modernization are combined, the particular style of

235

relationship between the different elementary ways of organization, will surely matter greatly. We must leave the further development of theory about these things to future research.

Our definition of modernization does not escape from the contradictions embedded in the history of the concept. But the tensions inherent in a notion of reform that rests on three clusters of strategies can be helpful in understanding paradoxes of modernization and devising ways to avoid bad surprise. We offer a requisite variety model to provide the general form for particular explanations of the unanticipated and/or unintended consequences of modernization. Requisite variety is needed for success, both to balance a reform across the three strategies of modernization and in the institutional forms of social organization that are sometimes required to counterbalance them. Cultivation of such variety in modernization reform may pull modernization away from the streamlined vision of control held by many of its earlier proponents; control of the natural environment, society, economic development, the state, and even the future. But by relinquishing the idea that we can control everything, we just might be able to control some outcomes, some of the time.

Bibliography

6, P. (1997). *Holistic Government*. London: Demos.

—— (2003). 'Institutional Viability: A Neo-Durkheimian Theory', *Innovation: The European Journal of Social Science Research*, 16(4): 395–415.

—— (2004). *E-governance: Styles of Political Judgment in the Information Age Polity*. Basingstoke: Palgrave Macmillan.

—— —— and Raab, C. (2010). 'Information Sharing Dilemmas in Public Services: Using Frameworks from Risk Management', *Policy and Politics* advance online publication DOI: 10.1332/030557310×488466.

——, Bellamy, C., Raab, C., and Warren, A. (2006). 'Partnership and Privacy: Tension or Settlement? The Case of Adult Mental Health Services', *Social Policy and Society*, 5: 237–48.

——, Glasby, J., and Lester, H. E. (2007). 'Incremental Change without Policy Learning: Explaining Information Rejection in English Mental Health Services', *Journal of Comparative Policy Analysis*, 9(1): 21–46.

——, Leat, D., Setzler, K., and Stoker, G. (2002). *Towards Holistic Governance: The New Reform Agenda*. Basingstoke: Palgrave.

Abbate, J. (1999). *Inventing the Internet*. Cambridge, Mass.: Massachusetts Institute of Technology Press.

Aboba, B. and Davies, E. (2007). 'Reflections on Internet Transparency', informational RFC 4924, July, see http://dret.net/rfc-index/reference/RFC4924.

—— —— and Elwyn, D. (2007). *Reflections on Internet Transparency*. Internet draft document publ. by the Internet Engineering Task Force (IETF). Available at: http://tools.ietf.org/pdf/draft-iab-net-transparent-05.pdf.

Acheson, D. (1998). *Independent Inquiry into Inequalities in Health*. London: Stationery Office.

Alesina, A., and Spolaore, E. (2003). *The Size of Nations*. Cambridge, Mass.: Massachusetts Institute of Technology Press.

Anderson, B. A. (2004). 'Unintended Population Consequences of Policies', *Population and Environment*, 25(4): 377–90.

Anderson, M. (2004). 'Spamming for Dummies: A Cautionary Tale', *The Register* (27 July). Available at: http://www.theregister.co.uk/2004/07/27/spamming_for_dummies/.

Anderson, R., Böhme, R., Clayton, R., and Moore, T. (2008). *Security Economics and the Internal Market*. Report for the European Network and Information Security

Agency (ENISA). Available at: http://www.enisa.europa.eu/doc/pdf/report_sec_econ_&_int_mark_20080131.pdf.

Anderson, R., Brown, I., Dowty, T., Inglesant, P., Heath, W., and Sasse, A. (2009). 'Database State'. York: Joseph Rowntree Reform Trust. Available at: http://www.jrrt.org.uk/uploads/database-state.pdf.

Anderson, R. M. (1995). 'Patient Empowerment and the Traditional Medical Model: A Case of Irreconcilable Difference?', *Diabetes Care*, 18: 412–15.

Andrews, R. (2004). 'Analysing Deprivation and Local Authority Performance: The Implications for CPA', *Public Money and Management*, 24(1): 19–26.

Andrews, R., Boyne, G. A., and Enticott, G. (2006). 'Performance Failure in the Public Sector: Misfortune or Mismanagement?', *Public Management Review*, 8(2): 273–96.

Andrews, R., Boyne, G. A., Law, J., and Walker, R. M. (2005). 'External Constraints on Local Service Standards: The Case of Comprehensive Performance Assessment in English Local Government', *Public Administration*, 83(3): 639–56.

Arnason, J. P. (2000). 'Communism and Modernity', *Daedalus*, 129(1): 61–90.

Ascher, W. (1983). 'New Development Approaches and the Adaptability of International Agencies: The Case of the World Bank', *International Organization*, 37(3): 415–39.

Ashby, W. R. (1956). *An Introduction to Cybernetics*. London: Chapman & Hall.

Atkinson, A., Burgess, S., Croxson, B., Gregg, P., Propper, C., Slater, H., and Wilson, D. (2004). *Evaluating the Impact of Performance-Related Pay for Teachers in England*. Working Paper 04/113, Centre for Market and Public Organisation, University of Bristol, 61 pp.

Audit Commission (2001). *Change Here*. London: Audit Commission.

—— (2002). *A Picture of Performance: Early Lessons from Comprehensive Performance Assessment*. London: Audit Commission.

—— (2005). *CPA The Harder Test*. London: Audit Commission.

—— (2009a). *Comprehensive Area Assessment*. London: Audit Commission.

—— (2009b). *Final Score*. London: Audit Commission.

Austin, C. (2008). 'Resourceful, Resilient and Respected', in T. Leunig *et al.*, *Billion Passenger Railways: Lessons from the Past, Prospects for the Future*, pp. 6–9. London: Association of Train Operating Companies. Available at: http://www.atoc-comms.org/admin/userfiles/Billion%20Passenger%20Railway%20090408.pdf.

Ayres, R. (1983). *Banking on the Poor: The World Bank and World Poverty*. Cambridge, Mass.: Massachusetts Institute of Technology Press.

Bahmueller, C. F. (1981). *The National Charity Company: Jeremy Bentham's Silent Revolution*. Berkeley, Calif.: University of California Press.

Bar-Joseph, U., and Sheaffer, Z. (1998). 'Surprise and its Causes in Business Administration and Strategic Studies', *International Journal of Intelligence and Counterintelligence*, 11(3): 331–49.

Barlow, J. P. (1996). *A Declaration of the Independence of Cyberspace*. 8 Feb. Available at: http://w2.eff.org/Censorship/Internet_censorship_bills/barlow_0296.declaration.

Barzelay, M. (2000). *The New Public Management: Improving Research and Policy Dialogue*. Berkeley, Calif.: University of California Press.

Beck, U. (1992). *Risk Society: Towards a New Modernity*. London: Sage.

—— (2006). 'Living in the World Risk Society', *Economy and Society*, 35(3): 329–45.

—— (2009). *World at Risk*. Cambridge: Polity Press.

Beer, S. (1966). *Decision and Control*. London: Wiley.

Bell, D. (1976a). *The Coming of Post-Industrial Society: A Venture in Social Forecasting*. Harmondsworth: Penguin.

—— (1976b). *The Cultural Contradictions of Capitalism*. New York: Basic Books.

Bendix, R. (1977). *Nation-Building and Citizenship*. Berkeley, Calif.: University of California Press.

Beniger, J. (1991). 'Information Society and Global Science', in C. Dunlop and R. Kling (eds.), *Computerization and Controversy: Value Conflicts and Social Choices*, pp. 383–97. London: Academic Press.

Berg, A. (1987). *Malnutrition: What can be Done? Lessons from World Bank Experience*. Washington, DC: World Bank.

Berners-Lee, T. (1989). 'Information Management: A Proposal'. Available at: http://eil.bren.ucsb.edu/~frew/courses/esm595k/documents/Information_Management_A_Proposal.pdf.

—— (1998). 'The World Wide Web: A Very Short Personal History'. Available at: http://www.w3.org/People/Berners-Lee/ShortHistory.html.

—— Hendler, J., and Lassila, O. (2001). 'The Semantic Web: A New Form of Web Content that is Meaningful to Computers will Unleash a Revolution of New Possibilities', *Scientific American* (17 May). Available at: http://www.si.umich.edu/~rfrost/courses/si110/readings/in_out_and_beyond/semantic_wcb.pdf.

—— (2005). Keynote paper to the British Computer Society (BCS) 'Web Science' Workshop, London, 12–13 Sept.

Bertelli, A., and John, P. (2010). 'Government checking government: how performance measures expand distributive politics', *Journal of Politics*, 72: 1–14.

Betts, R. K. (1982). *Surprise Attack*. Washington, DC: Brookings Institution.

—— (1989). 'Surprise, Scholasticism, and Strategy: A Review of Ariel Levite's *Intelligence and Strategic Surprises*', *International Studies Quarterly*, 33(3): 329–43.

Bichard, M. (1999). 'Performance Management: Civil Service Reform', A Report to the Meeting of Permanent Heads of Departments, Sunningdale. London: Cabinet Office, 30 Sept.–1 Oct. Ref: CABI-5195/9912/D4. Available at: http://www.enap.gov.br/downloads/ec43ea4fcivilservice_publicmanagement.pdf.

Binder, S. (2002) 'Injuries among Older Adults: The Challenge of Optimizing Safety and Minimizing Unintended Consequences', *Injury Prevention*, 8(4): iv2–iv4.

Black, C. (1966). *The Dynamics of Modernization*. New York: Harper & Row.

Blair, T. (1998). *The Third Way: New Politics for the New Century*. London: Fabian Society.

Blomberg, T., Yeisley, M., and Lucken, K. (1998). 'American Penology: Words, Deeds, and Consequences', *Crime, Law and Social Change*, 28: 269–86.

Blumenthal, M. S., and Clark, D. D. (2001). 'Rethinking the Design of the Internet: The End-to-End Arguments vs. the Brave New World', *ACM Transactions on Internet Technology*, 1(1): 70–109.

Bogason, P. (2005). 'Postmodern Public Administration', in E. Ferlie, L. E. Lynn, and C. Pollitt (eds.), *The Oxford Handbook of Public Management*, pp. 234–56 (ch. 10). Oxford: Oxford University Press.

Boudon, R. (1982). *The Unintended Consequences of Social Action*. Basingstoke: Macmillan.

Boyne, G. A. (2002). 'Concepts and Indicators of Local Authority Performance: An Evaluation of the Statutory Frameworks in England and Wales', *Public Money and Management*, 22(2): 17–24.

—— (forthcoming). 'Performance Management: Does it Work?', in R. Walker, G. A. Boyne, and G. Brewer (eds.), *Public Management and Performance: The State of the Art*. Cambridge: Cambridge University Press.

—— James, O., John, P., and Petrovsky, N. (2008). *Does Public Service Performance Affect Top Management Turnover?* Discussion Paper 0802, Economic and Social Research Council Public Services Programme. Available at: http://www.publicservices.ac.uk/wp-content/uploads/dp0802-final.pdf.

—— —— —— —— (2009a). 'Democracy and Government Performance: Holding Incumbents Accountable in English Local Governments', *Journal of Politics*, 71(4): 1273–84.

—— —— —— —— (2009b). 'Leadership Change and Government Performance: Political and Managerial Succession and the Performance of English Local Governments', Paper to the 59th Political Studies Association Annual Conference, Manchester, Apr.

—— —— —— —— (2010). 'Does Political Change Affect Senior Management Turnover? An Empirical Analysis of Top-Tier Local Authorities in England', *Public Administration*, 88(1): 136–53.

Braithwaite, R. (1956). *Scientific Explanation*. Cambridge: Cambridge University Press.

Brannan, T., Durose, C., John, P., and Wolman, H. (2008). 'Assessing Best Practice as a Means of Innovation', *Local Government Studies*, 34(1): 23–38.

Branston, J. R. (2002). 'The Price of Independents: An Analysis of the Independent Power Sector in England and Wales', *Energy Policy*, 30: 1313–25.

Brennan, S. (2005). 'An Interview with Sir John Pattison', in S. Brennan, *The NHS IT Project*, pp. 190–4. Oxford: Radcliffe.

Brewster, C., Ciravegna, F., and Wilks, Y. (2001). 'Knowledge Acquisition for Knowledge Management'. Paper to the International Joint Conferences on Artificial

Intelligence (IJCAI-2001). Workshop on Ontology Learning held in conjunction with the 17th International Conference on Artificial Intelligence (IJCAI-01), Seattle, Aug.

—— Iria, J., Ciravegna, F., and Wilks, Y. (2005). 'The Ontology: Chimaera or Pegasus'. Paper to the Dagstuhl Seminar on Machine Learning for the Semantic Web, 13–18 Feb.

British Computer Society (2006). 'The Way Forward for NHS Health Informatics: Where Should NHS Connecting for Health Go from Here?'. Report, Manchester: BCS. Available at: http://www.bcs.org/upload/pdf/BCS-HIF-report.pdf.

British Transport Commission (1955). *Modernisation and Re-equipment of British Railways*. London: British Transport Commission.

Brooks, H. (1986). 'A Typology of Surprises in Technology, Institutions and Development', in W. C. Clark and R. E. Munn (eds.), *Sustainable Development of the Biosphere*, pp. 325–48. Cambridge: Cambridge University Press for the International Institute for Applied Systems Analysis.

Brooks, R. (2007). 'System Failure!', *Private Eye* (15 Mar.): 17–24.

Burnham, D. (1983). *The Rise of the Computer State*. London: Weidenfeld & Nicolson.

Butler, D. E., and King, A. (1965). *The British General Election of 1964*. London: Macmillan.

Byman, D. (2005). 'Strategic Surprise and the September 11 Attacks', *Annual Review of Political Science*, 8 (June): 145–70.

Cabinet Office (2005). *Transformational Government: Enabled by Technology*. Available at: http://www.cio.gov.uk/documents/pdf/transgov/transgov-strategy.pdf.

Capling, A., and Nossal, R. (2006). 'Blowback: Investor-State Dispute Mechanisms in International Trade Agreements', *Governance*, 19(2): 151–72.

Casalino, L. P. (1999). 'The Unintended Consequences of Measuring Quality on the Quality of Medical Care', *New England Journal of Medicine*, 341(15): 1147–50.

Castells, M. (1996). *The Rise of the Network Society*. Oxford: Blackwell.

—— (2001). *The Internet Galaxy: Reflections on the Internet, Business and Society*. Oxford: Oxford University Press.

—— (2009). *Communication Power*. Oxford: Oxford University Press.

Cerf, V. (2001). 'Beyond the Post-PC Internet', *In Commun. ACM* 44(9): 34–7.

—— (2009). 'Cloud Computing on the Internet', *Google Research Blog* (28 Apr.). Available at: http://googleresearch.blogspot.com/2009/04/cloud-computing-and-internet.html.

Cherkaoui, M. (2007). *Good Intentions: Max Weber and the Paradox of Unintended Consequences*. Oxford: Bardwell Press.

Chevalier, A., Peter, D., and Steven, M. (2003). *Teacher Pay and Performance*. Bedford Way Papers 19, London: Institute of Education, University of London.

Chiles, J. (2001). *Inviting Disaster: Lessons from the Edge of Technology*. New York: HarperCollins.

Christou, G., and Simpson, S. (2007). 'Gaining a Stake in Global Internet Governance: The EU, ICANN and Strategic Norm Manipulation', *European Journal of Communication*, 22(2): 147–64.

Churchman, C. W., Ackoff, R. L., and Arnoff, E. L. (1957). *Introduction to Operations Research*. New York: Wiley.

Clark, D. D. (1988). 'The Design Philosophy of the DARPA Internet Protocols', *Computer Communication Review*, 18(4): 106–14.

Clark, D., Partridge, C., Braden, R. T., Davie, B., Floyd, S., Jacobson, V., Katabi, D., Minshall, G., Ramakrishnan, K. K., Roscoe, T., Stoica, I., Wrocklawski, J., and Zhang, L. (2005). 'Making the World (of Communications) a Different Place', *ACM SIGCOMM Computer Communication Review*, 35(2): 91–6.

CLG (Communities and Local Government) (2008). *Local Government Finance Key Facts*. London: Department for Communities and Local Government.

Coiera, E. (2006). *Essentials of Telemedicine and Telecare*. Chichester: Wiley.

Carter of Coles, Lord (2008). *The Independent Review of Pathology Services*. London: Department of Health.

Collingridge, D. (1992). *The Management of Scale: Big Organizations, Big Decisions, Big Mistakes*. London: Routledge.

—— and Margetts, H. (1994). 'Can Government Information Systems be Inflexible Technology? The Operational Strategy Revisited', *Public Administration*, 72: 55–72.

Colomer, J. (2009) *The Science of Politics*. New York: Oxford University Press.

Corbridge, S. E. (1986). *Capitalist World Development: A Critique of Radical Development Geography*. London: Macmillan.

—— (1990). 'Post-Marxism and Development Studies: Beyond the Impasse', *World Development*, 18(5): 623–39.

Cracraft, J. (2003). *The Revolution of Peter the Great*. Cambridge, Mass., and London: Harvard University Press.

Craig, D., and Brooks, R. (2006). *Plundering the Public Sector*. London: Constable.

Craven, P., and Wellman, B. (1973). 'The Network City', *Sociological Inquiry*, 43: 57–88.

Creel, H. G. (1964). 'The Beginnings of Bureaucracy in China: The Origin of the Hsien', *Journal of Asian Studies*, 23(2): 155–83.

Cross, M. (2006). 'Computer Scientists Call for Audit of NHS IT Programme', *BMJ* 332(7547): 930.

Cunha, M. P., Clegg, S. R., and Kamoche, K. (2006). 'Surprises in Management and Organisation: Concept, Sources and a Typology', *British Journal of Management*, 17 (4): 317–29.

Cunningham, H., Humphreys, K., and Gaizauskas, R. (1997). 'GATE: A TIPSTER-based General Architecture for Text Engineering'. Paper to the TIPSTER Text Program (Phase III) 6 Month Workshop, DARPA, Morgan Kaufmann, California.

Dahrendorf, R. (1988). *The Modern Social Conflict*. London: Weidenfeld & Nicolson.

Dallek, R. (1999). *Flawed Giant: Lyndon Johnson and his Times, 1961–1973*. New York: Oxford University Press.

DeJean, J. (1997). *Ancients Against Moderns: Culture Wars and the Making of a Fin de Siècle*. Chicago: University of Chicago Press.

Delpierre, C., Cuzin, L., Fillaux, J., Alvarez, M., Massip, P., and Lang, T. (2004). 'A Systematic Review of Computer-Based Patient Record Systems and Quality of Care: More Randomized Clinical Trials or a Broader Approach?', *International Journal for Quality in Health Care*, 16: 407–16. Available at: http://intqhc.oxford-journals.org/cgi/content/full/16/5/407.

Department of Health (1998). *Information for Health*. London: Department of Health.

—— (2001). *Building the Information Core: Implementing the NHS Plan*. London: Department of Health.

—— (2002). *Delivering Twenty First Century IT Support for the NHS: National Strategic Programme*. London: Department of Health.

DfEE (Department for Education and Employment) (1999). *Teachers: Meeting the Challenge of Change. Technical Consultation Document on Pay and Performance Management*. London: DfEE.

—— (2000). *Recognising Progress: Getting the Most from your Data, Primary School*. London: DfEE, Oct.

Diamond, N., and Graham, H. D. (1997). *The Rise of American Research Universities: Elites and Challengers in the Postwar Era*. Baltimore, MD: Johns Hopkins University Press.

—— —— (2000). 'How should we Rate Research Universities?', *Change* (July/Aug.): 21–33.

Dichev, I. (2001). 'News or Noise? Estimating the Noise in the U.S. News University Rankings', *Research in Higher Education*, 42(3): 237–66.

Dijkstra, E. (1979). *On the Foolishness of Natural Language Programming*, http://www.cs.utexas.edu/users/EWD/transcriptions/EWD06xx/EWD667.html.

DiMaggio, P. J., and Powell, W. W. (1983). 'The Iron Cage Revisited: Institutional Isomorphism and Collective Rationality in Organizational Fields', *American Sociological Review*, 48(2): 147–60.

Dixon, A., Le Grand, J., Henderson, J., Murray, R., and Poteliakhoff, E. (2007). 'Is the British National Health Service Equitable? The Evidence on Socioeconomic Differences in Utilization', *Journal of Health Service Research and Policy*, 12: 104–9.

Dopson, S., and Waddington, I. (1996). 'Managing Social Change: A Process-Sociological Approach to Understanding Organisational Change in the National Health Service', *Sociology of Health and Illness*, 18(4): 525–50.

Douglas, M. (1970). *Natural Symbols*. London: Routledge.

—— (1992). *Risk and Blame: Essays in Cultural Theory*. London: Routledge.

—— and Wildavsky, A. (1982). *Risk and Culture*. Berkeley and Los Angeles, Calif.: University of California Press.

Dowling, B., and Richardson, R. (1997). 'Evaluating Performance-Related Pay for Managers in the National Health Service', *International Journal of Human Resource Management*, 8(3): 348–66.

Downe, J., and Martin, S. J. (2006). 'Joined up Policy in Practice? The Coherence and Impacts of the Local Government Modernisation Agenda', *Local Government Studies*, 32(4): 465–88.

Draper, F. D., and Pitsvada, B. T. (1981). 'ZBB: Looking Back After Ten Years', *Public Administration Review*, 41(1): 76–83.

Drezner, D. W. (2004). 'The Global Governance of the Internet: Bringing the State Back In', *Political Science Quarterly*, 119(3): 477–98.

Dunleavy, P., and O'Leary, B. (1987). *Theories of the State*. Basingstoke: Macmillan.

—— Margetts, H., Bastow, S., and Tinkler, J. (2006). *Digital-Era Governance: IT Corporations, the State and e-Government*. Oxford: Oxford University Press.

Dunn, E., Conrath, D., Bloor, W., and Tranquada, B. (1977). 'An Evaluation of Four Telemedicine Systems for Primary Care', *Health Services Research*, 1: 19–29.

Dunsire, A. (1978). *Control in a Bureaucracy*. Oxford: Robertson.

Durkheim, É. (1964). *The Division of Labor in Society*, tr. G. Simpson. New York: Free Press.

Edgerton, D. (1996). *Science, Technology and the British Industrial Decline*. Cambridge: Cambridge University Press.

Efficiency Unit (1988). *Improving Management in Government: the Next Steps*. Report to the Prime Minister. London: HMSO.

Eisenstadt, S. N. (2000). 'Multiple Modernities', *Daedalus*, 129(1): 1–29.

Ellwood, J. W. (2008). 'Challenges to Public Policy and Public Management Education', *Journal of Policy Analysis and Management*, 27(1): 172–87.

Elster, J. (2009). *Alexis de Tocqueville, the First Social Scientist*. Cambridge: Cambridge University Press.

Engels, F. (1880). 'Socialism: Utopian and Scientific', *Revue Socialiste* (Mar., Apr., and May).

Escobar, A. (1995). *Encountering Development: The Making and Unmaking of the Third World*. Princeton: Princeton University Press.

Espeland, W. N., and Sauder, M. (2007). 'Rankings and Reactivity: How Public Measures Recreate Social Worlds', *American Journal of Sociology*, 113(1): 1–40.

Evans, A. W. (2005). 'Railway Risks, Safety Values and Safety Costs', *Proceedings of the Institution of Civil Engineers*, 158 (Issue TR1; Feb). Available at: http://www.thomastelford.com/journals/DocumentLibrary/TRAN1580102.pdf.PDF.

Everett-Church, R. (1999). 'The Spam that Started it All', *Wired* (13 Apr.). Available at: http://www.wired.com/politics/law/news/1999/04/19098.

Evron, G. (2008). 'Cyber Crime: An Economic Problem'. *CircleID* (6 Sept.). Available at: http://www.circleid.com/posts/89610_cyber_crime_an_economic_problem/.

Faber, M., Manstetten, R., and Proops, J. L. (1992). 'Humankind and the Environment: An Anatomy of Surprise and Ignorance', *Environmental Values*, 1(3): 217–41.

FAO (Food and Agriculture Organization) (2008). 'Hunger on the Rise: Soaring Prices Add 75 Million People to Global Hunger Rolls', *FAO Newsroom*. Available at: http://www.fao.org/newsroom/EN/news /2008/1000923/index.html.

Fapohunda, E. (1988). 'The Nonpooling Household: A Challenge to Theory. A Home Divided: Women and Income in the Third World', in D. Dwyer and J. Bruce (eds.), *A Home Divided: Women and Income in the Third World Countries*, pp. 143–54. Stanford, Calif.: Stanford University Press.

Finder, A. (2001). 'At University of Kentucky, a Push to Aim Higher', *The New York Times* (1 Aug.): A19.

Fine, G. A. (2006). 'The Chaining of Social Problems: Solutions and Unintended Consequences in the Age of Betrayal', *Social Problems*, 53(1): 3–17.

Finer, S. (1997). *The History of Government from the Earliest Times*. Oxford: Oxford University Press.

Finnemore, M. (1997). 'Redefining Development at the World Bank', in F. Cooper and R. Packard (eds.), *International Development and the Social Sciences: Essays on the History and Politics of Knowledge*, pp. 203–27. Berkeley, Calif.: University of California Press.

Folger, R., and Cropanzano, R. (1998). *Organizational Justice and Human Resource Management*. Thousand Oaks, Calif.: Sage.

Fombrun, C. J. (1996). *Reputation: Realizing Value from the Corporate Image*. Boston, Mass.: Harvard Business School Press.

Fordham, M. (2006). 'Disaster and Development Research and Practice: A Necessary Eclecticism', in H. Rodriguez, E. Quaranteli, and R. Dynes (eds.), *Handbook of Disaster Research*, pp. 335–46. New York: Springer.

Foster, C. D. (1963). *The Transport Problem*. London: Blackie.

Franklin, J., Perrig, A., Paxon, V., and Savage, S. (2007). 'An Inquiry into the Nature and Causes of the Wealth of Internet Miscreants'. Paper to the ACM Conference on Computer and Communications Security, Alexandria, VA. Available at: http://www.cs.cmu.edu/~jfrankli/acmccs07/ccs07_franklin_eCrime.pdf.

Frederickson, H. G. (2001a). 'Getting Ranked', *Change* (Jan./Feb.): 49–55.

—— (2001b). 'Reflections on Ranking Master's Degrees in Public Affairs: The Search for Reputational Capital', *Journal of Public Affairs Education*, 7(2): 65–71.

Frissen, P. (1995). 'The Virtual State: Postmodernization, Informatization and Public Administration'. Paper to 'The Governance of Cyberspace' Conference, University of Teesside, 12–13 Apr.

Gains, F., Greasley, S., John, P., and Stoker, G. (2007). 'Failing to Resolve a Long-Standing Representative Crisis: Reforming English Local Government?'. Paper to the European Consortium of Political Research General Conference: *Citizen Engagement in Decentralised Structures*, Pisa, Sept. Available at: http://www.essex.ac.uk/ecpr/events/generalconference/pisa/papers/PP1128.pdf.

Gambetta, D. (1998). 'Concatenations of Mechanisms', in P. Hedström and R. Swedberg (eds.), *Social Mechanisms: An Analytical Approach to Social Theory*, pp. 102–24. Cambridge: Cambridge University Press.

Game, C. (2006). 'Comprehensive Performance Assessment in English Local Government', *International Journal of Productivity and Performance Management*, 55: 466–79.

Geist, M. (2003). 'Cyberlaw 2.0.', *Boston College Law Review*, 44(2): 323–58.

Bibliography

Genschel, P. (1995). *Standards in der Informationstechnik: Institutioneller Wandel in der Internationalen Standardisierung*. Frankfurt/Main: Campus.

George, S., Latham, M., Frongillo, E., Abel, R., and Ethirajan, N. (1993). 'Evaluation of Effectiveness of Good Growth Monitoring in South Indian Villages', *The Lancet*, 342(8867): 348–51.

Gerschenkron, A. (1962). *Economic Backwardness in Historical Perspective: A Book of Essays*. Cambridge, Mass.: Belknap Press of Harvard University Press.

Gerth, H., and Wright Mills, C. (1975). *From Max Weber*. New York: Oxford University Press.

Gibbons, S., and Machin, S. (2005). 'Valuing Rail Access Using Transport Innovations', *Journal of Urban Economics*, 57(1): 148–69.

Giddens, A. (1977). 'Functionalism: Après la Lutte', in A. Giddens, *Studies in Social and Political Theory*, pp. 96–129. London: Hutchinson.

—— (1990). *The Consequences of Modernity*. Cambridge: Polity.

—— (2003). 'The Third Way: The Renewal of Social Democracy', in A. Chadwick and R. Heffernan (eds.), *The New Labour Reader*, pp. 34–8. Cambridge: Polity.

—— (2006). *Sociology*, 5th edn. Cambridge: Polity.

—— and Pierson, C. (1998) *Conversations with Anthony Giddens: Making Sense of Modernity*. Cambridge: Polity.

Gillies, J., and Cailliau, R. (2000). *How the Web was Born: The Story of the World Wide Web*. Oxford: Oxford University Press.

Glennerster, H. (2002). 'United Kingdom Education 1997–2001', *Oxford Review of Economic Policy*, 18(2): 120–36.

Goldsmith, J., and Wu, Y. (2006). *Who Controls the Internet? Illusions of a Borderless World*. Oxford: Oxford University Press.

Google Enterprise Blog (2009). '2008: The Year in Spam', *Google Enterprise Blog* (26 Jan.). Available at: http://googleenterprise.blogspot.com/2009/01/2008-year-in-spam.html.

Gopalan, C. (1992). 'Growth Charts in Primary Child-Health Care: Time for Reassessment', *Indian Journal of Maternal and Child Health*, 3(4): 98–103.

Gormley, W. T., and Weimer, D. Q. (1999). *Organizational Report Cards*. Cambridge, Mass.: Harvard University Press.

Gouré, D. (1993). 'Is there a Military-Technical Revolution in America's Future?', *Washington Quarterly*, 16(4): 175–92.

Gourvish, T. R. (1986). *British Railways 1948–73: A Business History*. Cambridge: Cambridge University Press.

—— (2002). *British Rail 1974–97: From Integration to Privatisation*. Oxford: Oxford University Press.

Grantham, A. (2001). 'How Networks Explain Unintended Policy Implementation Outcomes: The Case of UK Rail Privatisation', *Public Administration*, 79(4): 851–70.

Gray, C. (1989). 'The Cyborg Soldier: The US Military and the Post-modern Warrior', in L. Levidow and K. Robins (eds.), *Cyborg Worlds: The Military Information Society*, pp. 43–73. London: Free Association Books.

Gregory, R. L. (1967). 'Origin of Eyes and Brains', *Nature*, 213: 369–72.

Guenier, R. (2002). 'The NHS National Programme for IT', *Computer Weekly* (25 July): 5.

Gunderson, L. H., Holling, C. S., Peterson, G., and Pritchard, L. (1997). *Resilience in Ecosystems, Institutions and Societies*. Discussion Paper, 92, Beijer International Institute for Ecological Economics. Stockholm: Beijer.

Habermas, J. (1985). 'Modernity: An Incomplete Project', in H. Forster (ed.), *Postmodern Culture*, pp. 3–15. London: Pluto Press.

Hacker, J. (2004). 'Review Article: Dismantling the Health Care State? Political Institutions, Public Policies and the Comparative Politics of Health Reform', *British Journal of Political Science*, 34: 693–724.

Hadari, S. A. (1989). 'Unintended Consequences in Periods of Transition: Tocqueville's "Recollections" Revisited', *American Journal of Political Science*, 33(1): 136–49.

Hafner, K., and Lyon, M. (1996). *Where Wizards Stay up Late*. New York: Simon & Schuster.

Hagan, K. J., and Bickerton, D. (2007). *Unintended Consequences: The United States at War*. London: Reaktion Books.

Hakewill, G. (1630). *An Apologie or Declaration of the Power and Providence of God in the Government of the World*. Oxford: William Turner Printer.

Halberstam, D. (1972). *The Best and the Brightest*. New York: Fawcett Crest.

Hall, P., and Soskice, D. (eds.) (2001). *Varieties of Capitalism: The Institutional Foundations of Comparative Advantage*. Oxford: Oxford University Press.

Hambridge, S. (1995). *Netiquette Guidelines*. Memo. RFC1855. Available at: http://www.faqs.org/rfcs/rfc1855.html.

Hamilton, P. (1991). *Max Weber: Critical Assessments*. London: Routledge.

Handley, M. (2006). 'Why the Internet Only Just Works', *BT Technology Journal*, 24. 119–29.

Harasim, L. M. (1994). 'Networlds: Networks as Social Space', in L. M. Harasim (ed.), *Global Networks: Computers and International Communication*, pp. 15–34. Cambridge: MIT Press.

Harriby, A. L. (1999). 'Progressivism: A Century of Change and Rebirth', in S. M. Milkis and J. M. Mileur (eds.), *Progressivism and the New Democracy*. Amherst, Mass.: University of Massachusetts Press.

Harriss, B. (1991). *Child Nutrition and Poverty in South India*. New Delhi: Concept.

Hassan, H. (1987). *The Postmodern Turn, Essays in Postmodern Theory and Culture*. Athens, OH: Ohio University Press.

Hassol, S. J., and Katzenberger, J. (eds.) (1995). *Elements of Change 1994, Part 2: Anticipating Global Change Surprises*. Aspen, CO: Aspen Global Change Institute.

Haubrich, D., and McLean, I. (2006). 'Assessing Public Service Performance in Local Authorities through CPA: A Research Note on Deprivation', *National Institute Economic Review*, 197(1): 93–105.

—— Gutierrez-Romero, R., and McLean, L. (2008). 'Performance and Deprivation in English Local Government: Correlations and Possible Implications'. Presentation to Oxford Policy Institute meeting, 'Institutions, Incentives and Public Sector

Performance', Oxford, 18 Jan. Available at: http://www.opi.org.uk/events/documents/JanuarysymposiumDirkHaubrich.pdf.

Heaver, R. (2002). *India's Tamil Nadu Nutrition Program: Lessons and Issues in Management and Capacity Development*. Washington, DC: World Bank.

—— (2006). *Good Work: But Not Enough of it. A Review of the World Bank's Experience in Nutrition*. Washington, DC: World Bank.

Heclo, H. (1975). 'OMB and the Presidency: The Problem of Neutral Competence', *The Public Interest*, 38: 80–98.

Heelas, P., Lash, S., and Morris, P. (eds.) (1996). *Detraditionalization*. Oxford: Blackwell.

Heery, E. (1998). 'A Return to Contract? Performance Related Pay in a Public Service', *Work, Employment and Society*, 12(1): 73–95.

Hennessy, P. (2001). *The Prime Minister: The Office and its Holders since 1945*. Basingstoke: Palgrave Macmillan.

Hesse, J. J., Hood, C., and Peters, B. G. (eds.) (2003). *Paradoxes in Public Sector Reform: An International Comparison*. Berlin: Duncker & Humblot.

Hewitt, C. (1972). 'Procedural Semantics', in R. Rustin (ed.), *Natural Language Processing (Courant Computer Science Symposium 8)*, pp. 180–98. New York: Algorithmics Press.

Hirschman, A. O. (1970). *Exit, Voice and Loyalty: Responses to Decline in Firms, Organisations and States*. Cambridge, Mass.: Harvard University Press.

—— (1991). *The Rhetoric of Reaction: Perversity, Futility, Jeopardy*. Cambridge, Mass.: Belknap Press, Harvard University Press.

Hobsbawm, E. J., and Ranger, T. (eds.) (1983). *The Invention of Tradition*. Cambridge: Cambridge University Press.

Holling, C. S. (1986). 'The Resilience of Terrestrial Ecosystems: Local Surprise and Global Change', in W. C. Clark and R. E. Munn (eds.), *Sustainable Development of the Biosphere*, pp. 292–317. Cambridge: Cambridge University Press for the International Institute for Applied Systems Analysis.

Hood, C. (1994). *Explaining Economic Policy Reversals*. Buckingham: Open University Press.

—— (1998). *The Art of the State*. Oxford: Oxford University Press.

—— (2006). 'Gaming in Targetworld: The Targets Approach to Managing British Public Services', *Public Administration Review*, 66(4): 515–21.

—— and Jones, D. K. (eds.) (1996). *Accident and Design: Contemporary Debates in Risk Management*. London: University College London Press.

—— and Peters, B. G. (2004). 'The Middle Aging of New Public Management: Into the Age of Paradox?', *Journal of Public Administration Research and Theory*, 14(3): 267–82.

—— Scott, C., James, O., Jones, G., and Travers, T. (1999). *Regulation Inside Government: Waste-Watchers, Quality Police and Sleaze-Busters*. Oxford: Oxford University Press.

Horrocks, I. (2005). 'Description Logics in Ontology Applications'. Proceeding at 14th International Conference, TABLEAUX 2005, Koblenz, 14–17 Sept. Available at *Lecture Notes in Computer Science: Automated Reasoning with Analytic Tableaux and Related Methods*, 3702: 2–13. Berlin and Heidelberg: Springer.

Huczynski, A. A. (1993). *Management Gurus*. London: Routledge.

Hume, L. J. (1981). *Bentham on Bureaucracy.* Cambridge: Cambridge University Press.

Huntington, S. (1968). *Political Order in Changing Societies*. New Haven, CT: Yale University Press.

—— (1971). 'The Change to Change: Modernization, Development and Politics', *Comparative Politics*, 3(3): 283–322.

—— and Nelson, J. (1976). *No Easy Choice: Political Participation in Developing Countries*. Cambridge, Mass.: Harvard University Press.

IDeA (Improvement and Development Agency) (2009). *Looking Back Moving Forward: Accounts of Council Improvement by Leading Politicians*. London: IDeA. Available at: http://www.idea.gov.uk/idk/aio/9374711.

IDS (Incomes Data Services) (1987). *Public Sector Pay: Review of 1986 and Prospects for 1987*. London: IDS.

—— (1988). *Public Sector Pay: Review of 1987 and Prospects for 1988*. London: IDS.

Inglehart, R. (1997) *Modernization and Postmodernization: Cultural, Economic and Political Change in 43 Societies*. Princeton, NJ: Princeton University Press.

—— and Weizel, C. (2005). *Modernization, Cultural Change and Democracy: The Human Development Sequence*. Cambridge: Cambridge University Press.

Inkeles, A., and Smith, D. (1974). *Becoming Modern: Individual Change in Six Developing Countries*. Cambridge, Mass.: Harvard University Press.

Inland Revenue (1988). *New Pay Arrangements in the Inland Revenue, Text of the Agreement between HM Treasury and the Board of the Inland Revenue (on behalf of the Official Side) and the Inland Revenue Staff Federation, 29 Jan 1988*. London: Her Majesty's Inland Revenue.

Isenberg, D. (1997). 'The Rise of the Stupid Network', *Computer Telephony* (Aug.): 16–26. Available at: http://www.hyperorg.com/misc/stupidnet.html.

James, O. (2009). 'Evaluating the Expectations Disconfirmation and Expectations Anchoring Approaches to Citizen Satisfaction with Local Public Services', *Journal of Public Administration Research and Theory*, 19(1): 107–23.

—— and John, J. (2007). 'Public Management at the Ballot Box: Performance Information and Electoral Support for Incumbent English Local Governments', *Journal of Public Administration Research and Theory*, 17(4): 567–80.

Janis, I. (1982). *Groupthink: Psychological Studies of Foreign Policy Decisions and Fiascoes*, 2nd edn. Boston, Mass.: Houghton Mifflin.

John, P., Ward, H., and Dowding, K. (2005). 'The Bidding Game: Competitive Funding Regimes and the Political Targeting of Urban Programme Schemes', *British Journal of Political Science*, 34(3): 405–28.

Johnston, K. H. (1949). *British Railways and Economic Recovery: A Sociological Study of the Transport Problem*. London: Clerke & Cockeran.

Bibliography

Joy, S. (1973). *The Train that Ran Away: A Business History of British Railways 1948–68*. London: Ian Allen.

Kagan, K. J., and Bickerton, I. J. (2007). *Unintended Consequences: The United States at War*. London: Reaktion.

Kaldor, M. (1999). *New and Old Wars: Organised Violence in a Global Era*. Cambridge: Polity Press.

—— (2001). 'Beyond Militarism, Arms Races and Arms Control'. Essay prepared for the Nobel Peace Prize Centennial Symposium, 6–8 Dec.

Kamath, S. (1992). 'Foreign Aid and India: Financing the Leviathan State', *Policy Analysis*, 170: 1–26.

Kapor, M., and Weitzner, D. J. (1993). 'Social and Industrial Policy for Public Networks: Visions for the Future', in L. Harasim (ed.), *Global Networks: Computers and International Communication*, pp. 299–310. London: MIT Press.

Katznelson, I., and Weingast, B. (eds.) (2005). *Preferences and Situations: Points of Intersection between Historical and Rational Choice Institutionalism*. New York: Russell Sage Foundation.

Kaufman, H. (1956). 'Emerging Conflicts in the Doctrines of Public Administration', *American Political Science Review*, 50: 1057–73.

Kempf, J. and Austein, R. (2004). 'The Rise of the Middle and the Future of End-to-End: Reflections on the Evolution of the Internet Architecture', *Request for Comments*. RFC3724. Available at http://www.faqs.org/rfcs/rfc3724.html.

Kershaw, I. (2007). *Fateful Choices: Ten Decisions that Changed the World, 1940–1941*. London: Penguin.

Kessler, I., and Purcell, J. (1993). 'Staff Pay Survey'. Discussion paper at Amersham International. Mimeo, Templeton College, Oxford.

Khaldûn, I. (1967 [1381]). *The Muqaddimah: An Introduction to History*, tr. F. Rosenthal, abr. N. J. Dawood. London: Routledge & Kegan Paul.

Khong, Y. F. (1992). *Analogies at War: Korea, Munich and the Vietnam Decisions of 1965*. Princeton, NJ: Princeton University Press.

Klein, R. (1998). 'Why Britain is Reorganizing its National Health Service: Yet Again', *Health Affairs*, 17: 111–25.

Kleiner, K. (2008). 'Happy Spamiversary! Spam Reaches 30'. *New Scientist* (25 Apr.). Available at: http://www.newscientist.com/article/dn13777-happy-spamiversary-spam-reaches-30.html.

Klitgaard, R. (1997). '"Unanticipated Consequences" in Anti-Poverty Programmes', *World Development*, 25(12): 1963–72.

Kolb, D. (1986). *The Critique of Pure Modernity: Hegel, Heidegger and After*. London and Chicago: University of Chicago Press.

Kuipers, B. J. (1977). *Representating Knowledge of Large-Scale Space*. Technical Report TR-418. Cambridge, Mass.: MIT Artificial Intelligence Laboratory.

Landel, D., and Marsden, D. (2005). *Performance Related Pay Policies for Government Employees: An Overview of OECD Countries*. Paris: OECD.

Latham, M. (2000). *Modernization as Ideology: American Social Sciences and 'Nation Building' in the Kennedy Era*. Chapel Hill, NC: University of North Carolina Press.

Latour, B. (1993). *We have Never been Modern*, tr. C. Porter. Cambridge, Mass.: Harvard University Press.

Leech, G., Garside, R., and Bryant, M. (1994). 'CLAWS4: The Tagging of the British National Corpus'. Paper to the 15th International Conference on Computational Linguistics, Kyoto. Available at: http://ucrel.lancs.ac.uk/papers/coling.html.

Leiner, B. M., Cerf, V. G., Clark, D. D., Kahn, R., Kleinrock, L., Lynch, D. C., Postel, J., Roberts, L., and Wolff, S. (2001). 'A Brief History of the Internet', *The Internet Society*. Available at: http://www.isoc.org/internet/history/brief.shtml.

Lessig, L. (1995). 'The Path of Cyberlaw', *Yale Law Journal*, 104(7): 1743–55.

—— (1998). 'Governance'. Keynote speech at the CPSR Conference on Internet Governance. http://cyber.law.harvard.edu/works/lessig/cpsr.pdf.

—— (2006). *Code*. 2nd edn. New York: Basic Books.

Leunig, T. (2006). 'Time is Money', *Journal of Economic History*, 66(3): 635–73.

Levidow, L., and Robins, K. (eds.) (1989). *Cyborg Worlds: The Military Information Society*. London: Free Association Books.

Levine, D. (ed.) (1971). *Simmel on Individuality and Social Forms*. Chicago: University of Chicago Press.

Levite, A. (1987). *Intelligence and Strategic Surprises*. New York: Columbia University Press.

—— (1989). '"Intelligence and Strategic Surprises" Revisited: A Response to Richard K. Betts's "Surprise, Scholasticism, and Strategy"', *International Studies Quarterly*, 33(3): 345–9.

Levy, M. (1966). *Modernization and the Structure of Societies: A Setting for International Affairs*. Princeton, NJ: Princeton University Press.

—— (1967). 'Social Patterns (Structures) and Problems of Modernization', in W. E. Moore and R. M. Cook (eds.), *Readings on Social Change*, pp. 189–208. Englewood Cliffs, NJ: Prentice Hall.

Lewis, D. (1972). 'General Semantics', in D. Davidson and G. Harman (eds.), *The Semantics of Natural Language*, pp. 169–218. Amsterdam: Kluwer.

Lewis, J. (1992). 'Gender and the Development of Welfare Regimes', *Journal of European Social Policy*, 2(3): 159–73.

Lipset, S. M. (1959). 'Some Social Requisites of Democracy: Economic Development and Political Legitimacy', *American Political Science Review*, 53(1): 69–105.

—— (1981). *Political Man: The Social Bases of Politics*. Baltimore, MD: Johns Hopkins University Press.

Longuet-Higgins, H. (1972). 'The Algorithmic Description of Natural Language', Proceedings of the Royal Society of London, Series B, *Biological Sciences*, 182: 255–76.

Louis, M. R. (1980). 'Surprise and Sense Making: What Newcomers Experience in Entering Unfamiliar Organisational Settings', *Administrative Sciences Quarterly*, 25(2): 226–51.

McCarthy, J., and Hayes, P. (1969). 'Some Philosophical Problems from the Standpoint of Artificial Intelligence', in B. Meltzer and D. Michie (eds.), *Machine Intelligence 4*, pp. 463–502. Edinburgh: Edinburgh University Press.

McConnell, B. W. (1997). *Governance and the Internet: The Internet as Paradigm*, pp. 71–84. Queenstown: Institute for Information Studies.

McDonough, P. M., Antonio, A. L., Walpole, M., and Perez, L. X. (1998). 'College Rankings: Democratized College Knowledge for Whom?', *Research in Higher Education*, 39(5): 513–37.

Machiavelli, N. (2003). *The Discourses on the First Ten Books of Titus Livy*, tr. L. J. Walker, rev. B. Richardson. Harmondsworth: Penguin.

Macmillan, H. (1933). *Reconstruction*. London: Macmillan.

Mahony, P., Menter, I., and Hextall, I. (2003). *The Impact of Performance Threshold Assessment on Teachers' Work: Summary Report*. Roehampton, University of Surrey, Research Report on ESRC project (ESRC 0002239286).

Makinson, J. (2000). *Incentives for Change: Rewarding Performance in National Government Networks*. London: Public Services Productivity Panel, HM Treasury.

Malamud, C. (1992). *Exploring the Internet: A Technical Travelogue*. Englewood Cliffs, NJ: Prentice Hall.

Maor, D. (1999). 'Teachers-as-Learners: The Role of a Multimedia Professional Development Program in Changing Classroom Practice', *Australian Science Teachers' Journal*, 45(3): 45–50.

Margetts, H. (1999). *Information Technology in Government: Britain and America*. London: Routledge.

Marsden, D. (2007). 'Individual Employee Voice: Renegotiation and Performance Management in Public Services', *International Journal of Human Resource Management*, 18: 1263–78.

—— and Belfield, R. (2007). 'Pay for Performance Where Output is Hard to Measure: The Case of Performance Pay for School Teachers', *Advances in Industrial and Labor Relations*, 15: 1–37. Available at: http://cep.lse.ac.uk/pubs/download/dp0747.pdf.

—— and French, S. (1998). *What a Performance: Performance Related Pay in the Public Services*. London: Centre for Economic Performance Special Report, London School of Economics. Available at: http://cep.lse.ac.uk/pubs/download/special/performance.pdf.

—— and Richardson, R. (1994). 'Performing for Pay? The Effects of "Merit Pay" on Motivation in a Public Service', *British Journal of Industrial Relations*, 32(2): 243–62.

Martin, S. J. (2008). *The State of Local Services*. London: Department of Communities and Local Government.

—— Downe, J., Grace, C., and Nutley, S. (2009). 'Evaluating Organizational Effectiveness: The Utilization and Validity of Whole Authority Assessments',

Evaluation, 16 (forthcoming). Available at: http://www.publicservices.ac.uk/wp-content/uploads/evaluation-evaluating-organizational-effectiveness.pdf.

Mascie-Taylor, C., and Rosetta, L. (2009). 'Factors in the Regulation of Fertility in Deprived Populations', *Annals of Human Biology*, 36(5): 642–52.

Mason, E., and Asher, R. (1973). *The World Bank since Bretton Woods*. Washington, DC: Brookings Institution.

Megaw, J. (1982). *Inquiry into Civil Service Pay: Report of an Inquiry into the Principles and the System by which the Remuneration of the Non-Industrial Civil Service should be Determined*. Cmnd 8590, London: HMSO.

Mencher, J. (1988). 'Women's Work and Poverty: Women's Contributions to Household Maintenance in Two Regions of South India', in J. Bruce and D. Dwyer (eds.), *A Home Divided: Women and Income Control in the Third World*, pp. 99–119. Stanford, Calif.: Stanford University Press.

Merton, R. K. (1936). 'The Unanticipated Consequences of Purposive Social Action', *American Sociological Review*, 1(6): 894–904.

—— (1968). *Social Theory and Social Structure*. 2nd edn. New York: Free Press.

MessageLabs (2008). 'MessageLabs Intelligence: 2008 Annual Security Report'. Available at: http://www.messagelabs.co.uk/intelligence.aspx.

Meyer, M., and Gupta, V. (1994). 'The Performance Paradox', in B. M. Straw and L. L. Cummings (eds.), *Research in Organizational Behavior*, vol. 19, pp. 309–69. Greenwich, CT: JAI Press.

Miller, W. W. (1996). *Durkheim, Morals and Modernity*. London: UCL Press.

Ministerial Taskforce on the NHS Summary Care Record (2006). *Report of the Ministerial Taskforce on the NHS Summary Care Record*. Available at: http://www.connecting forhealth.nhs.uk/resources/policyandguidance/care_record_taskforce_doc.pdf.

Monnet, J. (1978). Memoirs. Tr. by R. Mayne. London: Collins.

Moore, B., Jr. (1966). *Social Origins of Dictatorship and Democracy: Lord and Peasant in the Making of the Modern World*. Boston, Mass.: Beacon Press.

Moore, G., Willemain, T., Bonnano, R., Clark, W., Martin, R., and Mogielnicki, R. (1975). 'Comparison of Television and Telephone for Remote Medical Consultation', *New England Journal of Medicine*, 292(14): 729–32.

Moran, M. (1999). *Governing the Health Care State*. Manchester: Manchester University Press.

—— (2003). *The British Regulatory State: High Modernism and Hyper-Innovation*. Oxford: Oxford University Press.

Morgeson, F. P., and Nahrgang, J. D. (2008). 'Same as it Ever was: Recognizing Stability in the Business Week Rankings', *Academy of Management Learning and Education*, 7(1): 26–41.

Morrison, H. (1933). *Socialisation and Transport: The Organisation of Socialised Industries with Particular Reference to the London Passenger Transport Bill*. London: Constable.

—— (1938). *British Transport at Britain's Service*. London: British Labour Publications.

Morrison, H. (2009). 'An Impossible Future: John Perry Barlow's "Declaration of the Independence of Cyberspace"', *New Media and Society*, 11(1–2): 53–72.

Moynihan, D. P. (1969). *Maximum Feasible Misunderstanding: Community Action in the War on Poverty*. New York: Free Press.

Nabarro, D., and Chinnock, P. (1988). 'Growth Monitoring: Inappropriate Promotion of an Appropriate Technology', *Social Science and Medicine*, 26(9): 941–8.

Nahar, S., Mascie-Taylor, C. G. N., and Ara Begum, H. (2009). 'Impact of Targeted Food Supplementation on Pregnancy Weight Gain and Birth Weight in Rural Bangladesh: An Assessment of the Bangladeshi Integrated Nutrition Program (BINP)', *Public Health Nutrition*, 12(8): 1205–12.

NAO (UK National Audit Office) (1989). *Manpower Planning in the Civil Service*. Cmnd 398, London: HMSO.

National Performance Review (NPR) (1993). *From Red Tape to Results: Creating a Government that Works Better and Costs Less*. Washington, DC: Government Printing Office.

National Research Council (1995). *Research-Doctorate Programs in the United States: Continuity and Change*. Washington, DC: National Research Council.

Nelson, W. W. (1987). 'Cheap or Efficient: An Examination of English Elementary Education during the Era of Payment by Results', Ph.D. thesis, University of Iowa.

Newberry, S. (2002). 'Intended or Unintended Consequences? Resource Erosion in New Zealand's Government Departments', *Financial Management and Accountability*, 18: 309–30.

Nguyen, D. T., and Alexander, J. (1996). 'The Coming of Cyberspace Time and the End of the Polity', in R. Shields (ed.), *Cultures of Internet: Virtual Spaces, Real Histories, Living Bodies*, pp. 99–124. London: Sage.

Nicholson, D. (2008). 'Oral Evidence in Public Accounts Committee', *The National Programme for IT in the NHS: Progress*. HC153, Ev. 1–20. London, TSO.

Nirenburg, S., and Wilks, Y. (2001). 'What's in a Symbol: Ontology, Representation and Language', *Journal of Theoretical and Empirical AI*, 13(1): 9–23.

NUT (UK National Union of Teachers) (1999). *Teaching at the Threshold: The NUT Response to the Government's Green Papers. Meeting the Challenge of Change—England, the Best for Teaching and Learning—Wales*. London: National Union of Teachers, Mar.

Obama, B. (2009). Inaugural speech. Available from White House at: http://www.whitehouse.gov/the_press_office/president_barack_obamas_inaugural_address/.

O'Connor, J. S. (1993). 'Gender, Class and Citizenship in the Comparative Analysis of Welfare State Regimes: Theoretical and Methodological Issues', *British Journal of Sociology*, 44 (3): 501–18.

Office of Rail Regulation (2007). *Station Usage Figures for 2006–7*. Available at: http://www.rail-reg.gov.uk/server/show/nav.1529.

Officer, L. H. (2009). 'Purchasing Power of British Pounds from 1264 to Present', *Measuring Worth*. Available at: http://www.measuringworth.com/ppoweruk/.

Olivier de Sardan, J. P. (2005). *Anthropology and Development: Understanding Continuity and Social Change*. London: Zed Books.

Opp, K.-D. (2002). 'When do Norms Emerge by Human Design and When by the Unintended Consequences of Human Action?', *Rationality and Society*, 14(2): 131–58.

Owen, D. (2008). *In Sickness and in Power: Illness in Heads of Government during the Last 100 Years*. London: Methuen.

Owen, Sir G. (1999). *From Empire to Europe*. London: Harper Collins.

Parsons, C. (2007). *How to Map Arguments in Political Science*. Oxford: Oxford University Press.

Parsons, T. (1966). *Societies: Evolutionary and Comparative Perspectives*. Englewood Cliffs, NJ: Prentice-Hall.

—— (1967). *Sociological Theory and Modern Society*. New York: Free Press.

—— (1971). *The System of Modern Societies*. Englewood Cliffs, NJ: Prentice-Hall.

Perkin, H. (1969). *The Origins of Modern English Society 1780–1880*. London: Routledge & Kegan Paul.

—— (1989). *The Rise of Professional Society: England since 1880*. London: Routledge.

—— (1996). *The Third Revolution: Professional Elites in the Modern World*. London: Routledge.

Perry, J. L. (1995). 'Ranking Public Administration Programs', *Journal of Public Administration Education*, 1(2): 132–5.

Poissant, L., Pereira, J., Tamblyn, R., and Kawasumi, Y. (2005). 'The Impact of Electronic Health Records on Time Efficiency of Physicians and Nurses: A Systematic Review', *Journal of American Medical Information Association*, 12: 505–16.

Pollitt, C. (2003). 'Joined-up Government: A Survey', *Political Studies Review*, 1(1): 34–49.

—— and Bouckaert, G. (2004). *Public Management Reform: A Comparative Analysis*. 2nd edn. Oxford: Oxford University Press.

—— Van Thiel, S., and Homburg, V. (eds.) (2007). *The New Public Management in Europe: Adaptation and Alternatives*. London: Palgrave Macmillan.

Post, D., and Johnson, D. R. (1996). 'Law and Borders: The Rise of Law in Cyberspace', *Stanford Law Review*, 48: 1367.

Post, D. G. (1998). 'The "Unsettled Paradox": The Internet, the State, and the Consent of the Governed', *Indiana Journal of Global Legal Studies*, 5(2): 521–43.

Preston, A. (2006). *The War Council: McGeorge Bundy, the NSC and Vietnam*. Cambridge, Mass.: Harvard University Press.

Preston, F. W., and Roots, R. I. (2004). 'Introduction: Law and its Unintended Consequences', *American Behavioural Scientist*, 47(11): 1371–5.

Priestley, R. (1955). *Report: Royal Commission on the Civil Service 1953–55*. Parliamentary Papers, Session 1955–6, vol. xi, Cmnd 9613, London: HMSO.

Provos, N., McNamee, D., Mavrommatis, P., Wang, K., and Modadugu, N. (2007). 'The Ghost in the Browser: Analysis of Web-Based Malware'. Google. Available at: http://www.usenix.org/events/hotbots07/tech/full_papers/provos/provos.pdf.

Pryke, R., and Dodgson, J. (1975). *The British Rail Problem: A Case Study in Economic Disaster*. Boulder, CO: Westview.

Przeworski, A., and Limongi, F. (1997). 'Modernization: Theories and Facts', *World Politics*, 49(2): 155–83.

Bibliography

PTC (Public Services, Tax and Commerce Union) (1996). *Whatever Happened to a National Civil Service?* London: PTC.

Pullen, W. (1993). 'Strategic Shocks: Managing Discontinuous Change', *International Journal of Public Sector Management*, 6(1): 30–9.

Putnam, H. (1975). *Mind, Language and Reality.* Cambridge: Cambridge University Press.

Pyle, D., and Greiner, T. (2003). 'India: Country Perspectives', in S. Gillespie, M. McLachlan, and R. Shrimpton (eds.), *Combating Malnutrition: Time to Act*, pp. 111–20. Washington, DC: World Bank.

Rao, N. (2002). 'Labour and Education: Secondary Reorganisation and the Neighbourhood School', *Contemporary British History*, 16(2): 99–120.

Ratanawijitrasin, S., Soumeraib, S. B., and Weerasuriya, K. (2001). 'Do National Medicinal Drug Policies and Essential Drug Programs Improve Drug Use? A Review of Experiences in Developing Countries', *Social Science and Medicine*, 53: 831–44.

Read, P. P. (1993). *Ablaze.* London: Secker & Warburg.

Reed, D. P., Saltzer, J. H., and Clark, D. (1998). *Active Networking and End-to-End Arguments.* Available at: http://web.mit.edu/Saltzer/www/publications/endtoend/ANe2ecomment.html.

Reidenberg, J. R. (1998). 'Lex Informatica: The Formulation of Information Policy Rules through Technology', *Texas Law Review*, 76(3): 553–84.

Revelli, F. (2008). 'Performance Competition in Local Media Markets', *Journal of Public Economics*, 92: 1585–94.

Rhodes, R. A. (1997). *Understanding Governance: Policy Networks, Governance, Reflexivity and Accountability.* Buckingham: Open University Press.

Richardson, R. (1999). *Performance Related Pay in Schools: An Assessment of the Green Papers.* Report for the National Union of Teachers. London: NUT.

Roberfroid, D., Lefèvre, P., Hoerée, T., and Kolsteren, P. (2005). 'Perceptions of Growth Monitoring and Promotion Among an International Panel of District Medical Officers', *Journal of Health, Population and Nutrition*, 23(3): 207–14.

Rodriguez, D. A., Targa, F., and Aytur, S. A. (2006). 'Transport Implications of Urban Containment Policies: A Study of the Largest Twenty-Five US Metropolitan Areas', *Urban Studies*, 43(10): 1879–97.

Rogers, E. M. (1995). *Diffusion of Innovations.* 4th edn. New York: Free Press.

Rose, R. (1977). 'Implementation and Evaporation: The Record of MBA', *Public Administration Review*, 37(1): 64–71.

Ross, S. E., and Lin, C. T. (2003). 'The Effects of Promoting Patient Access to Medical Records: A Review', *Journal of American Medical Information Association*, 10: 129–38.

Rostow, W. W. (1960). *The Stages of Economic Growth: A Non-Communist Manifesto*, ch. 2, pp. 4–16. Cambridge: Cambridge University Press.

Roth, G., and Schlucter, W. (1979). *Max Weber's Vision of History: Ethics and Methods.* Berkeley, Calif.: University of California Press.

Royal Commission on Transport (1931). *Final Report: The Coordination and Development of Transport.* Cmnd 3751 (Sir Arthur Griffiths-Boscawen), London: HMSO.

Russell, A. L. (2006). '"Rough Consensus and Running Code" and the Internet-OSI Standards War', *IEEE Annals of the History of Computing* (July–Sept.): 48–61.

Rustow, D. A. (1968) 'Modernization and Comparative Politics: Prospects in Research and Theory', *Comparative Politics*, 1(1): 37–51.

Rustow, W. (1962). *Political Development: The Vanishing Dream of Stability*. Washington, DC: Brookings Institution.

Saltzer, J. H., Reed, D. P., and Clark, D. (1984). 'End-to-End Arguments in System Design', *ACM Transactions on Computer Systems*, 2(4): 277–88.

Salus, P. H. (1995). *Casting the Net: From Arpanet to Internet and Beyond*. Reading, Mass.: Addison-Wesley.

Santos, B. S. (2001). 'Toward an Epistemology of Blindness: Why the New Forms of "Ceremonial Adequacy" Neither Regulate Nor Emancipate', *European Journal of Social Theory*, 4(3): 251–79.

Schank, R. (1972). 'Conceptual Dependency: A Theory of Natural Language Understanding', *Cognitive Psychology*, 3(4): 552–631.

Schechter, M. (1988). 'The Political Roles of Recent World Bank Presidents', in L. Finkelstein (ed.), *Politics in the United Nations System*, pp. 350–84. Durham, NC: Duke University Press.

Schick, A. (1973). 'A Death in the Bureaucracy: The Demise of Federal PPB', *Public Administration Review*, 33(2): 146–56.

Schneider, L. (1971). 'Dialectic in Sociology', *American Sociological Review*, 36(4): 667–78.

Schneider, S. H., Turner, B. L., and Garriga, H. M. (1998). 'Imaginable Surprise in Global Climate Science', *Journal of Risk Research*, 1(2): 165–85.

Schwartz, B. (1972). 'The Limits of "Tradition versus Modernity" in Categories of Explanation: The Case of the Chinese Intellectuals', *Daedalus*, 101(2): 71–88.

Schwarz, M. and Thompson, M. (1990). *Divided we Stand*. Hemel Hempstead: Harvester Wheatsheaf.

Scott, J. C. (1998). *Seeing like a State: How Certain Schemes to Improve the Human Condition have Failed*. New Haven, CT: Yale University Press.

Sculley, J. (1991). 'The Relationship between Business and Higher Education', in C. Dunlop and R. Kling (eds.), *Computerization and Controversy: Value Conflicts and Social Choices*. London: Academic Press.

Secretaries of State (1989). *Working for Patients*. Cmnd 555, London: HMSO.

Select Committee of the House of Lords on Science and Technology of the House (2007). 5th Report. Vol. i (HL Paper 165-I) (2006–07). London. Available at: http://www.publications.parliament.uk/pa/ld200607/ldselect/ldsctech/165/16502.htm.

Select Committee on the Nationalised Industries (1960). *Report with Proceedings (British Railways)*. Parliamentary session 1959–60 (254).

Select Committee on the National Industries (1961). *The Financial and Economic Obligations of the Nationalised Industries*. 1961 White Paper. Cmnd 1337. London: HMSO.

Sellar, W. C., and Yeatman, R. J. (1930). *1066 and All That*. London: Methuen.

Service, E. R. (1975). *Origins of the State and Civilization: The Process of Cultural Evolution*. New York: Norton.

Shah, R. C., and Kesan, J. P. (2003). 'The Privatization of the Internet's Backbone Network'. Paper to the National Science Foundation. Available at: http://www.governingwithcode.org/journal_articles/pdf/Backbone.pdf.

Sieber, S. (1981). *Fatal Remedies*. New York: Plenum.

Silberman, B. (1993). *Cages of Reason: The Rise of the Rational State in France, Japan, the United States and Great Britain*. Chicago: University of Chicago Press.

Simmel, G. (1955). *Conflict and the Web of Group-Affiliations*, tr. K. H. Wolff and R. Bendix. New York: Free Press.

Smithson, M. (1988). *Ignorance and Uncertainty: Emerging Paradigms*. New York: Springer.

Spar, D. L. (1999). 'Lost in (Cyber)Space: The Private Rules of Online Commerce', in C. Cutler, T. Porter, and V. Haufler, *Private Authority and International Affairs*, pp. 31–52. Albany, NY: Suny Press.

Spärck Jones, K. (2004). 'What's New about the Semantic Web?'. Paper at ACM SIGIR Forum.

Specter, M. (2007). 'Damn Spam: The Losing War on Junk E-mail', *The New Yorker* (6 Aug.). Available at: http://www.newyorker.com/reporting/2007/08/06/070806fa_fact_specter.

Sridhar, D. (2007). 'Economic Ideology and Politics in the World Bank: Defining Hunger', *New Political Economy*, 12(4): 499–516.

—— (2008). *The Battle Against Hunger: Choice, Circumstance and the World Bank*. Oxford: Oxford University Press.

Star, S. L., and Griesemer, J. R. (1989). 'Institutional Ecology, "Translations" and Boundary Objects: Amateurs and Professionals in Berkeley's Museum of Vertebrate Zoology, 1907–39', *Social Studies of Science*, 19: 387–420.

Steinberg, P. F. (2007). 'Causal Assessment in Small-N Policy Studies', *Policy Studies Journal*, 35(2): 181–204.

Steward, J. (2003). 'Sobig.a and the Spam you Received Today'. *SecureWorks* (21 Apr.). Available at: http://www.secureworks.com/research/threats/sobig.

Stinchcombe, A. L. (1986). 'Rationality and Social Structure: An Introduction', in A. L. Stinchcombe, *Stratification and Organisation: Selected Papers*, pp. 1–32. Cambridge: Cambridge University Press.

Stoker, G. (2004). *Transforming Local Governance: From Thatcherism to New Labour*. Basingstoke: Palgrave Macmillan.

Stone-Gross, B., Cova, M., Cavallaro, L., Gilbert, B., Szydlowski, M., Kemmerer, R., Kruegel, C., and Vigna, G. (2009) 'Your Botnet is My Botnet: Analysis of a Botnet Takeover'. http://www.cs.ucsb.edu/~seclab/projects/torpig/torpig.pdf.

Strauss, L. (1995). *Thoughts on Machiavelli*. Chicago: University of Chicago Press.

Streets, D. G., and Glantz, M. H. (2000). 'Exploring the Concept of Climate Surprise', *Global Environmental Change*, 10: 97–107.

Sztompka, P. (1993). *The Sociology of Social Change*. Oxford: Blackwell.

Taylor, F. W. (1967). *The Principles of Scientific Management*. New York: Norton.

Teasley III, C. E. (1995). 'The Bad (U.S.) News Ranking of MPA Programs', *Journal of Public Administration Education*, 1(2): 136–41.

Tenner, E. (1996). *Why Things Bite Back: Technology and the Revenge Effect*. London: Butterworth.

Therborn, G. (2000). 'Modernization Discourses, their Limitations and their Alternatives', in W. Schelkle, W.-H. Krauth, M. Kohli, and G. Elwert (eds.), *Paradigms of Social Change: Modernization, Development, Transformation, Evolution*. Frankfurt and New York: Campus Verlag and St Martin's Press.

Thomas, R., and Martin, J. (2006). 'The Underground Economy: Priceless', *Login* (Dec.). Available at: http://usenix.org/publications/login/2006-12/openpdfs/cymru.pdf.

Thompson, M. (1993). *Pay and Performance: the Employee Experience*. IMS Report, 218. Brighton: Institute of Manpower Studies.

—— and Wildavsky, A. (1986). 'A Cultural Theory of Information Bias in Organisations', *Journal of Management Studies*, 23(3): 273–86.

—— Ellis, R. J., and Wildavsky, A. (1990). *Cultural Theory*. Boulder, CO: Westview Press.

Tilly, C. (ed.) (1975). *The Formation of National States in Western Europe*. Princeton, NJ: Princeton University Press.

—— (1984). *Big Structures, Large Processes, Huge Comparisons*. New York: Russell Sage Foundation.

—— (1992). *Coercion, Capital and European States, AD 990–1992*. Oxford: Blackwell.

—— (1996). 'Invisible Elbow', *Sociological Forum*, 11(4): 589–601.

Timmerman, P. (1986). 'Mythology and Surprise in the Sustainable Development of the Biosphere', in W. C. Clark and R. E. Munn (eds.), *Sustainable Development of the Biosphere*, pp. 436–53. Cambridge: Cambridge University Press for the International Institute for Applied Systems Analysis.

Tipps, D. C. (1973). 'Modernization Theory and the Comparative Study of Societies: A Critical Perspective', *Comparative Studies in Society and History*, 15(2): 199–226.

Tirole, J. (1994). 'The Internal Organisation of Government', *Oxford Economic Papers*, 46(1): 1–29.

Tocqueville, A. de (1949). *L'Ancien Régime et la Révolution*. Oxford: Clarendon Press.

Toennies, F. (1887). *Gemeinschaft und Gesellschaft*. Leipzig: Fues's Verlag; 8th edn. Leipzig: Buske, 1935 (repr. Darmstadt: Wissenschaftliche Buchgesellschaft, 2005). Tr. C. P. Loomis, *Community and Society*. Ann Arbor: Michigan State University Press, 1957.

Toffler, A. (1970). *Future Shock*. London: Pan Books.

—— (1980). *The Third Wave*. New York: Bantam Books.

—— (1990). *Power Shift*. New York: Bantam Books.

Tomlinson, J. (1997). *Democratic Socialism and Economic Policy: The Attlee Years, 1945–1951*. Cambridge: Cambridge University Press.

Tracy, J., and Waldfogel, J. (1997). 'The Best Business Schools: A Market-based Approach', *Journal of Business*, 70(1): 1–31.

Trieshmann, J. S., Dennis, A. R., Northcroft, C. B., and Niemi, A. W. (2000). 'Serving Multiple Constituencies in the Business School: MBA Programs Versus Research Performance', *Academy of Management Journal*, 43(6): 1130–41.

Tuchman, B. W. (1984). *The March of Folly: From Troy to Vietnam*. London: Abacus.

Tunbridge, R. (1965). *The Standardization of Hospital Medical Records*. London: HMSO.

Tuohy, C. (1999). *Accidental Logics: The Dynamics of the Health Care Arena in the United States, Britain and Canada*. New York: Oxford University Press.

United States Department of Commerce (1998). Management of Internet Names and Addresses (White Paper). http://www.icann.org/en/general/white-paper-05jun98.htm.

Uttam, J. (2006). 'Korea's New Techno-Scientific State', *China Report*, 42(3): 257–68.

Valauskas, E. J. (1996). 'Lex Networkia: Understanding the Internet Community', *First Monday*, 1(4). Available at: http://outreach.lib.uic.edu/www/issues/issue4/valauskas/index.html.

Van Creveld, M. (1999). *The Rise and Decline of the State*. Cambridge: Cambridge University Press.

Van Eeten, M. J., and Bauer, J. M. (2008). *Economics of Malware: Security Decisions, Incentives and Externalities*. STI Working Paper Series (2008/1) JT03246705. Paris: OECD. Available at: http://www.oecd.org/dataoecd/53/17/40722462.pdf.

Van Hollen, C. (2003). *Birth on the Threshold: Childbirth and Modernity in South India*. Berkeley, Calif.: University of California Press.

Ventriss, C. (1995). 'The Rating System: Determining What Constitutes a Quality Program', *Journal of Public Administration Education*, 1(2): 142–53.

Vernon, R. (1979). 'Unintended Consequences', *Political Theory*, 7(1): 57–73.

Verweij, M., and Thompson, M. (eds.) (2006). *Clumsy Solutions for a Complex World: Governance, Politics and Plural Perceptions*. Basingstoke: Palgrave Macmillan.

Vijayaraghavan, K. (1997). 'India: The Tamil Nadu Nutrition Project. A Case Study of the Communication Component: Nutrition Education for the Public'. Paper to the United Nations Food and Agriculture Organization (FAO)'s Expert Consultation, Rome.

Wagner, P. (2008). *Modernity as Experience and Interpretation: A New Sociology of Modernity*. Cambridge: Polity Press.

Waldman, A. (2002). 'India's Poor Starve as Wheat Rots'. *New York Times* (2 Dec.). Available at: http://www.nytimes.com/2002/12/02/international/asia/02FARM.html?pagewanted=all

Walker, J. (2003). 'The Digital Imprimatur: How Big Brother and Big Media can Put the Internet Genie Back in the Bottle', *Knowledge, Technology and Policy*, 16(3): 24–77. Available at: http://www.fourmilab.ch/documents/digital-imprimatur.

Wall, D. S. (2005). 'Digital Realism and the Governance of Spam as Cybercrime', *European Journal on Criminal Policy and Research*, 10(4): 309–35.

Walton, R. E., and McKersie, R. B. (1965). *A Behavioral Theory of Labour Negotiations: An Analysis of a Social Interaction System*. New York: McGraw-Hill.

Wanless, D. (2002). *Securing our Future Health: Taking A Long-Term View*. London: HM Treasury.

Ward, R. and Rustow, D. (eds.) (1964). *Political Modernization in Japan and Turkey*. Princeton, NJ: Princeton University Press.

Weber, M. (1968). *Economy and Society: An Outline of Interpretive Sociology*. New York: Bedminster.

Webster, C. (2002). *The National Health Service: A Political History*. Oxford: Oxford University Press.

Weick, K. E. (1995). *Sense Making in Organisations*. London: Sage.

—— (2001). *Making Sense of the Organisation*. Oxford: Blackwell.

—— and Sutcliffe, K. M. (2001). *Managing the Unexpected: Assuring High Performance in an Age of Complexity*. San Francisco, Calif.: Jossey-Bass.

Welch, D. A. (2005). *Painful Choices: A Theory of Foreign Policy Change*. Princeton, NJ: Princeton University Press.

Weldes, J. (1999). *Constructing National Interests: The United States and the Cuban Missile Crisis*. Minneapolis, MN: University of Minnesota Press.

Wellman, B. (1979). 'The Community Question: The Intimate Networks of East Yorkers', *American Journal of Sociology*, 84 (Mar.): 1201–31.

Werle, R. (2002). 'Internet @ Europe: Overcoming Institutional Fragmentation and Policy Failure, in J. Jordana (ed.), *Governing Telecommunications and the New Information Society in Europe*, pp. 137–58. Cheltenham: Edward Elgar.

White, H. (2005). 'Comment on Contributions Regarding the Impact of the Bangladesh Integrated Nutrition Project', *Health Policy and Planning*, 20(6): 408–11.

White, L., Jr. (1968). *Medieval Technology and Social Change*, paperback edn. Oxford: Oxford University Press; 1st publ. 1962.

Whitten, P. S., Mair, F. S., Haycox, A., May, C. R., Williams, T. L., and Hellmich, S. (2002). 'Systematic Review of Cost Effectiveness Studies of Telemedicine Interventions', *British Medical Journal*, 324: 1434–7.

Wiener, N. (1948). *Cybernetics*. New York: Wiley.

Wildavsky, A. (1988). *Searching for Safety*. New Brunswick, NJ: Transaction Publishers.

Wilks, Y. (2005). 'What would a Wittgensteinian Computational Linguistics be like?' Paper at the International Congress on Pragmatics, Garda, Italy.

—— (2008). 'The Semantic Web: Apotheosis of Annotation, But What are its Semantics?', *IEEE Intelligent Systems*, 23(3): 41–9.

Williams, H. (ed.) (2009). *In our Time: The Speeches that Shaped the Modern World*. London: Quercus.

Willis, E., Malloy, M., and Kliegman, R. M. (2000). 'Welfare Reform Consequences for Children: The Wisconsin Experience', *Pediatrics*, 106: 83–90.

Willman, P., Bryson, A., and Gomez, R. (2006). 'The Sound of Silence: Which Employers Choose No Employee Voice and Why?', *Socio-Economic Review*, 4(2): 283–300.

Wilson, D., and Game, C. (2006). *Local Government in the United Kingdom*. 4th edn. Basingstoke: Palgrave Macmillan.

Wilson, W. (1941). 'The Study of Administration', *Political Science Quarterly*, 56(4): 481–506.

Wirtz, J. (2006). 'Responding to Surprise', *Annual Review of Political Science*, 9: 45–65.

Wohlstetter, R. (1962). *Pearl Harbour: Warning and Decision*. Stanford, Calif.: Stanford University Press.

Wolfson, M., and Hourigan, M. (1997). 'Unintended Consequences and Professional Ethics: Criminalization of Alcohol and Tobacco Use by Youth and Young Adults', *Addiction*, 92(9): 1159–64.

Woods, N. (2006). *The Globalizers: The IMF, the World Bank, and their Borrowers*. Ithaca, NY: Cornell University Press.

Woods, W. (1975). 'What's in a Link: Foundations for Semantic Networks', in D. Bobrow and A. Collins (eds.), *Representation and Understanding: Studies in Cognitive Science*, pp. 35–82. New York: Academic Press.

Wootton, R. (2001). 'Telemedicine', *BMJ* 323: 557–60.

World Bank (2006). *Repositioning Nutrition as Central to Development*. Washington, DC: World Bank.

World Bank, Operation Evaluation Department (OED) (1995). *Tamil Nadu and Child Nutrition: A New Assessment*. Washington, DC: OED.

Wragg, E. C., Haynes, G. S., Wragg, C. M., and Chamberlin, R. P. (2001). *Performance Related Pay: the Views and Experiences of 1,000 Primary and Secondary Head Teachers*. Teachers' Incentive Pay Project, Occasional Paper, 1. Exeter: University of Exeter.

Zegart, A. B. (2007). *Spying Blind: The CIA, the FBI and the Origins of 9/11*. Princeton, NJ: Princeton University Press.

Zittrain, J. (2006). 'The Generative Internet', *Harvard Law Review*, 119: 1974–2040.

—— (2008). *The Future of the Internet, and How to Stop it*. London: Penguin Books.

Index

Index

Index

'Scientific Management' movement 185
Scott, James C. 14, 41, 42, 43, 232
  Seeing like a State 5, 35–6, 132
Second World War 54–5
Sellar, W. C., and Yeatman, R. J. 102
Semantic Web (SW) 101, 106–12, 116, 224,
  230, 231
Service, E. R. 28–9
Sieber, Sam 5, 12
Siegel, Martha 94
Silberman, B. 38
Simmel, Georg 9, 13, 32, 45
6, P. 12
Skype 104
Smith, Adam: *Treatise of Human Nature, A* 12
Smith, D. *see* Inkeles, A., and Smith, D.
Sobig internet virus 97
social mobility 21, 29, 31
social networking 103, 104
social sciences 17–18, 46, 48
Society Policy Association 21
Soviet Union 5–6, 12 *see also* Russia
specialization 27, 40
  administration 38
  and professionalization 31
  railways 232–3
  technology 34, 41
  universities, American 233
  university and college ranking 74–5
Specter, M. 95
speech recognition 103
speed 156–7
  railways 156, 157, 159–64, 167, 233
Stalin, Joseph 33
standardization 26, 29, 43
  administration 38
  bureaucracy 35, 41
  education 170
  internet 230–1
  National Health Service (NHS) 139, 146,
    153–4, 231–2
  railways 232
  telecommunication networks 84
Stanford University AI Lab 103–4
State University of New York Albany 75
Stedeford Advisory Group Inquiry into rail
  investment 174
Stinchcombe, A. L. 49
Strong Local Leadership - Quality Public Services
  (White Paper) 208
surprise
  definition of 51
  and internet 103, 104, 116, 230, 231
  and policies, consequences of 53

and risk 55–6
  typologies of 48
sustainable development 34
Syracuse University, Maxwell School of
    Citizenship and Public Affairs 74

TCP/IP internet protocol suite 84, 86, 90
TPP (computing firm) 152
Taft, President William 21
Tamil Nadu (India)
  agriculture 126
  gender inequality 130, 131
  illiteracy 127, 128
  religion 126
Tamil Nadu Integrated Nutrition Project
    (TINP) 120, 125–32, 136–7, 231
targets 177, 195, 206
Taylor, Frederick Winslow 185
teachers
  pay 191, 192–3, 229
  performance 195–7, 200, 201
teamworking 41–2, 229
technological development 37–8
technological revolution 22
technology
  applications 16
  computers 102–4 *see also* internet
  military 34
  and modernization 22, 23, 27, 34–5, 41
  rail travel 159–60, 233
  and 'second Renaissance' 30
technoutopians 87, 230
telecommunication networks:
    standardization bodies 84
  see also cell phones; Skype
telemedicine 145
Teletext 103
Tenner, Edward: *Why Things Bite Back* 16
texting 103
Thatcher, Margaret 150, 186
The Spine network 149, 150, 152
Therborn, G. 25
Thomas, R., and Martin, J. 98
Thompson, M. *see* Schwarz, M., and
    Thompson, M.
Tilly, Charles 34
timetables, rail 157
Tipps, D. C. 25, 27
Tirole, J. 187–8
Tocqueville, Alexis de 13, 15, 45
Toennies, Ferdinand 9, 29
Toffler, Alvin 23, 30
Torpig botnet 98
Tracy, J., and Waldfogel, J. 79